CREATING EFFECTIVE MANUALS

JEAN d'AGENAIS
*Worker's Compensation
Board of Ontario
and George Brown College
of Applied Arts
and Technology*

JOHN CARRUTHERS
*Worker's Compensation
Board of Ontario
and George Brown College
of Applied Arts
and Technology*

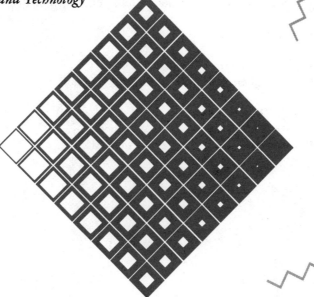

Published by

U20

SOUTH-WESTERN PUBLISHING CO.

CINCINNATI   WEST CHICAGO, IL   DALLAS   PELHAM MANOR, NY   PALO ALTO, CA

PREFACE

In the past few years there has been an ever-increasing push in industry and government for better documentation of systems, policies, standards, and procedures. This documentation, which is needed in nearly every sizable organization, is usually in the form of manuals, and the number of manuals being produced by these organizations is continually on the rise. Unfortunately, little has been done to control and standardize this proliferation.

Over this same period, text processing and word processing systems have become commonplace in business. These two trends, the demand for good documentation and the technology to produce it efficiently, have resulted in the need for instruction on how to develop high quality manuals. The goal of *Creating Effective Manuals* is to make the complex job of writing and producing manuals as simple as possible. The book is addressed to manuals writers and their management and to anyone else involved in manuals production.

Thus, *Creating Effective Manuals* has four objectives:

1. To give management an awareness of the need for high quality manuals and a cohesive manuals program.
2. To provide comprehensive standards for writing a manual and for setting up and maintaining an efficient manuals program.
3. To demonstrate to writers how to write clear, consistent material for their manuals.
4. To show "how" and not just "what" to do in all phases of manuals design and development.

Creating Effective Manuals is therefore a practical, nontheoretical text which takes the reader step-by-step through all stages of manuals production. Diagrams, examples, tables, charts, and illustrations are placed liberally throughout the text to ensure that the points made are clear. The methods documented in the text can be used for any manual, no matter what the subject matter, the organization, or the industry.

Creating Effective Manuals can be used in two ways. It can be read through from start to finish and the principles implemented en masse. Or, since the chapters represent separate functions of manuals development, one chapter can be a helpful reference on its own.

A chapter-by-chapter description of the contents follows:

- Chapter 1, "INTRODUCTION," establishes a perspective, defines terms, shows how to cost your manuals, and shows how to sell the idea of quality manuals to management.

- Chapter 2, "PLANNING AND PREPARATION," discusses all the activities which must be done before actually writing a manual, such as setting standards, designing a manual page, planning the manuals hierarchy, and setting up the manuals team.

- Chapter 3, "ORGANIZATION," presents the processes of gathering material, setting up a table of contents, and establishing a numbering system, and describes a framework for all manuals.

- Chapter 4, "WRITING STYLE," demonstrates good manuals writing style and standards, explains how to handle certain problem situations, and shows how to test the readability of your writing.

- Chapter 5, "LAYOUTS," describes each of the layouts used in manuals writing in detail, with particular emphasis on Caption, Matrix, Playscript, and Illustration layouts.

- Chapter 6, "PRODUCTION," discusses all aspects of the physical production of manuals including media, typing standards, the draft, critique and approvals processes, and printing.

- Chapter 7, "HOUSING," presents binder technology in layperson's terms, and demonstrates the importance of visual identity, then shows how to maximize their impact in binders.

- Chapter 8, "DISTRIBUTION," describes a straightforward distribution system, which can be adapted to either manual or automated methods.

- Chapter 9, "MAINTENANCE," includes topics such as revisions, amendments, directives, user education, writers' files, audits, and responsibilities.

We would like to acknowledge the contribution made to this book by our colleague and friend Murt Howell, forms expert, whose own textbook on forms management will become the outstanding work in the field. Murt served as our forms consultant and assisted in the critique of the manuscript. Thanks are also due to: Ian Gill for technical assistance; Sandra Gayle Ashby for word processing expertise; John Field and John Chisling of Weldo Plastics for information on binder technology; Trevor Harrison of Trevor Harrison Records Management and Carl Kemp-Jackson of Kemp-Jackson and Associates for starting us in the manuals field; and our students at George Brown College of Applied Arts and Technology in Toronto and the Worker's Compensation Board of Ontario, who provided a sounding board and critique committee for most of the material in this text.

Jean d' Agenais
John Carruthers

CONTENTS

"Comrade Moronski, orders were buildink space shuttle, *not* shovel!"

INTRODUCTION

1.1

ESTABLISHING A PERSPECTIVE
▼

Has your organization built any space shovels lately? Are your employees and associates guided by oral information only? Obviously such was the case with poor Comrade Moronski—and we know what's going to happen to him!

There's no doubt about it, oral communication becomes garbled in the telling. To prove this point, issue an oral policy statement. Then sit back and wait for its return via the office grapevine. When your message returns, you may not recognize it. For instance, the British, who don't mind poking a bit of fun at themselves, tell this World War II story of a message relayed by radio from their front lines: The communiqué said, "Send reinforcements, we are going to advance." By the time the message had gone through several relays and had reached headquarters, the message had become, "Send three and fourpence, we are going to a dance!"

This text is not about the oral transmission of information, but about the most effective written communication devices an organization can have: *manuals*. Today there are many reasons why written communication in the form of manuals is necessary, particularly in the business community. Some of these reasons are more subtle than Comrade Moronski's plight; others are less subtle. Time management, for instance, is one of the more obvious reasons. Often the effects of mismanaging time are known, while the causes remain elusive. Consider the following scenario:

> Harry arrived at work one morning to find a note left by his boss which asked him to explain the new order form to the sales staff. Unfortunately, Harry had never seen the new form before and it looked very complicated. Nevertheless, Harry began to fill in a sample to show the staff. It then occurred to him that his best source of information for filling out the form would be Joe in the Systems Department, since Joe had designed the new order entry system. So, off Harry went to Joe's office.

> After the usual chit-chat: "How about a coffee?" "How's the family?" etc., Harry let Joe know that he couldn't understand the new form. An hour or so later, Harry, a little less confused but not totally enlightened, returned to his office to complete his sample for the staff.

> Harry called the sales staff together. Of the staff of nine, two were on call and one was off sick. Undaunted, Harry explained the form to the remaining six. His lecture was understood by three of the six staff members, all of whom could have figured out the form's use by themselves. The other three went away with only a vague idea about the form's use. Of these three, two were knowledgeable and conscientious enough to go to Joe; that is, to hear it from the horse's mouth. The net result of all this interaction was that only five of the nine people who had to use the form now knew how to do so, and only after considerable time and effort. Furthermore, this wasn't the end; Harry hadn't yet presented the form to those who were absent.

It would have been much easier if Harry's new form had been introduced properly—via a procedure and an illustration in the sales manual. Harry's boss could have saved the time of writing the note to Harry; Harry could have saved the time of interviewing Joe and of meeting with the sales staff; Joe could have avoided three interviews to explain the form; and the sales staff could have saved the time of meeting with Harry and the time of interviewing Joe.

The basic principle underlying this example is that if somebody has a question that needs an answer, it requires that person's time and that of another person when the matter is not properly documented. If the answer is documented, only the questioner's time is required. Time wasted by seeking undocumented information is inefficient for any organization. It increases costs tremendously. Some of these costs, called the costs of operating without manuals, are listed here.

- Supervisory staff spend more time than necessary answering questions.
- The answers to such questions may be incomplete or inaccurate, possibly resulting in costly errors and more work.
- Management is often required to perform low-level tasks.

- Performance levels for staff are inconsistent.
- Training of staff requires more time and is more difficult.
- Steps in procedures or, in some cases, whole procedures are omitted or inconsistently applied.
- Duplication of effort is difficult to avoid.
- Time is lost in decision making; wrong decisions are made more often.
- Supervisory staff are not consistent in applying the same standards.
- In the absence of manuals, the organization's efforts to keep its people well-informed must take the form of bulletins, memos, and directives, all of which must be filed somewhere. Thus, staff must maintain their own records management system to keep up-to-date.
- Individual employees may take it upon themselves to write their own unauthorized manuals.

An example of some of the more subtle or hidden costs that occur when operating without manuals is presented in the following story.

> It was Jean's first day on the job. She was hired straight out of high school by a company that made steel gadgets and widgets in varying sizes. She was to be the new costing clerk although she was not advised as to the disposition of the previous costing clerk.
>
> Jean was taken to her desk in a dark corner. On it was a machine with what seemed like hundreds of buttons and a handle on the side—a comptometer; an in-basket with a stack of invoices a mile high; and an out-basket which was empty. Jean had never seen an invoice before, much less a comptometer.
>
> Her instructions were, "Just figure out those invoices." Jean was confused and frightened since no one showed her what to do. She envisioned being held responsible for the cost of millions of ¼- and ⅛-inch widgets. Jean wrestled with the comptometer for hours, gave up on that, and tried to do the sums manually. She surrendered after an hour or so and began fearfully to glance around. No one seemed to notice her plight. Finally someone who looked important stopped at her desk. "Well?" he asked. Jean tearfully admitted that she could not do the job. She was then told to go home. It wasn't even lunchtime.

This was the most shameful thing that had ever happened to Jean. The real shame, however, was the company's, for they had wasted and would probably continue to waste their time interviewing and hiring. They allowed a situation where costly mistakes could be made and they gave Jean the wrong impression of the working world.

One of the more subtle reasons why we need written communication is to cope with the effects of change. Harry's problem with the form was a direct result of change: a new computer system. Jean's first job was a direct result of change: Jean from school to work; the company from one employee to another.

Change, as told by Alvin Toffler in his book *Future Shock*, is happening exponentially. One need only look at the technological changes that have occurred in the last decade or so to comprehend the scope of their effects on modern society: new drugs, new forms of medical treatment, new legislation, new office and manufacturing equipment, etc. It is a well-established fact that any kind of change causes insecurity and stress. However, there are two methods of reducing these effects of change: (1) Attack the cause and reduce or eliminate any unnecessary changes; (2) Try to cope effectively with the changes as they occur. In business, written communication, especially in the form of manuals, does both by documenting changes and introducing them in an acceptable and understandable form. This reduces the surprise factor and in turn minimizes the magnitude of the changes. If Harry had received an update to his sales manual which explained and illustrated the form, it would have been much easier for Harry to explain the new order form to the sales staff. If Jean had been provided with an illustration of the comptometer and with written procedures for using it, it would have been a less frightening day and she may have remained on the job.

There is no reason to limit the discussion to an organization's internal manuals. Today, in the competitive high-tech fields of systems hardware and software, for example, the packaging of a software or hardware product may give one organization the competitive edge it needs to gain or retain the Number 1 position in the marketplace. An integral, but often forgotten, part of the total product concept is user documentation. In an era of the "corporate image," an organization's product image can be enhanced or diminished by what is written about the product, how it is written, and how it is presented to product users. The image an organization's documentation promotes, be it good or bad, lingers on. The end result should be a manual in which the information is quickly found and easily understood, whether it is an internal manual or an external manual.

1.2
OBJECTIVES AND ADVANTAGES OF MANUALS

Manuals should be used whenever personnel must be trained, when routine activities must be followed, and when decisions must be made. Any organization of any size—hospitals, schools, service industries, government, engineering, data processing, manufacturing, purchasing, marketing, sales, etc.—can use a manual of some kind. The list is virtually endless.

MANUALS AS MANAGEMENT RESOURCES

Manuals are basically management resources which classify and document the activities and policies of an organization. The objectives of manuals are to

- state and clarify policy
- define duties, responsibilities, and authority
- formalize operations thereby ensuring uniform treatment of repetitive tasks
- provide standards against which workers and their superiors can measure their performance
- provide information to employees, customers, or anyone else who needs it

- provide an open and established line of communication between management and staff thereby allowing for consistent methods of introducing new policies and procedures
- educate users.

Of these objectives, the first two are of prime importance to upper management, for if management does not have its policies and procedures documented effectively it has none. An organization cannot expect its employees to guess what is expected of them. In these times of high unemployment, employees also cannot be expected to accept dismissal lightly for not following undocumented procedures or for making errors when management has not done its part. Employees are beginning to fight tenaciously to hold onto their jobs. Cases of wrongful dismissal brought against employers are now becoming commonplace in our courts, to the extent that there are even lawyers who specialize in representing dismissed employees. So, it's more important than ever before to put it in writing.

Even though manuals cost money to produce and maintain, the organization saves time and money because of the

- reduction of time to find solutions to problems
- reduction of training time for new, temporary, promoted, or contract staff
- reduction of costly errors
- improved utilization of staff.

MANUALS AS
EMPLOYEE RESOURCES

It is apparent then that manuals benefit management. However, manuals also provide benefits to employees. They

- help employees do better jobs and thereby improve morale
- keep staff up-to-date and knowledgeable about the organization
- provide continuity by preserving policy through changes in personnel
- provide consistency in relations between staff and supervisors
- convince those employees who must see it in writing
- guarantee uniform, accurate measures of performance
- reduce stress when changes are introduced
- give employees confidence and settle arguments
- eliminate guesswork and save memory effort
- make the new employee feel more comfortable with his or her job
- assist employees in determining career objectives within the organization.

With regard to the latter point, which to some may seem slightly esoteric, note the following story:

A young vice-president in the banking business claims that his meteoric rise in the organization was due to his use of the company's policy and procedure manuals. When first hired as a management trainee, he didn't wish to wait years to be trained in each and every facet of the business. So, outside of his normal working hours, he methodically went through every manual in the organization. By the time he was finished, he not only knew the company's history and policies, but he was familiar with all the procedures followed in every department. He was therefore able to analyze what was going on around him, to speak knowledgeably in staff meetings, and to make unexpected and good recommendations—all of which did not go unnoticed.

So far, the discussion has centered on the purposes and advantages of all manuals. To make the most of these advantages, a specific manual must meet its users' requirements and must satisfy the objectives agreed upon for it by users, writers, and management. This aspect of manuals is often overlooked.

Writers of manuals must ensure that the users are satisfied with the manuals they receive. To accomplish this, the users' needs must be taken into account. It is the writers' responsibility to determine these needs, and they must be astute interviewers to do so, for users may not necessarily tell all when first asked. The possible reasons for this are varied. For example, some users may assume that the interviewer has a thorough knowledge of their department and a complete understanding of the procedures to be written. Some may be afraid that their jobs may change, or they may be worried that someone will discover that they are not doing their jobs efficiently. Other users may be concerned that their power will be usurped. There are many reasons why users may not be completely open with interviewers. Unfortunately, interviewers may never know that these reasons exist; they may only be aware of resistance.

To fulfill user requirements and to offset possible resistance, it is important that the writing of manuals be a team effort and that the team include users at all levels: management, line supervisors, and staff.

1.3
SCOPE AND DEFINITIONS
▼

Before we go any further, let's stop and establish the scope of this book. This can best be done by defining some of the terms which will be used. This, in turn, will also identify many of the topics which will be dealt with in detail.

DEFINITION: MANUAL
◆

A *manual* is a structured, easily referenced collection of any or all of the following: policy statements; operating procedures; illustrations (forms, equipment, etc.); standards; organization charts; systems documentation (e.g., flowcharts, decision tables, data flow diagrams, etc.); price lists; catalogs; and information that pertains to the activities of an entity such as an individual, firm, association, agency, or institution.

TYPES OF MANUALS
◆

In this text, no attempt is made to distinguish among types of manuals. The distinctions usually made are between policy, procedure, and training manuals; or internal (operations) and external (user) manuals; or sometimes administrative, technical, systems, and marketing manuals. If you want to put only policy in a manual or to develop a separate training manual, that's fine. The guidelines and standards offered in this text can be applied to any manual.

DEFINITION:
DESIGN AND DEVELOPMENT
◆

When referring to a manual's *design and development*, the reference is to six activities:

1. Planning and Preparation—everything that must be done before material is collected
2. Organization—determining and organizing manual content, data gathering, and analysis
3. Writing—choosing an appropriate writing style, following writing standards, and writing in the appropriate layout
4. Production—printing, housing, etc.
5. Distribution—who gets the manual, how, and why
6. Maintenance—keeping the manual up-to-date

Each of these activities comprises a chapter of this text. (Writing and production have actually been divided into two chapters each.) Therefore, the discussion will become progressively more detailed after Chapter 1.

DEFINITION:
THE MANUALS TEAM
◆

The *manuals team* is comprised of those individuals who provide input and who write, edit, type, distribute, maintain, and use a manual.

DEFINITION:
MANUALS WRITERS
◆

Manuals writers are those individuals who plan, and in most cases perform, the aforementioned activities. Manuals designers and manuals writers encompass procedure writers, policy analysts, technical writers, standards analysts, methods analysts, etc. Thus, when referring to any or all of these functions, the term manuals writers will be used rather than attempting to distinguish one specific function from another. There tends to be a large overlap anyway.

A *Tab* is a major or primary division of a manual. Tabs are separated by tab dividers.

A *Section* is a secondary division of a manual; i.e., a Tab may be broken down into several Sections.

Subjects are tertiary divisions of a manual; i.e., a Section may consist of several Subjects.

Tabs, Sections, and Subjects, as well as the application of a numbering system, are described in Chapter 3, "Organization."

DEFINITION: *LAYOUT AND PAGE FORMAT*

Layout is the way in which text is laid out or presented on the manual page. The term is used extensively in advertising, publishing, and printing. In the advertising industry, for instance, layout artists plan and design the text and graphics of their advertisements in such a way as to make them attractive or compelling to the consumer. Similarly, manuals writers use layouts as a technique to make the text and graphics of a manual more attractive and compelling to its users.

Many manuals writers mistakenly refer to layout as format or page format. The term *page format* describes the physical attributes of the manual page—for example, the masthead, page number, and date are all part of page format. How the text is applied to the page is layout.

DEFINITION: READABILITY AND *RETRIEVABILITY*

Readability refers to the degree of ease with which text is read and understood.

Retrievability refers to the degree of ease with which material can be found in a manual.

1.4 ## COSTING YOUR PRESENT MANUALS

How much do your manuals cost per year? Most people think of these costs as the

- cost of salaries
- cost of printing (for new or replacement copies)
- cost of binders (for new copies)

These are certainly the up-front costs. But what about the hidden cost—the cost of referencing the manual? This includes both the retrieval cost and the reading cost. A short explanation of both of these costs will help you to understand the importance of a well-indexed and easy-to-read manual.

RETRIEVABILITY

Manuals are used about 95 percent of the time for referencing and about 5 percent of the time for general reading, most of which is required in the training of new staff. Because referencing time is so high, it is essential that the retrieval of information be made as simple as possible so that little time is wasted in seeking this information.

A number of devices are used to gain rapid access to the information in a manual. Each is mentioned briefly here and discussed in greater detail later.

The first of the retrieval devices are *indices*. A good index is vital because to find information one must first look in the index. There can be as many as four types of indices in a manual.

- Alphabetic keyword index
- Table of contents
- Forms index
- Reports index

By far the most important of these is the alphabetic keyword index or the alpha subject index, as it is often called. This is a must for every manual. The keywords consist of subject titles and captions arranged in alphabetical order.

A good index can make a table of contents almost redundant; however, it certainly does no harm to have both. The table of contents is arranged in the same sequence as the documents in the manual, thereby giving the users a bird's-eye view of the manual's organization.

Forms indices and reports indices are only necessary if the number of forms and reports exceeds six or more. Reports can be statistical or technical documents, feasibility studies, position papers, etc. These reports may either be scattered throughout the manual, wherever they are applicable, or placed in an appendix, if they are of a supplementary nature.

The next important retrieval device is a good numbering system. The numbers should be placed so that they are highly visible on each page. A six-digit numbering system that is easy to understand and use is recommended. In this system each set of two-digit numbers represents a level in the hierarchy (i.e., Tabs, Sections, Subjects) of the manual. For example, 02–04–05 would represent the fifth Subject in the fourth Section in the second Tab of the manual.

There are three more retrieval devices—one which is purely physical and two which are organizational. The physical retrieval devices are the *tab dividers*. Each major division, or Tab, within a manual is separated from the next major division by a tab divider which is numbered 01, 02, 03, etc. Indices and appendices dividers are a different color from the numbered dividers, making it easy to find this material. The organizational retrieval devices are overviews and captions. *Overviews* are located at the beginning of each Section of the manual and "overview" the contents of the Section. They list and briefly describe each Subject within the Section and show the location number at which a particular Subject can be found. *Captions* are keywords which are located in the margins and which highlight text.

Proper use of all these retrieval devices allows users to find the Subject they desire in a matter of seconds.

READABILITY

Readability is one of the most important factors in developing good manuals. Poor writing and/or poor layout increase reading time and user costs. Manuals are a major reference source for policies and procedures. They should therefore tell the users what to do without the unnecessary loss of time.

The largest factor in the hidden costs of manuals is readability. If a page is difficult to understand, the reader must take extra time to determine the meaning. When this time is multiplied by the number of readers who must read the page, the total time and thus costs are greatly increased. It is therefore necessary to perfect a clear, simple, and concise writing style.

Presentation or layout of the text must also be considered. Solid pages of narrative offer little relief to the readers, whereas the effective use of white space, captions, illustrations, etc., is more appealing, helps the users focus in on the information sought, and maintains the users' attention.

COSTS OF
REFERENCING

Needless to say, if your manuals do not have all the retrieval devices mentioned and if they are poorly written, they may be costing your company a bundle. You can cost your manuals by first conducting a test and then applying the data derived from the test to a formula.

If you are about to rewrite any of your manuals, the current costs should first be analyzed. The costing process should also be used on an ongoing basis so that savings can be measured and recorded after a manual has been rewritten. Use the following procedure:

1. Choose at random a Subject from one of your manuals and make up a simple question about the Subject.
2. Ask a sample group of users in your organization to be guinea pigs for your test. Your group should include about 12 individuals who are from different departments. They should have diverse job descriptions and varying degrees of responsibility. Note: You should test the participants individually in order to keep accurate records.
3. Ask each participant to find the Subject you have chosen.
4. Record the amount of time in minutes taken by each participant to find the Subject.

5. Request that participants read the Subject to complete comprehension. This means that they must be able to answer a simple question about the Subject without having to look back at it. A few words of assurance to participants (e.g., "Take as long as necessary.") may be in order.

6. Record the length of time it takes each user to read and understand the Subject. Then ask your question to ensure that complete comprehension has been achieved.

7. Determine an average of the times taken by users to: (1) find the Subject (retrievability) and (2) understand the Subject (readability). For example:

Average Retrieval Time = 2 Minutes
Average Comprehension Time = 17 Minutes

8. Determine the number of references made to the manual in one year as follows:

Number of Manual Locations	×	Average Number of Users per Location	×	Average Number of References per User per Year	=	Total Annual References

For example:

20 Locations × 4 Users × 50 References = 4,000 Annual References

9. Figure out the average salary per minute of the employees who use the manual. For example:

$9 per Hour = 15¢ per Minute

10. Apply the information gleaned from Steps 7, 8, and 9 to the following formula to find the current annual reference costs.

Average Number of Minutes per Reference	×	Estimated Annual References	×	Cost per Minute	=	Annual Reference Costs

For example:

2 × 4,000 × $0.15 = $ 1,200 (to retrieve)
17 × 4,000 × $0.15 = $10,200 (to read)

$11,400 (annual reference costs)

The foregoing example illustrates that each year this particular manual costs the organization $11,400. This figure was based on very conservative estimates of approximately 15 references per working day (4,000 total references divided by 260 working days per year) and $9 per hour as an average wage. The retrieval and reading times in the example are high and indicate that the manual has either substandard or no retrieval devices and is written poorly.

These reference costs are not going to disappear when a manual has been organized and written to the standards suggested. On the contrary, if you had no reference costs you would have no one referencing your manuals. Therefore, the ideal to achieve is

1. Less time to retrieve and read each reference to comprehension (which will *reduce* your reference costs)
2. More users referencing manuals more often (which will *increase* your reference costs)

Even though the costs of retrieving and reading are hidden, they are easy to quantify. However, there are other factors which are more difficult to quantify. They are:

- errors made as a result of references to poorly written manuals
- errors made as a result of not referencing the manuals
- time taken by employees and supervisors to come up with the answers to questions which should be documented.

When you have rewritten several manuals according to the standards recommended, you can cost the rewritten manuals and compare the new costs with the old costs. This comparison should be done on the basis of an equal number of references for each manual, even though more references are made to the better manuals. You will be surprised at the difference—a difference which will represent a savings to you each year. What is really remarkable is that the costs incurred in producing good manuals are not so much greater than the costs incurred in producing poor manuals.

1.5
ESTIMATING PRODUCTION COSTS OF MANUALS
▼

The production costs of manuals vary widely from one organization to another. One company may pay top salaries for writers and spare no expense for printing and housing in order to produce high quality manuals, while another company may spend as little as possible. Nevertheless, the cost components will be the same for all manuals.

- Gathering material
- Organizing material
- Interviewing
- Analyzing procedures
- Writing
- Preparing illustrations
- Editing
- Proofreading
- Keying (either on a typewriter or a word or text processor)
- Typesetting and/or printing
- Graphics (forms, illustrations, tables, photographs, etc.)

- Medium (paper, microfiche)
- Binders and tab dividers
- Distribution
- Maintenance

The costs associated with writing-related activities (from gathering material to proofreading) are usually the heaviest because of the number of work hours expended. Maintenance, as with any system or equipment, is ongoing and may consist of some or all of the other components. The costs in total, particularly when you make the supreme effort to produce all your manuals at once, say within one year, will seem steep. But these costs must be likened to those of any other system or piece of equipment which is considered to be a capital expenditure—and like them, they must be amortized. The difference between a manual and a system or piece of equipment, however, is that the manual never becomes obsolete if it is properly maintained, whereas systems and equipment, even if they are maintained, do become obsolete. So, once you have established the cost of a manual, spread this cost over the life of the manual.

The first step in estimating the production costs of new manuals is to determine volume. The term "new" is used because that is the norm. However, you could also apply these methods to discover the production costs of existing manuals. The questions to be answered are:

- How many manuals will be developed?
- How many pages will each manual have?
- How many copies of each manual will be distributed?
- How often will the manuals be updated?

Manual pages consist of document pages and control document pages. *Control document pages* are such items as an alphabetic index, a table of contents, etc. To estimate the number of document pages in a manual, allow an average of three pages per Subject. To estimate the number of control document pages, take 15 percent of the estimated document pages. Each of the control documents in a manual will be explained and illustrated later.

Once you have a fixed page count, the guidelines of junior writer: 1 page per day, intermediate writer: 2–3 pages per day, and senior writer: 4–5 pages per day can be applied to calculate the total number of work days required to produce the manual. These figures include everything on our list from gathering material to proofreading. Writing costs can then be obtained by multiplying work days by writers' costs per day. This can be formalized as follows:

$$\text{Manual Cost} = \frac{\text{Number of Days}}{\text{to Produce}} \times \frac{\text{Cost of Writers}}{\text{per Day}}$$

These elements of the formula can be broken down further.

$$\frac{\text{Number of Days}}{\text{to Produce}} = \frac{\text{Manual Pages}}{\text{Production per Day}}$$

Production per day is the total output of the writing team, keeping in mind the production rates for junior, intermediate, and senior writers. The cost of writers per day can be calculated by using whatever method you use to determine their salaries—hourly, daily, or weekly rates. Take a look at a simple example.

Suppose you wish to figure the cost of an estimated 378-page manual. You need it done in a hurry so you assign one senior writer, two intermediate writers, and one junior (trainee) writer to the project. First, figure out how long it will take to produce the manual.

$$1 \times \text{Junior Rate} = 1.0 \text{ Page per Day}$$
$$2 \times \text{Intermediate Rate} = 5.0 \text{ Pages per Day}$$
$$1 \times \text{Senior Rate} = 4.5 \text{ Pages per Day}$$

$$\text{Team Rate} \quad 10.5 \text{ Pages per Day}$$

Now, using the following formula:

$$\text{Number of Days to Produce} = \frac{\text{Manual Pages (Document Pages} \times 115\%)}{\text{Production per Day}}$$

incorporate the following figures:

$$\frac{378 \text{ Pages} \times 1.15}{10.5 \text{ Pages per Day}} = 41.4 \text{ Days.}$$

Next calculate the writing costs per day. For the sake of simplicity, say the rates are:

$$\text{Junior Writer} = \$75/\text{Day}$$
$$\text{Intermediate Writer} = \$100/\text{Day}$$
$$\text{Senior Writer} = \$150/\text{Day, then,}$$
$$\text{Cost of the Writers per Day} = (1 \times \$75) + (2 \times \$100) + (1 \times \$150)$$
$$= \$75 + \$200 + \$150$$
$$= \$425.$$

So, putting the figures into the following formula:

$$\text{Manual Cost} = \text{Number of Days to Produce} \times \text{Cost of Writers per Day,}$$

the result is

$$42 \times \$425 = \$17,850.$$

The costs associated with the other tasks can readily be calculated once the page count is known. Typesetters, printers, and binder manufacturers, for instance, will give you very accurate estimates of their prices.

Distribution and maintenance costs must not be overlooked either. For example, if your manuals need to be sent to branches in other cities, mailing and shipping charges must be considered. Maintenance costs can be estimated using the 20 percent revision rule: If you have no other measure, 20 percent of your manual will be revised (Subjects added, changed, or deleted) each year. For example, with a 378-page manual, you can assume that 75 pages or so will be written or rewritten each year.

1.6

RETURN ON INVESTMENT

▼

Unfortunately, measuring returns is not as simple as calculating the costs of manuals. For instance, you know that there will be considerable savings to any organization which documents its procedures, thereby resulting in

* activities performed and decisions made with fewer errors
* time saved to perform these activities and to make sound decisions expeditiously.

But how do you actually quantify these savings? Provided you have a measurable output, you can take a stab at it. For example, suppose your inside sales staff makes 500 calls a day and the issuance of a new manual allows them to increase the number of calls to 530 calls a day. This means a 6 percent increase in effectiveness. Or, perhaps your costing clerks can handle six new items a day instead of the previous five; that means a 20 percent increase in effectiveness. You can also measure the reduction of training time for new staff, which translates into increased productivity over a shorter period of time. In any event, whenever you can measure an increase in productivity or effectiveness or a savings in time or money as a result of issuing a manual, you can translate that increase into cash benefits.

For example, suppose your support staff budget (salaries) is $1 million and you produce a manual that costs $20,000. Then to recover the expense incurred in producing the manual, you would need an increase in effectiveness from your support staff of only 2 percent ($20,000 divided by $1 million). Any increase in effectiveness that is greater than 2 percent would provide cost benefits. Using the same manual and salary costs, Table 1–1 shows what 3 percent, 4 percent, etc., would provide in cost benefits.

Percentage Increase in Effectiveness	Dollar Benefits Over Manual Costs
3%	$ 10,000
4	20,000
5	30,000
10	80,000
15	130,000

TABLE 1-1
COST BENEFITS
OF MANUALS

Keep in mind that this justifies the manual solely on the basis of an increase in effectiveness. It does not take into account any additional revenue which accrues through this increase in efficiency nor any internal company benefits. For instance, when sales calls were increased from 500 to 530 a day, it is probable that the company experienced some additional revenue from those 30 extra calls—a quantifiable benefit of the sales manual. It is not the aim of this text, however, to teach cost/benefit analysis, but to allow you to see examples of how you might calculate the returns on your investment in manuals.

1.7
A CENTRALIZED MANUALS PROGRAM
▼

Since a manual saves time and money, it follows, then, that a complete manuals program will be even more beneficial. It also follows that the more manuals you produce, the more costs you incur. One could glibly say that manuals are "cheaper by the dozen;" but they are not, unless a genuine effort is made to control all phases of design and development. As in any production environment, costs can be greatly reduced by ensuring that standards are employed and monitored while still maintaining high quality. A centralized program can ensure this.

A *centralized manuals program* is an organized effort to plan, organize, write, produce, distribute, and maintain all the manuals within an organization. Often there is a lack of communication and direction within large organizations. For instance, manuals writers from the same organization may not know one another, or may not even be aware that similar manuals projects exist in other departments. It is therefore suggested that all people who are involved in the preparation of manuals within a company get together and coordinate their activities by establishing a centralized manuals program.

Definite cost benefits can be assured if management commits itself to a centralized manuals program. But before this happens, certain questions about the program must be answered: What exactly are the program's objectives and responsibilities? Under whose auspices should the program fall? These questions are often overlooked. Management should address these questions constructively in light of the organization's needs.

Manuals are designed and developed like any other business system. Each stage, from planning to maintenance, must have its milestones and checkpoints. For example, most organizations have an accounting department and a systems department. And, just as it is unheard of to allow individual employees to write their own paychecks or to develop their own computer systems, so it should be with manuals. Employees must not be allowed to develop their own manuals as they see fit; they must be given a set of standards to follow. Management must ensure that manuals are accorded the importance they deserve. A commitment to a centralized manuals program goes a long way to accomplishing this. Remember, manuals document the philosophy, history, policies, and procedures of the organization. They are an important vehicle of communication.

THE PROGRAM'S OBJECTIVES

Two major objectives of a centralized manuals program are:

1. to analyze and meet the present and future manuals requirements of the entire organization
2. to establish valid standards for the development of these manuals.

Thus, a cohesive manuals program ensures that procedures throughout the organization are analyzed, authored, and edited; properly approved by management; produced, housed, distributed, and maintained; all in a uniform manner.

The economic benefits of such an operation are readily apparent. Fewer analysts/writers are required; production and housing costs are lower; the manuals are of higher quality; and they are easier to maintain.

WHERE DOES THE MANUALS PROGRAM FIT IN THE ORGANIZATION?

There is no definitive answer to this question, although everyone in the organization will have his or her ideas about where the program belongs. Most will believe that it should fall under their auspices, but the most likely candidates are Systems, Standards, Forms, Communications, Records Management, and Education. Each organization will have to come to its own decision based upon its needs and resources.

Answers to the following questions may help you decide where the manuals program fits in your organization. A shift of resources to accommodate the program may be required.

Where in the Organization Is the Talent to Run the Program? Talent may be broken down into two categories: skills and knowledge. Although it would be desirable to resource the manuals program with employees who have both skills and knowledge, skills must be considered of primary importance for they take years (of education and/or experience) to develop. Knowledge of the organization can be gained much more quickly, particularly by employees who possess the skills listed in Table 1–2.

Skills	Knowledge
Analytical	Policy
Organizational	Expediting the Program
Writing	Administration
Interviewing	Manual Systems (procedure)
Technical	Computer Systems (procedure)

TABLE 1-2
SKILLS AND KNOWLEDGE
OF EMPLOYEES IN A
MANUALS PROGRAM

Who Has the Physical Resources (Hardware, Software, Space)? Who Wants to Administer the Program? Who Has the Most to Gain from Controlling the Manuals Program? The last two questions may seem facetious upon first reading, but consider the psychological overtones. Positive results are most likely to occur when someone wants to do something, particularly if there is something to be gained.

In order to determine exactly where the manuals program fits in an organization, that organization will have to come to its own decision based upon its own needs, its own resources, and the factors mentioned.

1.8
WRITING A MANUALS REPORT FOR MANAGEMENT
▼

It has been proven that management commitment is needed for the successful implementation of any administrative program. If management has not recognized the need for manuals or if you have manuals but no centralized program which ensures their quality, then a manuals report can often pave the way to obtaining management commitment.

The type of report you write will depend on whether your organization has manuals or not. The difference between the reports is:

A. The management of a company that has no manuals may need to be convinced of their importance
B. The management of a company that has manuals may need to be convinced of the need for a manuals program or manuals standards

In either case (A or B), before the report is written a thorough investigation should be done in order to present a report which contains facts and not just hypotheses. The facts to be investigated and reported, as well as the report's content, will be quite different, depending upon which report is to be written. For this reason the following guidelines have been established for investigating and outlining your report.

INVESTIGATION GUIDELINES AND CHECKLIST FOR REPORT A
(the organization that has no manuals)

The following points should be considered before preparing your report.

1. Why is a manuals project now being considered?
2. What factors prompted the issue?
3. Has management ever considered a manuals program before? If yes, why wasn't it initiated?

4. Are there any unofficial manuals in the organization? If yes, who wrote them? Why were they written? Are they used? Are they kept up-to-date? By whom?

5. What written documentation is used for training?

6. Consider the entire organization and identify the areas where day-to-day operating procedures are required. Establish how many manuals are required in each area. For example, Finance could require Accounts Receivable, Accounts Payable, Payroll, and General Ledger manuals. The relationship of these and the other manuals to each other can conveniently be shown on an organization chart.

7. Investigate outside organizations which have successful manuals programs. If you don't know of any, ask of local professional organizations such as the Association for Systems Management (ASM) or the Association of Records Managers and Administrators (ARMA). You can also call a few of the larger companies in your area and ask if they have a manuals program. If they do, they will probably be delighted to show off their work and to share their experiences with you and your management. Ask them the following questions:

   • Did they initiate their own program or was it installed for them by consultants?
   • If consultants installed the program, is the organization pleased with the program?
   • What resources (employees and time) are required to maintain the program?

8. Investigate the costs of operating without manuals in your organization. Consider the following:

   • training time of staff
   • utilization of staff
   • the length of time it takes new or promoted employees to operate efficiently and at full potential
   • costly errors (time and money) which could have been avoided if documentation had existed.

   For more details, refer to Section 1.2 "Objectives and Advantages of Manuals."

9. Estimate the costs of operating with manuals. Consider Section 1.5 "Estimating Production Costs of Manuals."

OUTLINE FOR
REPORT A

A report prepared for an organization that has no manuals should contain the following information.

1. A complete reorganization and rewrite
2. Structural changes; e.g., a new numbering system
3. Cosmetic changes; e.g., a new page design
4. Enhancements such as an alpha subject index

Costs. Show the costs for each alternative solution.

Benefits. Describe the benefits of each alternative.

Recommendations. Choose the best alternative solution and justify it.

Implementation. Describe a plan for implementation.

OTHER GENERAL REMINDERS

For either report (A or B), supporting documentation is a must. Use illustrations liberally to help describe the text. For example, if you decide you want a new manual page, illustrate the old page and the proposed new page (See Chapter 2). Explain and illustrate the controls tab (to be discussed in Chapter 3). Make your report convincing.

FOLLOWING UP THE REPORT

No report should be distributed without following it up with the same energy and enthusiasm that went into its development. The recipients of the report should be advised by a covering memo that you will:

* make a manuals presentation which will describe the basic concepts of the report
* schedule a meeting to discuss ideas, opinions, and a course of action.

Remember, your main concern is to get people interested and excited about your ideas. You want to receive as much input as possible from all areas of the organization. If you make your readers feel that their opinions are wanted, they will get involved and there will be a better chance of getting approval for your program.

1.9
DEVELOPING A MANUALS PRESENTATION FOR MANAGEMENT
▼

The problem with a lot of presentations is that they are bor-r-r-ing! Nobody wants to attend a presentation where someone either reads what has already been written in a report or just stands there and talks about it. You've got to put pizzazz into your presentation! First, you must decide what the content of the presentation should be and then you must decide the best means of presenting it. Here are a few suggestions.

CONTENT
◆

A presentation should be like a well-planned full-course dinner; the ingredients should be fresh and colorful, no course should be too heavy, and each course should lead smoothly into the next. Planning is the key, and your plan should be based on the concept that effective presentations are visual; otherwise, why have the presentation?

Prepare an outline of the presentation based on the report you have written. Expand the outline in point form to include the basic or key concepts that you want to get across. Try to use different phrases from those used in the report. Use examples or analogies which are meaningful to your audience.

Decide which parts of the presentation should be oral and which parts should be visual. For instance, you may want to introduce your presentation by briefly describing the events which prompted the report. This would not require visual support. However, if you describe the numbering system recommended for manuals or the page design, layouts, or typing standards, you should have illustrations to support your explanation. Decide where the use of diagrams, illustrations, and charts are most effective. These may be taken directly from the report or they may be entirely new.

Put yourself in the shoes of your audience. Pretend you know nothing about manuals and that you have not read your report. Ask yourself whether the material in your presentation hangs together. Is there too little material or too much? Is the approach positive? Are you selling your ideas to the audience?

HOW TO PRESENT
THE MATERIAL
◆

The way you present material will influence your audience's response. The following methods are suggested.

Overhead Transparencies. The use of overhead transparencies (foils) and an overhead projector is highly recommended. Slide presentations are slick but costly, whereas overheads can be made much more cheaply and with little loss of effectiveness. Some points to remember when preparing overheads are:

1. Use bold print. Typefaces on typewriters are not good enough. Use dry-transfer lettering, such as Geotype or lettering machines, although hand-drawn print is perfectly acceptable, providing it is neat. Print should be large enough so that everyone in your audience can see it without straining. Experiment with foils and the projector.
2. Don't put too much information on any one foil. Your facts should be in point form. Rule of thumb: Use a maximum of 10 lines of print per foil.
3. Illustrations and charts should be drawn to the full size of the foil. Only one chart or illustration should appear on each foil.

4. Use color on your foils—either to highlight or to accentuate points. Alcohol-based colored pens, especially made for overheads, allow the color to project onto the screen. These pens come in a wide variety of colors and thicknesses and can be purchased at most art or office supply stores.

5. Insert a little humor wherever possible. However, you must take care that the humor is not offensive to anyone in the audience. Illustrations are best for the inclusion of humor.

Speaking. Practice your presentation in the room in which you will speak and in front of a chosen few who should sit at the back of the room. This will give you an idea of how loudly you must speak. If you have to strain to be heard, get a microphone.

Emphasize important words, particularly adjectives. For example, if you are discussing *big* savings, emphasize "big." Verbally underscore it. You cannot convince your audience that there are substantial savings if you, yourself, do not sound convinced. A weak, timorous voice would be a complete denial.

Body Language. Body language plays a big part in influencing the audience one way or another. You know how nervous you, as part of an audience, feel if the speaker is nervous. Thus, the best way to reassure your audience is to stand firmly, feet slightly spread. This will prevent you from rocking back and forth. The hands must also be under control: no fists, no hand wringing (holding a pointer can help), no grasping at clothes, and no hands in your pockets. Hand gestures should be made for emphasis.

Eye Contact. Eye contact with your audience is absolutely necessary. One of the problems that many inexperienced speakers encounter is that they are not told how to make eye contact. They scan the room from left to right and back again, trying to include as many people as possible in their gaze. The results can be disastrous. Scanning can put the eyes out of focus, which can cause dizziness or disorientation and which can cause the speaker to forget what he or she is saying. The eyes must be focused properly for the brain to work. Focus on one face at a time and speak to that person for a few seconds or until the thought being expressed is finished. Then move to the next face until you have spoken to every person in the room. If you have someone in the room whom you feel you are losing or not convincing, concentrate more of your attention on that person by talking directly to or smiling at that person, but not to the extent of producing uneasiness.

Whether or not you have done any public speaking before, you will be nervous. This is not only natural, but beneficial. It gets the adrenalin flowing, which can be channeled into enthusiasm.

PREPARATION

The best way to allay your fears or nervousness is to be well prepared. Run through the presentation several times—first on your own to determine timing and then for your workmates to receive their feedback.

Make sure you have a room that accommodates your audience. Room temperature should be just right (66–67° Fahrenheit). The room should be well ventilated. Nonsmokers may wish to be separated from smokers. The lighting should not be so dark that people can't see you or that people go to sleep. It should not be so light that your overheads don't show up to best advantage. Sunlight should not shine in anyone's face nor glare off the walls, the screen, or the furniture. If you have venetian blinds, turn them up, not down.

Be certain your equipment works properly and is placed conveniently. If everything is well organized, it will boost your confidence. There should be no physical barriers (e.g., a lectern) between the speaker and the audience for these create psychological barriers and thereby make the audience feel as though the speaker is removed or isolated from them. Do not address your audience from the back of the room while running the projector. It is extremely important that the audience be able to see your face. If you stand behind your audience they may be torn between their desire to look at the screen and their desire to see your face while you are talking. Place yourself in front of your audience and place your overhead or slide projector and viewing screen so that you never cross in front of them. See Figure 1–2 for an example.

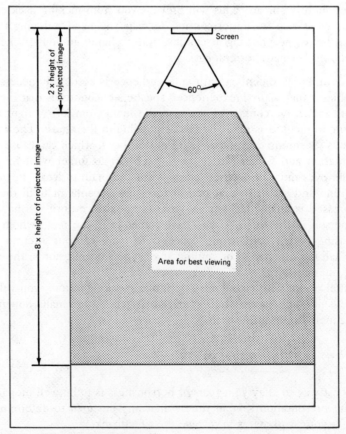

FIGURE 1-2   PRESENTATION SETUP

An alternative to the layout in Figure 1–2 is to place the screen in a front corner of the room. This avoids the blocked view which sometimes results from centrally placed projectors. Keep in mind, though, that wherever you place the screen, the projector must be at right angles to it. Otherwise, the image will be distorted. When the equipment is placed in the corner of the room, you have the freedom to move about without blocking the view of the audience. You can place the foils on the projector without crossing through the path of light, and you can walk to the side of the screen to point to specific information without passing through the light. The use of a pointer enables you to indicate items on the screen without reaching across it.

One last word: Check out your facilities half an hour or so before starting your presentation to make sure that everything is set up properly. This gives you time to add or remove chairs, to provide ashtrays, to adjust the lighting and the temperature of the room, and to do whatever else needs to be done.

PLANNING AND PREPARATION

2

2.1
THE IMPORTANCE OF PLANNING

In Chapter 1, the activities associated with the design and development of manuals were categorized into the following phases:

1. Planning and Preparation
2. Determining and Organizing Content
3. Writing
4. Production
5. Distribution
6. Maintenance

Whether you produce 1 manual or 50 manuals, the phases will be the same. Furthermore, the success of Phases 2 through 6 will depend on the successful fulfillment of Phase 1.

Planning and preparation is an integral part of manuals development, but is one which is often neglected. Consider the results of a multi-story building erected without the aid of an architect's blueprints, or a computer system built without user design specifications. Of course, neither of these examples could occur, because in the first instance there are preventive laws and in the second instance users would not allow it. However, for some reason, people start writing manuals with no attempt at planning.

To give you an example, an experienced manuals writer in one organization received a call one day from a frantic young man in another organization.

"Please help me. I've got to get a document written, published, and distributed by tomorrow, and I don't know what document number I should assign to it."

"What is the Subject about? Where does it best fit in your manual's table of contents?" was the response from the experienced writer.

"Table of contents? We don't have one. In fact, we don't really have a manual yet. This is the first document," replied the young man.

It seems that the young man had been given an edict from management that a certain policy and procedure statement had to be introduced to their staff immediately. At the same time that management made this decision, they also questioned why they had no company manuals, and it was decided then and there that this would be the perfect time to start one. The document the young man was to write would be the first in a series. The organization's management was asking for the impossible. There was no preliminary table of contents, the staff had no binders in which to house the documents, no thought had been given as to what production methods would be used—in short, there was no plan.

It's difficult to imagine this sort of haphazard "planning" taking place for a new building or a computer system, but unfortunately it's often seen in producing a manual. People sometimes do not realize that a successful manual must also be carefully planned.

In most organizations manuals just evolve. Often, this evolutionary process results from the realization that some employees are indispensable because of the amount of knowledge they have. Companies soon recognize the need for documenting this knowledge so that they cannot be crippled by staff turnover, and they consequently realize that this lack of documentation is detrimental to their well-being. Therefore, companies set out to correct this deficiency by putting their procedures in black and white. Look at the following example of this type of evolutionary development of manuals.

WM Company, a leading widget manufacturer, grew rapidly. This growth began when the owner-president hired managers of sales and manufacturing along with the staff for each. Sales grew and these managers were promoted to vice-presidents.

Next, marketing, engineering, purchasing, and finance divisions were created and managers had to be hired for each new department. As the company acquired national status, these managers were also promoted to vice-presidents and the staffs for each of their departments continued to grow (see Figure 2–1).

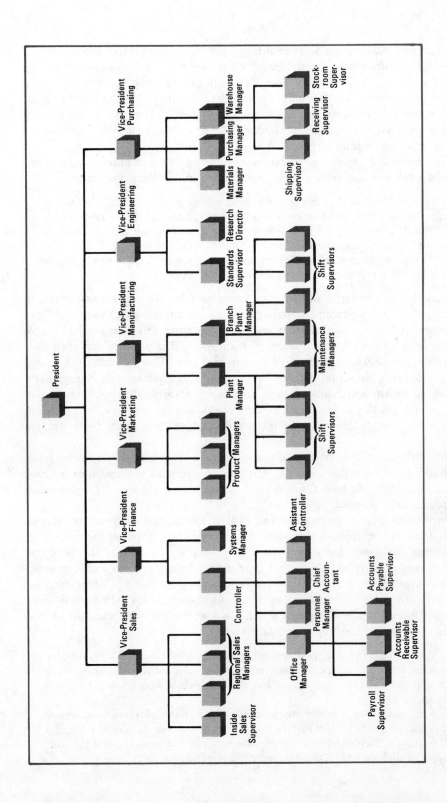

FIGURE 2-1   ORGANIZATION CHART FOR WM COMPANY

It became apparent to the supervisor of engineering standards that the company was growing so rapidly that soon no one would have a clue as to what anyone else was doing. So she had her staff document and develop a manual for this area. The systems manager saw the engineering department's manual and asked his staff to prepare one, too. In this way, the manuals at WM Company began to proliferate with no attention to planning, consistency, or standards. Everyone did his or her own thing and soon WM Company had a dozen poorly written, jargon-filled manuals.

Where does this process end? The answer is: it doesn't, unless steps are taken to end it. Fortunately, with a little planning and foresight, WM Company, and any other company, can prevent this uncontrolled proliferation and can achieve well-written, accessible information. As Peter Drucker said, "The only things that evolve by themselves in an organization are disorder, friction, and malperformance." The point is clear: order and high performance result from planning.

WM Company's manuals grew from the bottom up, but they could have developed from the top down. In *top-down evolution*, the organization's management realizes the need for policy and procedure documentation early on and orders a manual titled, for instance, *Administration*. The administration manual contains policy and procedures germane to the entire organization, and then follows with specific information about each of the organization's departments: systems, marketing, sales, etc. As these divisions of the manual become too large, they are removed and made into separate manuals for each department. This top-down evolution has a much greater chance of achieving organization-wide consistency than does the bottom-up approach. The reasons for this should be fairly obvious. With the top-down approach, you already have material written to some standard and there is a good chance that the manuals which are off-shoots of the original manual will achieve a degree of consistency, particularly with regard to appearance, content, and writing style.

2.2
PLANNING THE MANUALS HIERARCHY
▼

The top-down approach to manuals evolution is the best way of developing a plan for all manuals. The manuals hierarchy (see Figure 2–2) can be planned by calling the chief manual *Administration*. Under this administration manual will fall the manuals required by the functional divisions of the organization. These manuals can then be further subdivided. For instance, a finance manual might generate an accounting and data processing manual (remember the organization chart in Figure 2–1). The accounting manual, in turn, may be subdivided into accounts payable, accounts receivable, costing, and payroll manuals.

As you can see, the manuals hierarchy follows the organization chart almost exactly. There are good reasons for this which can best be illustrated by attempting to organize the hierarchy in a different way. Suppose, for instance, that the

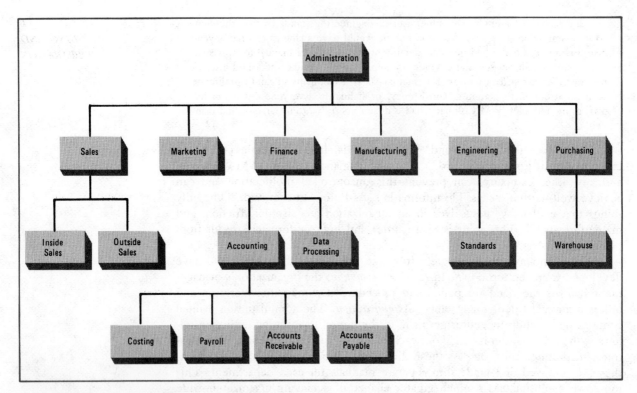

FIGURE 2-2   WM COMPANY MANUALS HIERARCHY

manuals hierarchy were organized along, say, process lines rather than functional lines. One process, then, might be to develop new products. Thus, one manual might contain all the procedures necessary for developing new products. These procedures could be as follows:

1. Marketing—to survey saleability of the new product
2. Engineering—to research the manufacturing feasibility of the new product
3. Accounting—to cost the new product
4. Purchasing—to evaluate the availability of raw materials for the new product
5. Manufacturing—to estimate production times and the number of units needed.

Now, if this case were taken to its logical conclusion, each person who had a hand in the development of a new product would need a copy of that process manual—i.e., the *New Product Development* manual. Thus, the same would be true for each of the other processes performed within the company. The net result of this type of hierarchical arrangement would be that each employee might have 10 to 20 different manuals on his or her desk, depending on how many different processes that particular employee was involved in.

How much simpler it would be if a hierarchy based on functional lines (like those shown in Figure 2–2) were adopted. In this case, an accounts receivable clerk, for example, would have an accounting manual or an accounts receivable manual only. Thus, each person would have a manual with only information pertinent to that individual and his or her functions. Retrieval time would be much less since each person would have all the information he or she needs in one manual rather than in several. Production costs for the manuals would also be less since there would be fewer manuals to produce.

So, having decided that the manuals are going to follow functional rather than process lines, the next thing to do is to plan and organize the content for the chief manual—i.e., the *Administration* manual. Once you have done that, you will have a much better idea as to how many more manuals will follow. Study Figure 2–2 to see how a manuals hierarchy would evolve based on the functions performed at WM Company.

2.3
BUILDING THE MANUALS TEAM
▼

Writers certainly play a leading part in developing manuals, but only with the support of the many other people in the organization who are involved in producing the manuals. A good manuals program requires teamwork, and all members of the team must be aware of their roles and the team's objectives.

In a manuals project certain members of the team will be active during all phases, while others will participate only when their expertise is required. The team may be resourced completely from within the organization, or some outside resources may be contracted. In some cases, team members may wear several hats or they may change hats throughout the project. Table 2–1 on page 34 lists members of the manuals team and their various responsibilities.

WRITER/EDITORS
◆

Who will write the manuals in your organization? Choosing the writer/editors for the manuals team may be the single most important aspect of planning and preparation. As you can see from the following list of responsibilities, writer/editors must be well-rounded individuals. They must:

- be self-starters
- have good planning and organizational skills
- deal pleasantly and effectively with people at all levels of the organization
- be good interviewers
- be analytical
- have good writing and editing skills.

The main things to consider in choosing your writers are: (1) How large will the project be? (2) Who in your organization has the foregoing characteristics that

The Manuals Team	
Team Members	**Responsibilities**
Management	Plans and supports the program Sets and clarifies policies Approves standards Supports standards Helps write documents Helps critique documents Approves documents
Writer/Editors	Help plan program Administer program Recommend standards Gather material Interview authors Organize material Analyze procedures Write and edit documents
Users	Help plan individual manuals Assist in gathering material Help write documents Help critique documents Update individual manuals
Support Staff	Assist in administration of program Support standards Key text Print Distribute manuals
Critique Committee	Critiques documents to ensure policy and procedures are correct

**TABLE 2-1
RESPONSIBILITIES OF
THE MANUALS TEAM
MEMBERS**

will enable them to be good writer/editors? and (3) How quickly do you want the manuals installed? Upon answering these three questions, you will see that you basically have two choices when selecting your writer/editors: permanent staffing or temporary (contract) staffing.

Perhaps a combination of permanent and temporary staff may prove best. However, each organization will have to make this decision for itself. Some factors to consider in making this decision are:

- Do people within your organization have the desired characteristics and are they free to devote their time to manuals development? (Writing manuals should not be considered part-time work.)
- Can these people be trained to write quality manuals? Are there courses available? Can your organization set up its own manuals program?
- Are there consultants available who produce quality manuals? What costs are associated with hiring these consultants?

If your company plans to produce four or more manuals which will require updates on a regular basis, be sure that you have permanent writers on the company staff. If proper care is taken in choosing these writers, this can be the most satisfactory solution.

If writers must be hired from outside the organization, it is a good idea to see each applicant's portfolio which may consist of nothing more than a manual that the applicant has developed; however, it will give you some idea of the applicant's abilities. A word of caution: many company manuals contain either proprietary or confidential information, so don't be too pushy about demanding to see an applicant's work. You must keep in mind that a potential employee who exhibits reticence in displaying a company's manual may be doing so out of loyalty and personal integrity—qualities you want your own employees to possess.

Now, whether you appoint people from within the organization or hire permanent writers, the next thing you must consider (unless your employees are skilled manuals writers already) is how best to train them as manuals writers. One way to do this is to send them to a seminar or a course on manuals writing. Another way to do this is to have them read and study this text. The preferred way would be to do both.

If you have an early deadline for producing your manuals and if you have the financial resources, then probably the best way to get the manuals project going is to hire consultants to do the job. There are numerous consultants in this field and, like any other "experts," there are good ones and there are bad ones. So a little research is in order. Most inquiries will be welcomed by reputable consulting firms. Two ways in which you can find out more about a consultant's abilities are: (1) Study the consultant's publications, including previous work in his or her field, and (2) Find out if the customers the consultant has served in the past were satisfied. Nearly all consultants will provide you with samples of their work, copies of their publications, and recommendations. Check these out carefully before committing yourself to a large expense.

After deciding to hire a consultant, a further decision must be made; that is, whether the consultant should write the manuals or train people within your organization to write them. You may consider utilizing both methods. Manuals are not static; they have to be maintained, reviewed, and revised as policies and procedures change and as new products, services, forms, etc., are introduced. New manuals may need to be developed as well. So it is a good idea to ensure that a few people in your organization have the know-how to continue the manuals program once the consultants have finished their current assignment. If this is not done, sometime down the road you will be back at square one.

One important point to keep in mind when hiring consultants is: Find out exactly what the consultants are promising, and get this promise in writing. This, of course, holds true for any type of consultant, not just the ones who write manuals. This means that consultants must give you a list of deliverables and their dates of delivery. Don't be satisfied with vague phrases such as "improve this," "reduce that," "enhance the other," etc. The consultants should be specific. If they can't give you specifics, chances are they themselves don't know what to deliver. Of course, you may be in a position to list the deliverables accurately. Then, all you want to know from the consultants is "How soon?" and "How much?"

It is worth mentioning that management also has deliverables. The writers (permanent or temporary) need certain items in order to perform their jobs. Management's deliverables are:

- information
- the organization's standards
- cooperation of, and access to, the staff
- adequate accommodation
- the necessary writing tools.

Management should also give their writers an overview of the organization's history, products, organizational structure, lines of command, policy statements, directives, and existing written procedures. If legislation is involved, copies of pertinent acts and statutes should be made available as well.

If you have design standards for your manuals, be sure that the writers are so instructed before they begin. This includes standards for organization, numbering, writing, illustrations, page design, and typing. In other words, give the writers all the facts they need to do the job.

The cooperation of, and access to, staff is particularly important if you have hired consultants to do the writing. The writers should feel free to contact and interview your staff when required. They must be able to see the organization's activities taking place. Your staff will cooperate much better with people they know than with total strangers, so introduce the writers to your staff.

The best way to get total cooperation is to call a meeting of your management and supervisory staff, and have the writers on the project explain exactly what the plans are and what the finished product will do for the company. Plans should be made to free up time, first for interviews and later for staff critiques of the first drafts. Time should also be allocated for team activity/status meetings, which will be the forum for problem solving and reporting.

Once the writing members of your team are chosen, determine where they will work and the tools they will need. Developing manuals is a relatively expensive proposition, but since this is only a small percentage of the total cost, do not scrimp in this regard. Your writers will require adequate space, preferably in an enclosed area with good lighting and air circulation. Their accommodations should be near your management staff, if possible. Tools needed will include reference works and office supplies such as those listed in Table 2–2.

Reference Works and Office Supplies

Reference Works	Dictionary Thesaurus Grammar books Secretary's handbook Financial reports Company documents Legislation etc.
Equipment and Office Supplies	Desks Typewriter, word processor, or text processor Telephone Pens and pencils Paper Dry-transfer lettering Tape Templates Erasers and corrective fluid Glue etc.

*TABLE 2-2
REFERENCE WORKS AND
OFFICE SUPPLIES FOR
MANUALS WRITERS*

CHOOSING THE CRITIQUE COMMITTEE

Subject matter written for manuals must be closely scrutinized before it is submitted to management for approval and publication. The writers of the policies and procedures are too involved to perform this important function objectively. Thus, it is important that a group of people who have had nothing to do with the actual production of the manual be appointed to critique the manuscript. Members of the critique committee must understand the value, scope, and objectives of their role as well as the benefits of their critique to the writers, users, and the organization as a whole.

What, exactly, is a critique? A *critique* is a form of constructive criticism from knowledgeable people, given with a view toward building and improving the text. Constructive criticism includes finding errors and helping to correct those errors as well as pointing out when a written statement is not presented clearly or when information is redundant or missing.

On the other hand, fault-finding, censure, and deprecation are insidious and psychologically destructive. Most people have been the recipients of *destructive criticism* at some point in their lives and know the frustration and anger it causes. In most instances, however, destructive criticism is not deliberate, but merely thoughtlessness, as shown in the following statements: "This is wrong," "You haven't explained this properly," etc. Such statements are ambiguous and ineffective. They only destroy morale, and they certainly don't help to improve anything.

The role of the critique committee is not just to proofread or criticize layout or style. Rather, it is to edit, instruct, and improve the manuscript to ensure that the policy statements and the procedures that are ultimately described in the manual are correct.

Members of the critique committee should be chosen for their knowledge of company policy and operating procedures. To ensure that the critique is thorough for all Subjects, a vertical cross-section of staff should be chosen; that is, staff who perform the activities, supervisors, and management. In addition to this, the subject matter of the manual should also determine who is to be a member of the critique committee. For instance, an employee of the accounting department in a hospital should not be asked to critique a procedure manual for the intensive care unit. Thus, because your critique group must be knowledgeable about the policy and procedure content of the manual, you may feel that a different critique committee is needed for each type of manual. For instance, if you are preparing four or five manuals for a bank, you may require four or five critique committees: one for the loans manual, one for the savings manual, one for the terminal operators manual, one for the mortgage manual, etc.

2.4
SETTING STANDARDS
▼

Standards for each phase of the manuals program need to be developed. Everybody recognizes the need for standards. However, developing them, adhering to them, and monitoring them is a different matter altogether. Two things are necessary to achieve success with standards:

1. There must be a commitment to the standards by all personnel.
2. The standards must be reasonable, flexible, and up-to-date.

These two necessities are interdependent. Commitment must start with top management and trickle down through the ranks. If the administrative personnel in an organization do not believe in standards, neither will their subordinates. Conversely, if the employees see that their supervisors and managers are committed to standards, there is a better chance that the employees will be committed as well. It's a two-way street. Therefore,

- Standards must be practical.
- Procedures to apply the standards must take into account all the necessary processing variations.
- The procedures for application of the standards must be reviewed and updated periodically.
- The standards must allow for a certain amount of deviation.

"Sorry, Thornton, according to Policies and Procedures you don't need a wastepaper basket."

THE GLOBE AND MAIL, *TORONTO*

FIGURE 2-3

Policies, standards, and procedures fit into a hierarchy. A *policy* states a goal in general terms; *standards* define what is to be accomplished in specific terms; and *procedures* tell us how to meet the standards. Look at the following example.

Policy: It is company policy to process insurance claims as quickly as possible.
Standard: Each claim must be processed within six working days of receipt.
Procedure: Day 1—Set up a manual file for correspondence, receipts, etc.
Day 2—Verify data.
Day 3—Adjudicate the claim.
Day 4—Enter data into the computer system.
Day 5—Print the check.
Day 6—Mail the check.

Figure 2–4 also illustrates this hierarchy of policies, standards, and procedures. It shows the standards and procedures that result from the policy, "Have a cohesive, consistent, and efficient manuals program."

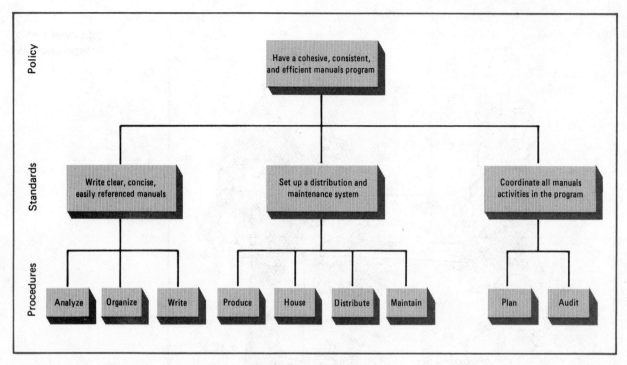

FIGURE 2-4   HIERARCHY OF POLICY, STANDARDS, AND PROCEDURES

2.5

INTERVIEWING—
TECHNIQUES AND TOOLS
▼

The *interview process* is an important method of gathering data when writing manuals. The writer must be certain to get all the facts; otherwise, the manual will suffer.

BARRIERS TO A GOOD INTERVIEW

Robert L. Kahn and Charles F. Cannell, in their excellent book *The Dynamics of Interviewing*, describe five physicians who agreed to tape-record interviews with their patients to see if they could learn anything that would help them in their practices.

When the tapes were played back, each doctor reacted similarly upon hearing his or her own interviews. They were embarrassed, astonished, and even angry at themselves. Their comments were: "I'm not letting the patient tell me what's wrong." "I'm using too much terminology—no wonder he can't understand me." "I'm answering my own questions for the patient!" "That's a good lead she gave me—why didn't I follow it up?"

Before hearing the tapes, each doctor had a different idea of what had occurred during the patient interviews. They all saw themselves as attentive, sympathetic listeners. Now, however, after hearing the tapes, they were interested in improving their interviewing techniques. Basically what the tapes showed was that all five physicians allowed or encouraged their patients to erect barriers which the physicians were not skilled enough to tear down.

There are two main barriers to successful interviews. These are language barriers and psychological barriers. *Language barriers* are due to vocabulary differences. These barriers are evident between different age groups, different geographical groups, and different nationalities. For example, people from different generations might refer to the same thing as being either "cool" or "hot stuff." Britons and North Americans have different meanings for words such as *homely, tube, lift,* and *dough. Psychological barriers* reflect the respondent's inability to answer questions due to such factors as memory failure, emotional forces, and lack of motivation. There isn't much you can do if a person cannot remember something, but you can ask him or her to make a note of it and call you if and when memory returns. As for emotional forces, unless you know the person very well, you probably won't even be aware that these forces are at work.

A particular barrier in the doctor-patient interviews was a lack of motivation on the part of the patients. The fault for this lack of motivation was the doctors'. *Motivational barriers* may be created by interviewers in three ways:

1. Trying too hard to impress.
2. Anticipating answers to questions which results in either (a) not listening to the actual answers or (b) supplying the answers (as one doctor did).
3. Defensiveness or resisting the idea of being "sold" something.

In order to motivate a respondent properly, the interviewer must acquire insight into the interactions which take place during an interview. This is a two-step process. The first step is for the interviewer to understand what forces motivate the respondent. The second step is for the interviewer to acquire the skills needed to put this knowledge to use.

In a business interview it may not be possible to overcome all the psychological barriers. However, the language and motivational barriers can be overcome or at least minimized. There are a number of things which may be done to accomplish this. These are:

1. *Be prepared.* Determine the goals of the interview. Write them down. Next, read all the relevant documentation and determine, in general, what the content of the interview will be. Arrive at a formal statement of the interview's objectives. Once you've determined the content, formulate specific questions. Test each question for its relevance and validity; make sure that no bias is evident. Open-ended questions are superior to closed questions. That is, ask "What types of books do you read?" not, "Do you like to read books?" In other words, avoid questions which can be answered with a yes or a no.
2. *Establish rapport with the respondent.* Prove to the respondent that you are willing to listen. An informal beginning goes a long way to achieving this

goal. Meet the interviewee on his or her own turf. Call the person by name. Ask the interviewee about the family, his or her activities, etc. This helps to break the ice and it softens those first few awkward moments. Be enthusiastic. Be positive.

FIGURE 2-5

3. *Make sure that all physical barriers are removed.* The physical surroundings must be comfortable and should not distract either party. Neither the interviewer nor the interviewee should be put at a psychological disadvantage

because of physical surroundings. For instance, a desk that is situated between the two participants can establish a superior-subordinate relationship which can ultimately affect rapport. A light should not shine in the face of one participant, while the face of the other participant is concealed in its shadow.

Time and interruptions are also physical barriers. Make sure that an appropriate amount of time is allotted for the interview, and do not allow any interruptions.

4. *Lay out the ground rules for the interview.* Prior to the interview, it is important that the interviewer let the respondent know the purpose of the interview. In addition to this, the respondent should know how the information gained from the interview will be used; what, in general, is expected of the respondent during the interview; and why the manuals project (or any other topic) is important and relevant.

5. *Be sincere.* Exhibit warmth, responsiveness, and genuine interest. Most people can spot insincerity. This insincerity will only cause resentment. The interviewer must be perceived by the respondent as being understanding and being appreciative of the respondent's point of view.

6. *The respondent must feel free from pressure or coercion.* The interviewer must not pass judgment on the respondent's ideas and opinions.

7. *Avoid complicated language.* For an interview to be successful, there must be a common base to the language used by the participants. This means that the interviewer must shift gears to mesh with the respondent, if necessary. The interviewer must be able to discuss the respondent's area of expertise in the respondent's own terms.

SUPPLEMENTING THE INTERVIEW QUESTIONS

Despite all your careful planning for the actual interview, you will need to supplement your questions by probing a little more deeply. Perhaps a question you ask will trigger another question that you hadn't thought of earlier. Perhaps the respondent's answer will provoke another question which, again, you hadn't thought of earlier. Or, perhaps the respondent's answer will be incomplete. Supplementing a question can be achieved in the following ways:

1. Indicate interest and understanding by nodding, smiling, or using phrases such as "uh huh," "I see," etc. Such phrases often encourage the respondent to tell more.

2. Use neutral phrases which indicate that more information is required: "Tell me more," "Why?" "Anything else?" etc.

3. Pause. This will encourage the respondent to fill in the empty space with further comments. Be careful with this technique, however. You must not allow the pause to go on for so long that it makes the respondent uncomfortable.

If the respondent's reply doesn't answer the question, accept the answer which has been given, but pose the question again; rephrase it. For example:

Interviewer: How did the game go?
Interviewee: We had a great time.
Interviewer: Well, it's wonderful that you enjoyed it so much. But did you win?

As shown in this example, how you pose your original and supplementary questions is of great significance. The answer desired by the interviewer was actually the result of the game, not how it went. Thus, the supplementary question would achieve the desired response.

Sometimes an interviewee may evade a question or will not give you an accurate response. For example:

Interviewer: Why do you want a new stereo system?
Interviewee: It's outdated.
Interviewer: Does it no longer perform well?
Interviewee: Well, it doesn't play loudly enough, and the turntable is slightly warped.

In the latter example, the reply to the interviewer's first question was quite general, almost evasive. Although the first answer may have been true, it was not specific. The interviewer recognized this and therefore posed the second question. The interviewer then received the detailed response needed.

When you have all your questions formulated, guess at a few of the evasions that might occur. Then try to reformulate the questions so that you receive the information you need. All of this seems like hard work, but the rewards are great.

TOLS

The most valuable tool for interviewing is the tape recorder. An inexpensive cassette recorder eliminates errors that may result from anticipation, faulty hearing, note-taking, or poor memory. Skill at shorthand is also a very helpful tool. Sketches, flowcharts, blackboards, and other visual aids also can be used as tools to help the interview. However, the most important tool is the right attitude!

The face-to-face interview is the best and most commonly used method of collecting data for manuals. However, two other tools can also be used to supplement the interview. These are observation and questionnaires. Observation should be used when describing particularly complex procedures: for example, those involving equipment or machinery. For instance, a procedure for documenting how to power a computer up or down should be observed to ensure that no steps are left out—that could have disastrous results. It may also be necessary to make sketches of the equipment and the positions of dials and switches. A pulp and paper mill on the west coast has an excellent method of recording particularly difficult start-up operations after equipment failures occur. Their methods analyst records the start-up with a camera and later the employees review the photographs to see if there might be better ways of handling the problems which occur. If a particular piece of equipment continues to fail, a camera is trained on the equipment full time to see if they can analyze the problems. Using a camera ensures that your observations are recorded permanently.

Questionnaires are used to obtain data from respondents who it would be impractical to interview personally, either because of their large number or because they are so far physically removed. Nevertheless, an attempt should still be made to interview some of the respondents to achieve the interaction which is lacking in a questionnaire. Just as preparation is the keynote of a good interview, so it is also with a good questionnaire. The difference between the two is that the questions in a written questionnaire *should* be designed for short answers, since in this case the respondents, lacking the crucial interaction, will quickly lose patience with what they perceive as essay-style questions.

2.6
DETERMINING THE MANUAL'S PHYSICAL REQUIREMENTS

▼

In order to plan for the latter stages of a manuals project—whether the project consists of the production of one manual or many manuals—thought must be given to the manual's physical requirements. Three questions may be asked:

1. Is there a requirement for the manual to be produced using a specific medium?
2. What design specifications and style of binder will be used?
3. How many manuals will be produced and distributed?

THE MEDIUM

◆

The majority of manuals are printed on paper, but there is no reason that they have to be. Manuals can be produced on microfilm, microfiche, computer files, or audio-visual cassettes.

Throughout this book, the assumption is sometimes made that the manuals under discussion are printed on paper. However, the same principles apply to other media as well.

Lately, there has been a lot of talk about the "paperless office." One effect of this concept could be the production of manuals on terminals with two data sets—one used as the master manual for approved documents and one used as the working copy for new material and revisions. Only the writer would have access to the working copy, and only once a policy or procedure had been approved would it be copied onto the master data set. Read-only access would then be allowed to those users who required the procedures to do their jobs. Users would only need to log on at the nearest terminal, call up the master alpha index, and key in the document number of the Subject required. It would still be necessary to print the material and store one copy on-site and one copy off-site for emergency back-up. Considering the cost of paper, a number of video display terminals in work areas may be the more economical position to take in the office of the future.

BINDER AND
DESIGN SPECIFICATIONS

◆

If your manual is to be produced on paper, the following physical aspects must be considered: binder specifications, cover design, type size and style, page design, tab dividers, etc.

Each of these items is discussed in Chapters 6 and 7. In addition to considering these physical requirements, however, you must take into account requirements unique to each department. Perhaps in one department a heavier-than-average paper is required for durability. If a manual in a particular department is to be referenced throughout the day, perhaps an easel-type binder is needed. (An *easel binder* is one that bends at the middle and can be stood up so that information can be easily seen.) Types of manuals which fit into this style of binding are secretarial guides, terminal operator manuals, laboratory manuals, and programming manuals.

HOW MANY MANUALS
TO PRODUCE AND DISTRIBUTE?

◆

Once you've chosen the medium, the binding requirements, the cover design, the page specifications, etc., you must determine the number of manuals to produce and distribute. In order to determine how many manuals to distribute, ask the question: Is this manual necessary to the employee's job or function? Once you have the answers, you will know how many manuals to produce and to whom your manuals should be distributed. Remember, that along with those employees who need the manual to perform their jobs, you should also provide those employees' supervisors with the same manuals. In other words, if the accounts receivable clerks need the accounting manual to perform their jobs, then the accounts receivable supervisor must have it as well. Similarly, if the accounts receivable supervisor also needs the manual to perform his or her job, then the accounting manager or whoever is the supervisor's boss should also have a copy of the manual.

2.7
PAGE DESIGN
AND FORMAT

▼

The design of the manual page is of crucial importance to manuals writers, typists, and ultimately the users of the manual.

Figure 2–6 illustrates the page used for the Nadir, Inc., policy and procedure manual. The *page format* or *page design* of this manual page has a number of limitations. In particular, this page, which is used throughout the entire organization, has not been designed to accommodate variable information. That is, no provision has been made on the *masthead*—the top of the page which contains preprinted information—for the department's name nor for the title of the man-

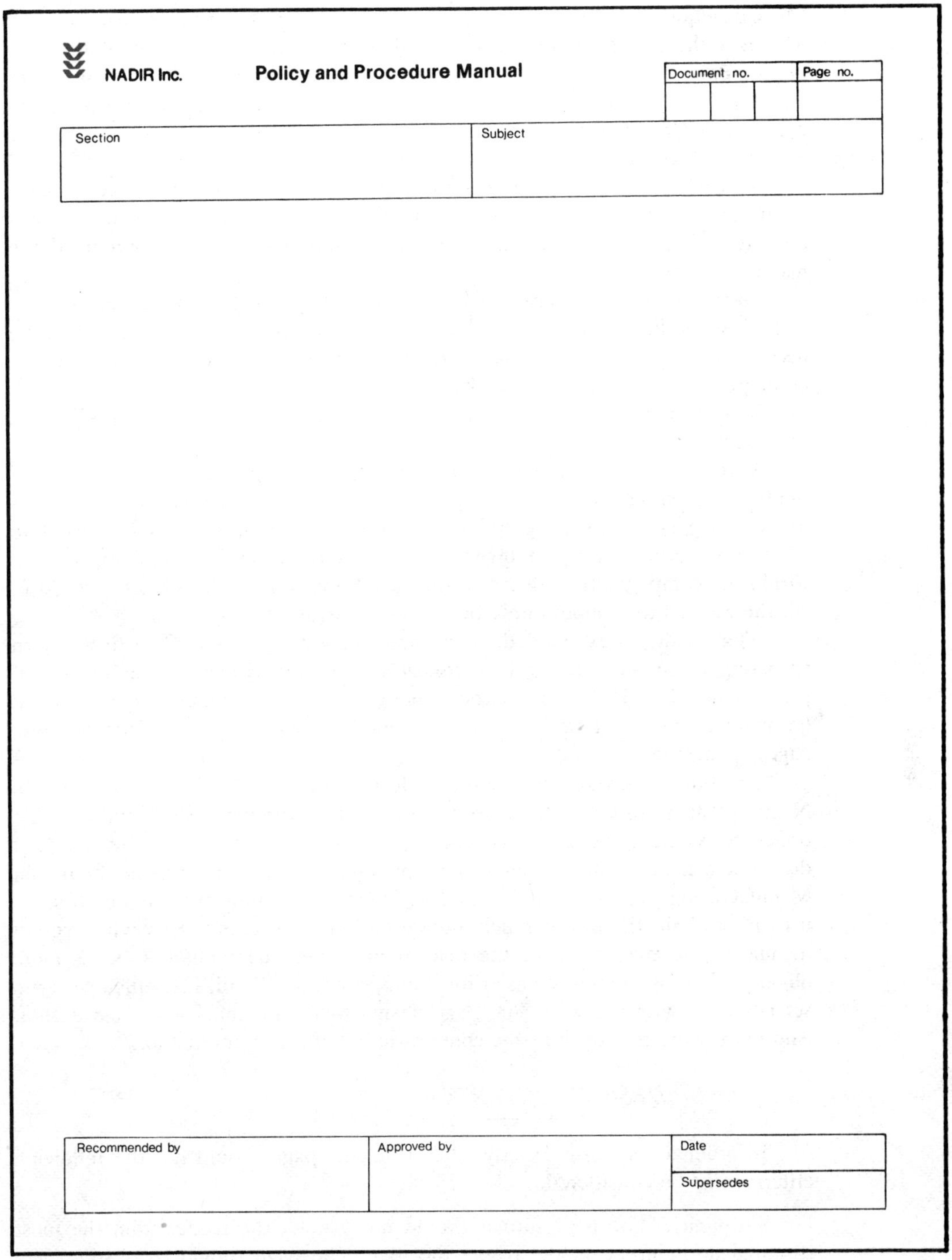

```
┌─────────────────────────────────────────────────────────────────────────┐
│  ☰                                                    ┌──────────┬──────────┐  │
│  ☰  NADIR Inc.    Policy and Procedure Manual         │Document no.│ Page no. │  │
│  ☰                                                    │     │    │    │     │  │
│                                                       ├─────┴────┴────┴─────┤  │
│  ┌──────────────────────────────────┬──────────────────────────────────┐    │
│  │ Section                          │ Subject                          │    │
│  │                                  │                                  │    │
│  │                                  │                                  │    │
│  └──────────────────────────────────┴──────────────────────────────────┘    │
│                                                                           │
│                                                                           │
│                                                                           │
│  ┌──────────────────────┬──────────────────────┬────────────────────────┐  │
│  │ Recommended by       │ Approved by          │ Date                   │  │
│  │                      │                      ├────────────────────────┤  │
│  │                      │                      │ Supersedes             │  │
│  └──────────────────────┴──────────────────────┴────────────────────────┘  │
└─────────────────────────────────────────────────────────────────────────┘
```

FIGURE 2-6   NADIR'S ORIGINAL PAGE DESIGN

ual. Consequently, this information has to be typed at the top of each page—wherever there is sufficient room. Furthermore, the arrangement of the pre-printed data hinders, rather than aids, retrievability. For example, the document number does not stand alone and cannot be seen at first glance. In addition, each set of two-digit numbers in the document number has to be typed in its own individual box (not easy to do) along with the page number.

The title, "Policy and Procedure Manual," is self-evident and redundant. It does not answer the simple questions: Policy for what and for whom? Procedure for what and for whom? The title should describe the content of the manual.

From a functional point of view, the use of typing guides (natural margins and tab stops) has not been considered. Therefore, the typed information can be inserted wherever the individual typist thinks it looks best. If the typist uses the outer perimeters of the masthead as guides, margin allowance is not sufficient for back-printing and punching, which means that every manual is bulkier than necessary.

As for the *foot*, or the bottom of the page, having signatures there can create the following situations: (1) Employees may phone the signators to ask questions or make suggestions; (2) Doubt can be raised concerning a policy or procedure when a signator leaves the organization or is transferred to another position within the company. In addition to this, the Supersedes field is worthless. After all, the manual user should only be concerned with what is current.

What Nadir, Inc., needed, then, was a new page design. The first step in preparing a new page design is to collect and analyze as many different manual pages as possible. If there is any one page particularly impressive, then it should be analyzed to see if there are any adaptable design elements. One of these pages appears in Figure 2–7.

The Four Star Manufacturing page design in Figure 2–7 is much better than Nadir's. It features a simple, open masthead; and although some of the rules are unnecessary and although space could have been utilized more effectively, it does not contain a lot of useless information. When comparing the Four Star Manufacturing page with the Nadir, Inc., page, notice how much more effective it is. First of all, the title is much more descriptive—it tells exactly what type of manual the item is. Second, the placement of the document number is more obvious, thereby making it easier for the user to find. Third, it is much easier to set tab stops with the Four Star page design than with the Nadir page design. And fourth, the foot of the page contains only pertinent information.

DESIGN CRITERIA

In order to establish exactly what a manual page should do, the following criteria must be considered.

Simplicity. The page format should not distract the reader from the most essential information on the page—the text. The page should be aesthetically pleasing.

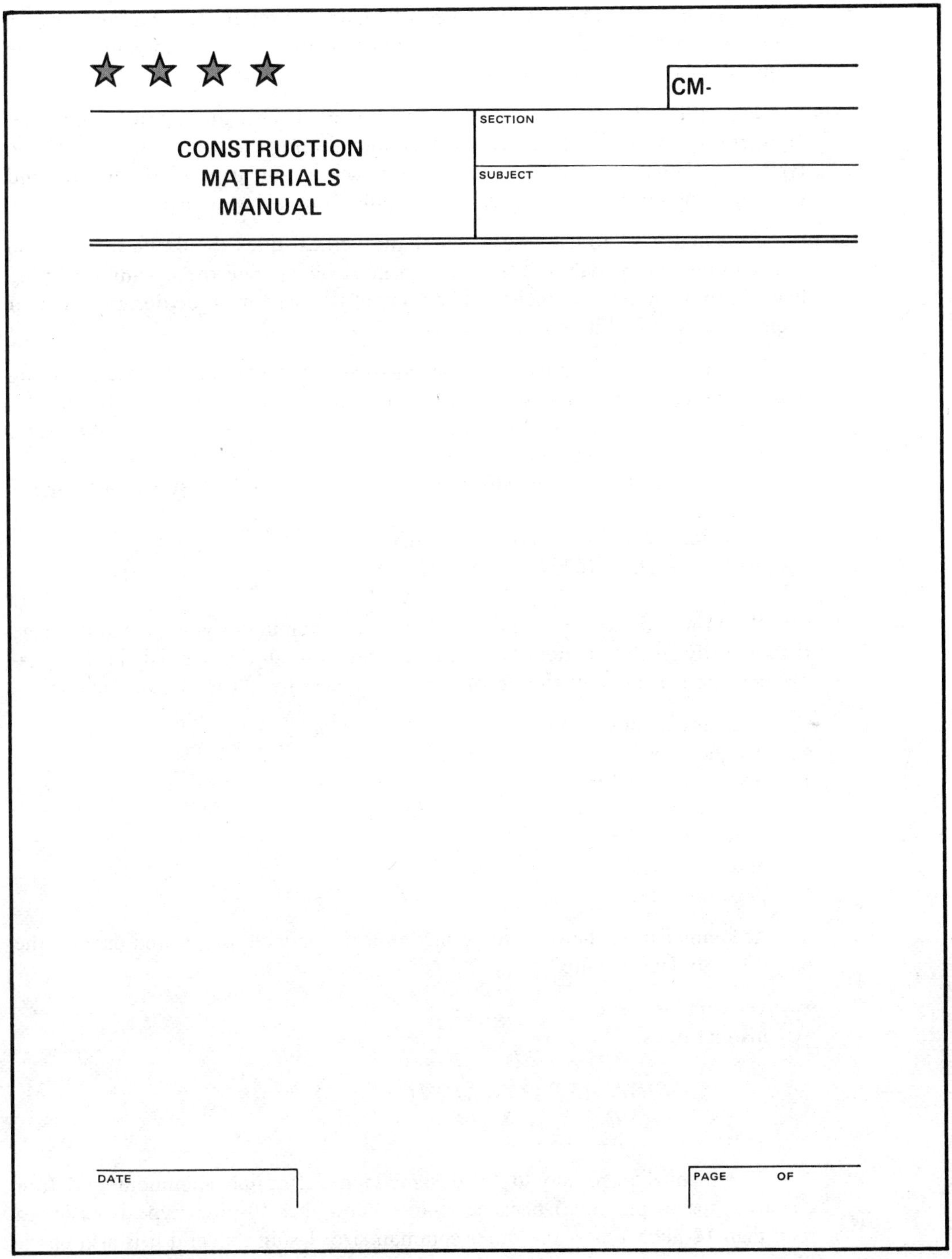

★ ★ ★ ★

CM-

CONSTRUCTION
MATERIALS
MANUAL

SECTION

SUBJECT

DATE

PAGE   OF

FIGURE 2-7   FOUR STAR'S PAGE DESIGN

Retrievability. There should be sufficient preprinted data on the page to offer immediate identification of the subject matter. The arrangement of the preprinted data must be logical.

Flexibility. The page must accommodate all variable identification data (department names, manual names, etc.) without altering the common format or the typing standards. The typing standards for each layout, particularly margins and tab stops, should not have to change radically from layout to layout.

Readability. The use of horizontal and vertical rules should be minimal, so as not to impede readability. The design must incorporate the optimum reading line of approximately 4½ inches. The body of the page must be designed so that there is plenty of white space.

Functionality. Margins must be adequate to accommodate back-printing and punching. The format should allow for a logical hierarchy of data. The design must use a minimum of space for the masthead and foot of the page, thereby leaving as much room as possible for the body of the page—for insertion of the text. The design must also incorporate prearranged tab stops for typing.

IDENTIFYING COMMON AND VARIABLE ELEMENTS

With these design criteria in mind, the next step in designing a manual page is to identify all the elements which are common to all the manuals in the organization, no matter what the department or subject matter is. These include

- company name
- company logo
- document number
- section title
- subject title
- date
- page number.

Accommodation then has to be made for the variable preprinted data on the page. These data include

- department names
- manual titles.

DESIGN ARRANGEMENT AND RATIONALE

The manual page should be designed on a 10-pitch alignment grid (ten character spaces per inch) because studies show that 10-pitch type is easier to read than 12-pitch type—the other common size. Using this grid it is also possible to create natural tab stops as part of the design for text typing.

The Masthead. The most important elements on the manual page are the document number, the section title, and the subject title.

Since the document number is the first thing the user seeks after looking in the subject index, it needs to be placed in the most conspicuous place: the top right-hand corner of the page (see Figure 2–8). Standing alone (with no boxes) and plenty of white space surrounding it, the number truly stands out. A typing dot indicates where to start typing the document number.

Section and subject titles are necessary to clarify what the number represents. For this reason they are positioned to be the next data elements seen by the user. The titles appear in their logical hierarchical order. There is sufficient space for the insertion of a 45-character section or subject title. In fact, there is enough space for a two-line title, although this is considered taboo. A good writer should be able to think of a two- or three-word title which can easily be indexed. The longest titles are those which include a form name and number.

The top left-hand corner of the masthead is reserved for information which does not affect retrievability. This includes the common organizational data which would be preprinted: company name and logo. Here, also, space is allowed for the variable preprinted data, namely department name (although there isn't one on the Nadir page) and manual title. The area used for the manual's title should accommodate a three-line title in the size of the type shown in Figure 2–8. One hairline rule divides the section and subject titles and one bold rule divides the masthead from the body.

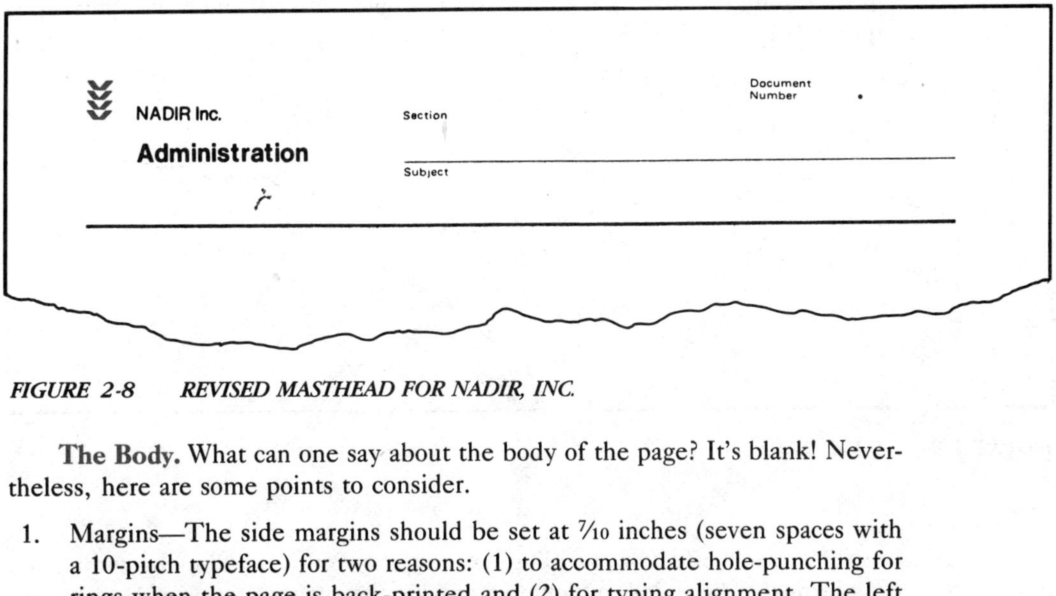

NADIR Inc.

Administration

Section

Subject

Document
Number

FIGURE 2-8   *REVISED MASTHEAD FOR NADIR, INC.*

The Body. What can one say about the body of the page? It's blank! Nevertheless, here are some points to consider.

1. Margins—The side margins should be set at $7/10$ inches (seven spaces with a 10-pitch typeface) for two reasons: (1) to accommodate hole-punching for rings when the page is back-printed and (2) for typing alignment. The left margin for typing is directly aligned with the left side of the company logo and with the left edge of the dividing line between the masthead and the body of the page. The typing of primary captions is begun here. The right margin for typing is aligned with the right edge of the dividing line be-

tween the masthead and the body. Typing is not extended beyond this margin.

2. Tab stops—The first tab stop, which will be used for secondary captions (discussed in Chapter 4), is aligned with the manual name. The tab stop for the body of the text is directly aligned with the preprinted fields: Subject and Section.

3. First and last typing lines—The first typing line for the text of any document is indicated by a typing dot which is placed 2⅙ inches from the top of the page. Although there is no typing dot at the bottom of the page, the last typing line for the text should be about half an inch above the date box.

The Foot. The foot of the page should contain the date and the page number only (see Figure 2–9). Because the date is not considered a vital piece of information since the material in a properly maintained manual always reflects current policy and/or procedure, it is located in the bottom left corner of the page. With the typist in mind, the date is placed so that it can be typed one space below the preprinted caption—starting at the left margin.

The page number is located in the lower right corner where it can be easily seen as the reader approaches the end of the copy. Because the number is always shown as 1 of 1, 2 of 5, etc., it acts as an instruction to the reader to either continue to the next page or stop. This page numbering system is also useful because it assures the user that all the pages are there. The page number is typed on the same line as the date and is aligned directly under the preprinted caption: Page.

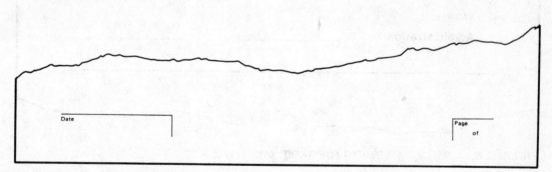

Date

Page

of

FIGURE 2-9   FOOT OF PAGE

The overall effect of providing these typing guides is uniformity throughout each manual. These design elements provide the typist with a simple and accurate method of setting margins and tab stops. Typing standards are discussed in detail in Chapter 6.

In Figure 2–10 the page format shows the margins, tab stops, and typing dots for the new Nadir, Inc., form. Figure 2–11 shows the same page with text.

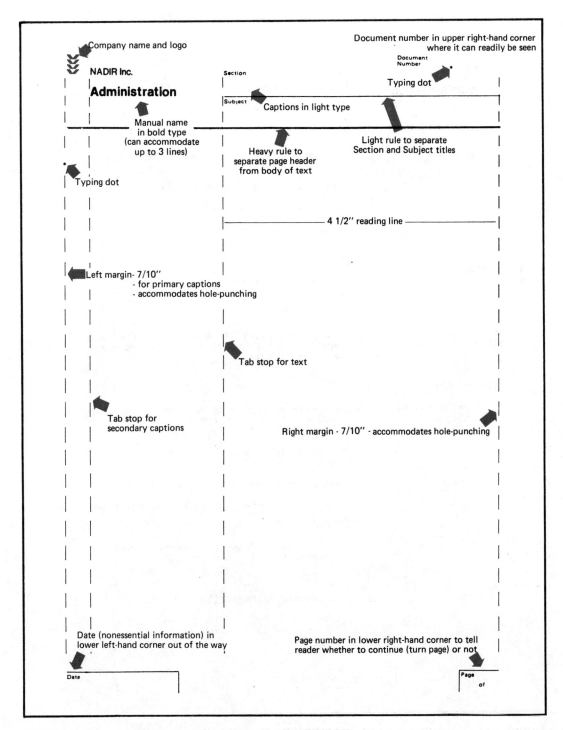

Company name and logo

Document number in upper right-hand corner
where it can readily be seen

Document
Number

NADIR Inc.

Section

Typing dot

Administration

Subject

Captions in light type

Manual name
in bold type
(can accommodate
up to 3 lines)

Heavy rule to
separate page header
from body of text

Light rule to separate
Section and Subject titles

Typing dot

———————— 4 1/2" reading line ————————

Left margin- 7/10"
- for primary captions
- accommodates hole-punching

Tab stop for text

Tab stop for
secondary captions

Right margin - 7/10" - accommodates hole-punching

Date (nonessential information) in
lower left-hand corner out of the way

Page number in lower right-hand corner to tell
reader whether to continue (turn page) or not

Date

Page
of

FIGURE 2-10   NADIR, INC.—NEW PAGE AND DESCRIPTION

54

NADIR Inc. **Administration**	Section Employee Benefits	Document Number 04-03-05
	Subject VACATION ENTITLEMENT	

LENGTH OF VACATION

All employees must take at least two weeks vacation per year.

Length of uninterrupted vacation may not

- be less than one week in length
- be longer than one year's entitlement.

ILLNESS DURING VACATION

If an employee is sick during vacation, a request may be made to deduct days sick from attendance credits. The equivalent number of days are reimbursed to vacation credits.

PAID HOLIDAY DURING VACATION

If a paid holiday (04-03-04) occurs during vacation, the day will not be deducted from vacation credits.

CASH PAYMENTS

Termination of Employment

Upon termination, cash payment for existing credits will be made according to Personnel policy (03-02-07).

Credit deficits must be repaid in cash by the employee.

In Lieu of Vacation

Cash payment (in part) may be made if

- an employee has sufficient accumulation

  and

- the required number of weeks of uninterrupted vacation are taken.

See example on Page 4.

Date
July 30, 19--

Page
3 of 4

FIGURE 2-11   NADIR, INC.—NEW PAGE WITH TEXT

UNIVERSAL INDEX

▼

If the number of manuals in your organization is increasing, you may experience some difficulty in discovering which manual you need in order to reference a particular query. True, once you've found the manual, the retrieval devices will speed you to the information. But how do you determine which manual you need? The answer is a *Universal* or *Combined Alphabetic Index*—which is a combination of the alphabetic keyword indices of all your manuals.

Unless you have an automated system which will alphabetize the entries for you, this Universal Index will likely remain a utopian ideal. A software package which would allow you to tag and locate whatever you want for the index while you are inputting your material on the keyboard would be very convenient. However, the amount of work needed to develop and maintain a Universal Index might not be justified if the index has to be constructed manually.

One thing to keep in mind if you are seriously considering a Universal Index is that each manual will require a unique identifier code. The reason for this is that you could have as many duplicated document numbers as you have manuals. In other words, your accounting manual may have a document number 02–03–04 and so might your marketing manual, etc. When issuing codes such as these there sometimes is a tendency to give department initials to distinguish one manual from another. For example, Systems Administration could be SA; Marketing could be MA; Accounting, AC; etc. However, the preferred method is to give the manual a two-character alpha prefix (in contrast to the department abbreviations) starting with AA and working systematically to ZZ. This would give 676 unique prefixes—more than enough for most organizations. If your organization is very unusual and you have more than 676 different manuals, you could have a three-character alpha code, allowing for 17,576 different prefixes.

The reason for assigning sequential rather than meaningful prefix codes is that you will eventually experience difficulty in assigning properly meaningful codes. For instance, if you've already called Systems Administration SA, what do you call Sales?—it will have to be SL or something similar. And what, then, if you need a Systems Library manual? In the long run, it's easier to start at AA and avoid the abbreviation headaches.

Alphabetic prefixes for manuals are preferred to numeric prefixes since there is no confusion over which digits represent the manual and which the Subject. Additionally, alphabetic prefixes allow for many more combinations than do numeric prefixes (676 vs. 100).

The alpha prefix should only appear in the Universal Index. It should not be printed in the subject index of the individual manual nor on the manual page. There are several reasons for not having the prefix on the manual page and in the individual manual's subject index. The main reason is that the prefix is not a retrieval device *within* the manual. In other words, once the user has the manual, the prefix is just extraneous information. The printing of the prefix may also hinder retrievability just by being there. When using word or text processors, codes can be inserted which will suppress or prevent printing of the prefix on the manual page and in each individual index and which will shadow print the prefix (double impression) to make it stand out in the Universal Index.

The Universal Index has a side effect which is quite beneficial. It will point to any duplication of subject matter. This is a common problem which often arises when the number of manuals in an organization increases; that is, repetition of Subjects in more than one manual. This repetition is wasteful in terms of the extra paper, duplication time, distribution and maintenance effort, and especially in the effort expended in actually writing the material. This reason alone may justify the creation of a Universal Index.

Another advantage of the Universal Index is apparent when it becomes necessary to revise information in Subjects that affect other Subjects or other manuals. A Universal Index will assist in retrieving those Subjects so that this activity can be carried out more efficiently.

While on the topic of documents affecting other documents, a few words about cross-referencing are in order. Cross-referencing between manuals, Tabs, Sections, or Subjects should be done only when it is absolutely necessary, because cross-referencing must be maintained. For example, if document number 02–02–03 references document number 02–02–04, the latter will probably also reference the former. Then, if the document number of either Subject is changed, the cross-reference will also have to be changed. If the text of either subject is amended, then both may have to be updated. This, if it's done too often, can become an administrative nightmare, particularly if you are not able to perform "search and change" functions automatically.

When cross-referencing between manuals is absolutely necessary, do not reference the document number. Reference only the subject title and the manual since the names of the manuals and Subjects will change less often than the document numbers. This will not cause users any undo hardship since all your manuals will have alphabetic subject indices. It will therefore take the users only a few extra moments to look up these Subjects in the index.

If you don't yet have the hardware and/or software with the facility to provide an automated Universal Index but are planning to acquire it, there are some requirements that the chosen system should have. It must

- be able to produce an alphabetic subject index for each manual
- be able to produce a combined alphabetic index for all (or a combination of) the manuals
- have "Bill of Materials" capability. This means that the system must be able to identify all procedures referenced in any other procedure
- have "Where Used" capability; that is, you must be able to tell the system to identify all procedures in which a procedure specified by you is referenced.

You may also wish to have your automated Universal Index available as a forms index and a reports index. The requirements would then be:

- to produce a numeric forms (reports) index for each manual
- to produce combined forms (reports) indices

- "Bill of Material" capability for procedures which reference forms (reports)
- "Where Used" capability for forms (reports) referenced in procedures.

2.9
MILESTONES
▼

In the past, large stones set at the edge of roads were marked to indicate distances in miles between two points of travel. Today, the word *milestone* indicates a significant event in the development of an endeavor, career, or lifetime.

When writing a manual, it is wise to set milestones to help plan activities, to budget time and costs, to control the project, and to set standards. These milestones, once established for the production of one manual, will remain the same no matter how often you travel the manuals development road. However, the time you take to travel to a particular milestone or to the end of a project may vary. To illustrate this, if you travel from home to work each day using the same route, the distance in miles will always be the same. However, if the traffic is particularly light one day, or if it rains or snows, the time it takes will differ. So it is with any project. The time you take will vary depending on the size of the manual you are writing and the size of your budget. Budget may be the chief factor, for the amount of money you have to spend will determine the size of your production team and the equipment and production methods you will use.

Manuals writers should set up a schedule to show the important milestones of a project. Arrival at a milestone indicates that a particular activity in the production of a manual has been completed, and variances from original estimates can then be tracked. Some of the more important milestones are indicated in the following list:

- Determining content
- Organization (preliminary table of contents)
- Writing
- Keying
- Proofreading and correcting
- Illustration preparation
- Index preparation
- Printing
- Distribution

Although each of these activities should be indicated on its own in the schedule, they may, in fact, be combined when they are actually carried out. Writing and keying the content of the manual are perhaps the best examples of when two activities may be combined. If manuals writers have good typing skills, and if a word processor or computer terminal (with text processing capabilities) is used, the combination of authoring and keying will decrease the total amount of time. It will also save time in the proofreading and correction stages, for the writers will be proofing and correcting simultaneously as they go along.

Some other activities may also overlap. For instance, there is no need to wait until *all* the content of a manual has been keyed before printing some of the documents. Writers can just begin writing the next document or producing illustrations. Similarly, all the documents need not be keyed and printed, or typed, before proofreading has begun. However, since it's faster to give the typist a number of documents at once, the work should be planned and batched accordingly.

There are some activities which must be completed before the subsequent activity can be begun. Printing is one of them. If you intend to publish the entire manual at one time, you should send all the documents to the print shop at one time rather than piecemeal. Similarly, if you intend to publish one Tab or one Section of the manual at a time, all the documents in the Tab or Section should be sent to the printer together. The same applies to distribution. All the assembly and distribution work is best done at one time.

MANUALS SCHEDULE

A *bar chart/calendar schedule* is one of the best formats for graphically showing the milestones (see Figure 2–12). Milestones are plotted at the outset of the

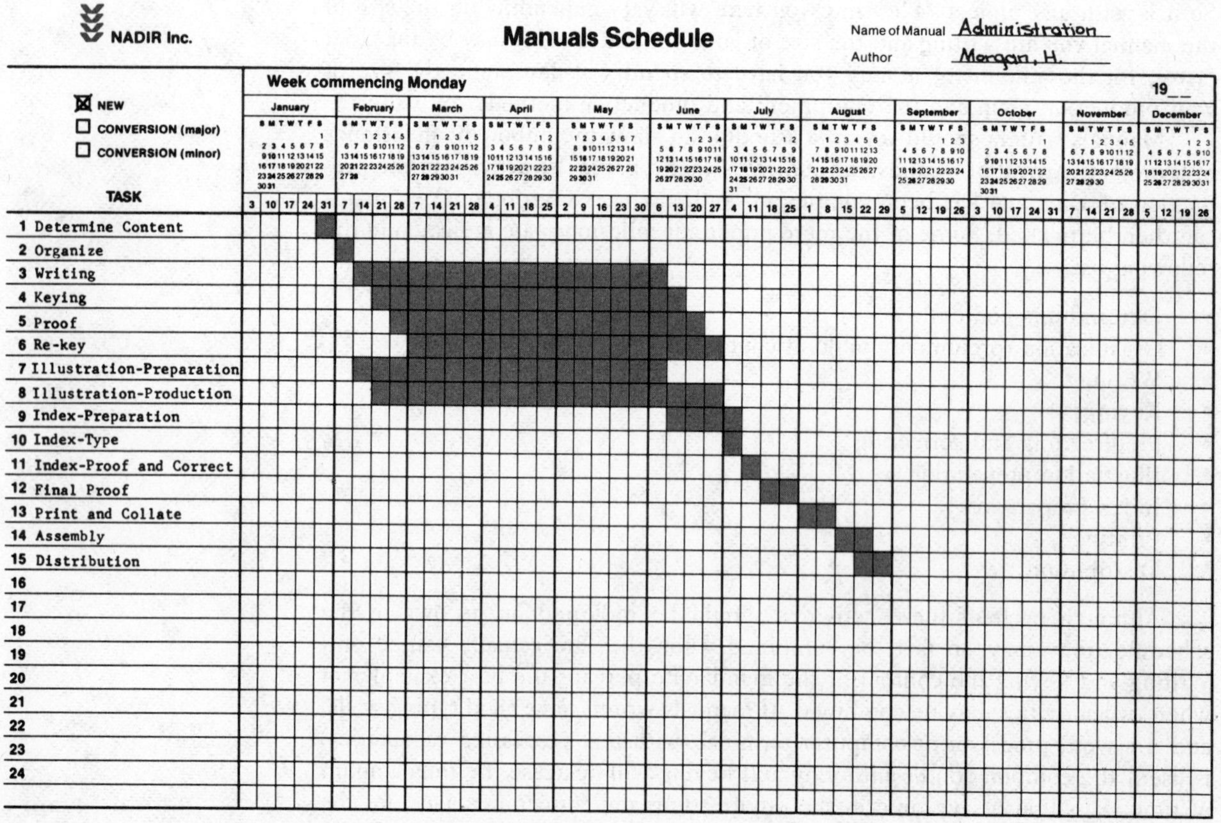

FIGURE 2-12   MANUALS SCHEDULE (FORECAST)

project as a forecast. Management should recognize that this forecast, especially for the first manual, should be flexible and subject to change. However, the more often these milestones are plotted, the more accurate the forecasts become. Volume (how many pages can be written and keyed per day) and skill levels of the entire team will become known factors because they are based on past experience.

Prepare one schedule for each manual showing the milestones and the forecasted time each activity will take. The schedule should be hung on a wall for the entire team to see and the actuals (actual times) should be recorded as the project progresses. This will show how far off target the forecast is and will thus assist in the preparation of the next schedule. The milestones on this schedule will also act as indicators for the ordering of supplies and equipment (lead times are always important) and the hiring of temporary staff, if required.

In Figure 2–12, the schedule for the writing of an administration manual is plotted. There is only one writer involved in its production. Note that the bar chart tasks represent elapsed time; they do not represent person-weeks of effort.

Setting and charting milestones can be justified from a psychological point of view. Knowing where you are and how far you have to go is important to a team. But this type of information should also be recorded and stored for use in future forecasts and for setting standards for the performance of tasks. You should record the obstacles which had to be removed or detoured in order to reach the milestone. If you are able to recognize where you went wrong in your forecast and the problems encountered, you may be able to permanently overcome those obstacles in future endeavors.

MANUALS
PROGRESS REPORTS

The *manuals progress report* is more specific than the manuals schedule. The manuals progress report summarizes production for each writer on the team. It can be used for several writers working on the same manual or on different manuals. The report can be completed weekly or monthly according to management's needs. Remember, the manuals progress report indicates where you are in relation to your schedule, but the schedule itself is only an estimate.

This report is easily maintained if you produce it electronically: i.e., on a word processor or on a computer terminal. It can be maintained by one individual or each author can maintain his or her own portion. In Figure 2–13, the report has been produced electronically and because of this, extra lines can be inserted in order to show notes for the figures shown. These lines can be deleted if not required the next time. If you were designing this form on paper, it would be advisable to leave space between each manual in case notes are required. Otherwise, a covering narrative may be needed.

With a report of this type, management can see at a glance how each manual in the project is going, how the writers are performing, problems that have occurred, and whether the project is on schedule.

WMC — MANUALS PROGRESS REPORT — Reporting Period: June 6 – 10, 19-- (5 workdays)

MANUAL: WRITER: START	COMPLETION DATE Orig. Est. DD,MM,YY	COMPLETION DATE Curr. Est. DD,MM,YY	PAGES AT COMPLETION Original Estimate New	Rev	Tot	Current Estimate New	Rev	Tot	PAGES COMPLETE (of Current Estimate) Report Period New	Rev	To Date New	Rev	Total	TIME ELAPSED (days)
-1-	-2-	-3-	-4-	-5-	-6-	-7-	-8-	-9-	-10-	-11-	-12-	-13-	-14-/-15-	-16-
AA H.J.A. 01.02.--	31.08.-- (152 work days)	31.08.--	149	315	464	315	90*	405	32	12	189	90	279/405 68.9%	94/152 61.8%
AB J.G.C. 02.05.--	31.10.-- (131 work days)	30.11.-- (175 work days)	0	250	250	**	312	312	29		29		29/312 9.3%	30/175 17.1%
AC M.H. 11.07.--	15.07.--	30.06.--	87	102	102	102	130	130	37		46		46/130 35.4%	13/38 34.2%
AD M.H. 25.07.--	30.09.--		*** 31		31									

*NOTE: Revised pages decreased when rewritten to standards. Project may be completed ahead of schedule but no change to completion date at this time.

**NOTE: New pages increased from 250 to 312 (24.8% increase). Further revisions to current estimates may be required if any new material comes to light. Now that analysis and organizational phases are complete, an increase in pages completed will occur in the next reporting period.

***NOTE: The Data Entry Manual (AD) has been in a maintenance mode for over one year. Approximately 31 new pages (6 documents describing Format Preparation) are scheduled to be written by M. Howell who is also assigned to the AC manual. A priority must be established by management.

FIGURE 2-13   MANUALS PROGRESS REPORT

The following is a description of each field illustrated in Figure 2–13.

Reporting Period. The exact dates which are being reported should be indicated clearly. If one of the days were a statutory holiday, report only four workdays.

Column 1: Manual, Writer, Start. *Manual* refers to the two-digit alpha code for the administration manual. The codes were described in Section 2.8 (Universal Index). No other manual will have this code.

Writer refers to the writer's initials. If by chance you have two employees with the same initials, you could add a number to them; e.g., H.J.A.1.

Start refers to the date that the gathering and organizing of material began. The standard expression for date used in this report is day.month.year.

Column 2: Completion Date—Original Estimate. Indicate in this field your original estimated date for completion of the manual.

Column 3: Completion Date—Current Estimate. If, during the writing stages, you have reason to revise your estimated date of completion, complete this field showing your new estimated date of completion.

Column 4: Pages at Start. This field represents the total manual pages, including controls, which exist at the beginning of the project or when progress reports are first introduced to the project.

Column 5: New Pages at Completion—Original Estimate. This field should indicate the number of new pages which will be written, including the control pages.

Column 6: Revised Pages at Completion—Original Estimate. This will be the same figure as in Column 4 unless you think that some of the Subjects or pages will be deleted, in which case the number will be lower. Of course, there is the possibility that the pages are so badly written that a complete rewrite is necessary. In this case, "O" should be filled in and explained in a note.

Column 7: Total Pages at Completion—Original Estimate. Insert the sum of Columns 5 and 6.

Column 8: New Pages at Completion—Current Estimate. If during the writing stages you discover additional material for the manual and this new material will change the number of pages, insert the new figure.

Column 9: Revised Pages at Completion—Current Estimate. This field should be the same as Column 6, unless it is discovered nearing completion that the number of revised pages will be fewer. This should be explained in a note as in the illustration.

Column 10: Total Pages at Completion—Current Estimate. This field should show the sum of Columns 8 and 9.

Column 11: New Pages Complete (of Current Estimate)—Report Period. Indicate the number of new pages completed during the report period.

Column 12: Revised Pages Complete (of Current Estimate)—Report Period. Indicate the number of revised pages completed during the report period.

Column 13: New Pages Complete (of Current Estimate)—To Date. Add the pages completed during the report period (Column 11) to those completed for previous reports. This is a running total.

Column 14: Revised Pages Complete (of Current Estimate)—To Date. Add the pages completed during the report period (Column 12) to those completed for previous reports.

Column 15: Total Pages Complete (of Current Estimate)—To Date. Add both new and revised pages completed to date; i.e., Columns 13 and 14. Show this figure over the total estimated (Column 10). Multiply this fraction by 100 to show the total time expended to date expressed as a percentage.

Column 16: Time Elapsed. Show the number of days expended on the project to date over the total number of days estimated to complete the project (Column 2). Multiply this fraction by 100 to show the total time expended to date as a percentage of completion.

2.10
TASK
CHECKLIST
▼

When you have carried a couple of manuals projects through from inception to installation and maintenance, you will get a better idea of the chronology that must be followed. This book is divided into chapters based on the functions performed in the manual production process. However, this does not mean that everything in Chapter 3 must be done before everything discussed in Chapter 4. Indeed, in some cases, particularly those involving outside sources—printers and binder suppliers—it may be necessary to order things many weeks in advance of the target date you have set for publication. This long lead time means that early on in the manuals project, you must start thinking about such things as how the manual is to be stored, distributed, and maintained. Obviously your distribution list must also be confirmed before you can order from outside suppliers.

Table 2–3 presents a task checklist in approximately chronological order for the completion of a manual from the ground up. This list should not be taken as binding nor should strict adherence to the chronology necessarily be followed. The important thing is to have a little foresight so that you don't find yourself twiddling your thumbs while you wait for someone else to finish a task which is holding you up.

Standards need to be set for each item on this list prior to executing the task itself. That way, the manuals developers don't have to think about how to perform the task every time and they can thus devote more energy to the development itself rather than *how* to do the development.

Task Checklist for the Production of Manuals

1. Gather material.
2. Organize material.
3. Create a working table of contents.
4. Set up a schedule.
5. Form a critique committee.
6. Investigate and choose a medium.
7. Design a manual page, title page, and cover.
8. Determine the distribution of the manual.
9. Determine the number of binders, tab dividers, and pages.
10. Order the binders, tab dividers, and paper.
11. Write the material—first draft.
12. Prepare illustrations.
13. Translate material to standards (typing, word processing, etc.)
14. Proofread and correct the first draft.
15. Prepare unnumbered documents (Amendment Record, Management Endorsement, etc.)
16. Critique the first draft.
17. Prepare second draft based on the critique.
18. Proofread and make changes for the second draft.
19. Critique second draft (and third and fourth, if necessary).
20. Obtain approvals.
21. Produce illustrations.
22. Prepare indices.
23. Arrange printing, collating, and punching.
24. Set up distribution system.
25. Set up channels for requesting revisions and processing amendments.
26. Set up master and control copies of the manuals.
27. Set up files for transmittals, original documents, approval forms, and archives documents.
28. Schedule reviews.
29. Schedule spot checks (audits) for manuals.
30. Schedule user education.
31. Distribute and maintain the manuals.

TABLE 2-3
CHRONOLOGICAL ORDER
FOR COMPLETION OF
MANUALS

ORGANIZATION

3

3.1
GATHERING SUBJECT MATERIAL
▼

All the preimplementation tasks have been completed: the team is established, the manuals to be written have been identified, the critique committees have been chosen. Now it's just a matter of getting started—a most critical period. However, manuals writers often find themselves stymied at this point. Where to start? How to start? These are the questions often asked. The best advice is to just dig in and follow some tried and true methods.

First you should gather all the available subject material. This activity often helps you to recognize anything that is missing. Furthermore, having something tangible in your hands with which to work offers a psychological benefit. Your sources for this activity are the

- files of the administrative and support staff of the involved department
- personnel department, which will provide you with job descriptions, organization charts, and policy documents
- systems department, which will provide you with flowcharts and/or data flow diagrams, and input and output documentation

- legal department, which will provide you with local by-laws or legislation which may affect policy and procedure
- manuals which already exist
- forms department, which will provide you with forms used by the individual departments.

You will no doubt think of other items to add to the following list of documentation: policy statements; operating procedures; illustrations of equipment; organization charts; floor plans; written standards; flowcharts or data flow diagrams; decision tables; brochures and catalogs; price lists; vendor-supplied documentation; and variable data forms and constant data forms. *Variable data forms,* which contain blank spaces to record, analyze, transmit, and store variable data, include form letters, envelopes, contracts, and letterheads. *Constant data forms* are preprinted without fill-in space or variable choice of data. They may include items such as business cards, instruction sheets, pamphlets, contract conditions, signs, notices, posters, and booklets.

READ AND INDEX

Reading all the gathered documentation may seem time-consuming at this stage, but it will help familiarize you with the subject matter which must later be written. This *read-in period* is similar to the indoctrination period during which newly hired employees familiarize themselves with the organization. Manuals writers also require a read-in period for each manual written. Read and index the material only—do not evaluate it yet.

Indexing at this point consists of assigning subject titles to the documentation you have gathered and writing the subject titles on index cards. Subject titles should be considered preliminary since they will change as more investigation is done. You may consider just making lists of the subjects you have identified, but it is much less time-consuming to write each subject title on an individual 3″ × 5″ index card. And as new subjects are identified, cards can simply be added. The cards can then be divided into like groups, and individual subjects or even entire groups can be shuffled about during this stage.

ORGANIZE

Organizing the material for one manual is much the same as organizing material for another manual. The methods are alike whether it be an accounting manual or a child-care manual.

Once you have listed all your subjects on the index cards, divide and group the subjects according to content. Beware! Do not divide the subjects by category of documentation; for example, into groups of forms, memos, flowcharts, etc. Thus, when the term *subject content* is used, it means *personnel* policies and procedures, *accounting* policies and procedures, *security* policies and procedures, etc.

The following example is used as a classroom exercise in organization. The assignment is to organize this partial list of subjects for a cookbook.

Table of Equivalents	Broiling
Braising	Buying Fish
Cuts of Meat	Roasting
Deep Frying	Salami Platter
Wiener Schnitzel	Variety, Color, and Texture of Hors
Sweet and Sour Pork	d'Oeuvres
Carving	Preparation for Freezing
Rack of Lamb	Thawed Food
Emergency Meals	Types of Freezers
Boiling	Storage of Eggs
Boning Fish	Table of Substitutions
Freezer Packaging and Wrapping	Flavors
Smoked Oysters	Ham Cornets
Baked Snapper	Guide to Freezing Times
Table of Measures	Cleaning Fish
Omelettes	Test for Freshness, Eggs
Methods of Cooking Meat	Steaming
Broiled Fillets of Sole	Lobster Thermidor
Egg Foo Yong	Pickled Herring
Unsuitable Foods for Freezing	Oysters Mornay
Quiche Lorraine	Ham and Onion Flan
Beef Wellington	Staples
Beef Stew	Herbs
Spices	Stuffed Mushrooms
Lamb Kebobs	Meal Planning

As you read through this list, you will begin to note potential categories of items. There may be items on the list with which you are not familiar, or which seem to have no relationship to others, or which seem to fit into more than one category. This is to be expected. You will find this is the case no matter what type of manual you are writing. However, try using the following categories for this example:

Seafood	Methods of Cooking
Meat	Eggs
Hors d'Oeuvres	General

The *General category* will contain everything that doesn't fit conveniently into one of the other categories. Keep in mind that this breakdown is only tentative and will undoubtedly change as organization is begun and input is received from others.

Assuming you have written each of the items listed on an index card, you will now be able to sort the cards into their appropriate categories. The result should look something like this:

Seafood

Cleaning Fish	Boning Fish
Buying Fish	Baked Snapper
Broiled Fillets of Sole	Lobster Thermidor

Meat

Methods of Cooking Meat
Cuts of Meat
Beef Wellington
Lamb Kebobs

Wiener Schnitzel
Sweet and Sour Pork
Rack of Lamb
Beef Stew

Hors d'Oeuvres

Variety, Color, and Texture
   of Hors d'Oeuvres
Smoked Oysters
Salami Platter

Pickled Herring
Oysters Mornay
Ham Cornets
Stuffed Mushrooms

Methods of Cooking

Braising
Deep Frying
Boiling

Steaming
Broiling
Roasting

Eggs

Storage of Eggs
Test for Freshness, Eggs
Omelettes

Egg Foo Yong
Quiche Lorraine
Ham and Onion Flan

General

Table of Equivalents
Carving
Emergency Meals
Guide to Freezing Times
Table of Measures
Unsuitable Foods for Freezing
Herbs
Spices

Freezer Packaging and Wrapping
Preparation for Freezing
Thawed Food
Types of Freezers
Table of Substitutions
Flavors
Staples
Meal Planning

The categorization you come up with may be slightly different from this. Purposely, a number of items have been inserted which might fit into more than one group. For example, Oysters Mornay could go into the Seafood group rather than Hors d'Oeuvres; Salami Platter could go into Meat rather than Hors d'Oeuvres; and Ham and Onion Flan could go into Meat rather than Eggs. It is largely a matter of personal choice.

Now that you have sorted each and every card under a major division, you can review these categories and add, delete, or recategorize them as you see fit. For example, originally Pickled Herrings and Smoked Oysters were under Seafood. It was decided these should be under Hors d'Oeuvres and the cards were rearranged accordingly. Similarly, Boning Fish and Cuts of Meat had been placed under General, but later were transferred to the Seafood and Meat categories, respectively.

During this exercise you will no doubt come up with other ideas, such as a major category which you have missed altogether or combining two or more major categories into one. Let your original categories remain intact until you have received input from the rest of the staff and until you have identified all possible subjects for the manual.

    Now that you have shuffled the Subjects around and categorized them, you should type up lists, double- or triple-spaced, with no more than one category per page.

    You should then let all the people involved with the manual have their first chance at adding subjects to the lists and making suggestions for reorganization. The best method of gathering all input is to distribute copies of your lists to all concerned. The lists will aid the others in understanding the method you are using to organize the material, and will help them to recall items that are missing. Advise everyone that you will be conducting a brainstorming session; allow them time to prepare for it. Each staff member should make a list of the activities he or she performs and of the forms used each day. These should not be described at this point, only identified. Even the simplest activities should be noted, such as taking telephone messages and filling in forms.

    During the actual brainstorming session, blackboards or flipcharts are extremely useful for jotting down subjects and activities. Again, the index cards will prove helpful because you may decide to do some major shuffling of subjects. It will probably take one or two weeks to determine the content of one manual for which no previous documentation has been written.

3.2
DIVIDING MATERIAL INTO TAB, SECTION, SUBJECT HIERARCHY

    You now have a fairly extensive list of subjects which you and your colleagues have divided into a number of major categories or primary divisions. These primary divisions of the manual are called *Tabs*. The name is easy to remember because it is between these major divisions that tab dividers will be inserted. At this point you will begin to break down each of the Tabs even further. Each Tab is broken down into secondary divisions called *Sections*. Each Section is then divided into tertiary divisions called *Subjects*.

    Usually each Tab in the manual will have a Section called "Introduction." The *Introduction Section* may contain any Subject which in itself is of an introductory nature, or any Subjects which do not seem to fit under any other classification, or Subjects that stand alone. If no Subjects of this nature exist, you do not need an Introduction Section.

    Looking back at the lists of primary divisions in the cookbook, a general division has been identified, which becomes the *General Tab*. This General Tab is always the first Tab of a manual and contains information which is of a general nature. In other words, if you were writing a data entry manual, the General Tab would contain information that affects the entire data entry department, such as administrative duties. The General Tab would also be a catch-all for Sections or Subjects that do not fit into any of the other Tabs.

Return to the cookbook and the major divisions that have already been identified. Classify and group the Subjects in the General division into like Subjects. Only two groups are readily identifiable: Freezing and Tables. But once the hierarchical structure of the manual and the content of the General Tab and Introduction Sections is understood, it becomes evident that one of the previously identified major divisions, Methods of Cooking, can also be included as a Section in the General Tab.

Consequently, the General Tab may look something like this:

Tab	Section	Subject
General	Introduction	Meal Planning
		Emergency Meals
		Table of Measures
		Table of Equivalents
		Table of Substitutions
	The Well-Stocked Kitchen	Staples
		Flavors
		Herbs
		Spices
	Cooking Methods	Roasting
		Boiling
		Deep Frying
		Braising
		Broiling
		Steaming
	Freezing	Types of Freezers
		Unsuitable Foods
		Preparation
		Packaging and Wrapping
		Guide to Freezing Times
		Thawed Food

- Tables may have been a Section on its own but the Subjects were placed under Introduction because there were only three tables and they were of an introductory nature.
- Meal Planning and Emergency Meals were two stand-alone Subjects (at this point in time), and so they, too, were placed in the Introduction.
- Carving was taken out of General and appears under the Meat Tab. It was decided that Carving was not general to the entire cookbook.
- The common characteristic of staples, flavors, herbs, and spices is that they are all necessary to a well-stocked kitchen, thereby prompting the creation of the Section with that name.

Each one of the primary divisions (Tabs) is studied in the same manner. No doubt you will amend, delete, and add as you progress into the writing stage. Remember—retain flexibility. Nothing should be set in stone.

3.3
THE
NUMBERING SYSTEM
▼

The importance of retrievability in manuals has been discussed and the point made that the alpha subject index is the key to the manual. However, the numbering system is the key to the key, for it is the *numbering system* which identifies each and every document.

There are two qualities which any numbering system for manuals must have: simplicity and flexibility. It must be simple so that the user of the manual can quickly retrieve the information required. And, because a manual is not static (it changes as policy and procedure changes), the numbering system must also be flexible. It must allow the writer to add pages, Subjects, or Sections, and delete them with as little disruption to other documents as possible. This is one reason why manuals are not permanently bound, but housed in loose-leaf binders.

The following numbering system, used and recommended by most authorities in the manuals field, is simple and flexible. Similar numbering systems are also used in many organizations all over the world for file systems and inventory control systems. Each document (Subject) is assigned a unique six-digit number which is divided into three sets of two digits each, separated by dashes (for example: 02–03–06). The first two digits represent the Tab (primary division), the second two digits represent the Section (secondary division), and the third two digits represent the Subject (tertiary division).

Tab	Section	Subject
02	03	06

This system allows for maximum flexibility: 99 Tabs within a manual, 99 Sections within a Tab, and 99 Subjects within a Section. Theoretically, you could have a total of 970,299 Subjects in any manual. However, it is most practical to try to limit a manual to a maximum of about nine Tabs; each Tab to about nine Sections; and each Section to about nine Subjects. Even this, if taken to its extreme, would mean a manual containing 729 Subjects, each of which could be several pages in length. Any manual which has more than 350 back-printed pages is unwieldy.

It is often asked whether six-digit numbers aren't difficult for users to remember. Wouldn't it be easier to use an alphanumeric mix? The answer to this is that no user should be expected to remember a document number for any longer than the length of time it takes to go from the alpha subject index to the document. However, users do become so familiar with their manuals (as they use them each day) that they do remember the document numbers or the number of the Tab in which the particular Subject is housed. The numbers seem to be easier to recite than an alphanumeric mix, and the more often the numbers are repeated aloud by the user, the more likely they will be remembered. But in any case it is not necessary to memorize document numbers since each Subject in the manual will be included in the index.

Not everyone will be able to adopt this numbering system at once. There may be some other system already in place, or there may be constraints placed upon you by management. In this case, get permission to try out the six-digit numbering system on one manual; when that works out, you can gradually convert your other manuals.

As for page numbering, the best system is to number each page within each Subject, for example: Page 1 of 5 or Page 3 of 4, so that the user will know when a page is missing and where the end of each Subject occurs. This modularity also reduces page number revisions. At all costs, avoid numbering your manual pages consecutively throughout the manual. Consecutive page numbering presents you with a Hobson's choice when revisions are required: you can either renumber the whole manual, or you can introduce page numbers such as 8A, 8B, etc. Either way, you'll have a maintenance nightmare.

Now apply the numbering system to the General Tab of the cookbook.

Tab	Section	Subject
01 General	01 Introduction	01 Overview (Discussed in 3.8)
		02 Meal Planning
		03 Emergency Meals
		04 Table of Measures
		05 Table of Equivalents
		06 Table of Substitutions
	02 The Well-Stocked Kitchen	01 Overview
		02 Staples
		03 Flavors
		04 Herbs
		05 Spices
	03 Cooking Methods	01 Overview
		02 Roasting
		03 Boiling
		04 Deep Frying
		05 Braising
		06 Broiling
		07 Steaming
	04 Freezing	01 Overview
		02 Types of Freezers
		03 Unsuitable Foods
		04 Preparation
		05 Packaging and Wrapping
		06 Guide to Freezing Times
		07 Thawed Food

Other Tabs such as Hors d'Oeuvres, Meat, and Seafood would be numbered in a similar fashion, the difference being that the Tab numbers change (e.g., Hors d'Oeuvres—Tab 02, Meat—Tab 03, Seafood—Tab 04, etc.). There is one last step to be performed before the cookbook table of contents is established. That is to add in certain preassigned document numbers and prescribed text headings, as described in the following sections of this chapter.

THE FRAMEWORK
OF THE MANUAL
▼

Since one aim of a manuals program is consistency, all the manuals within an organization should be designed so that they are as alike as possible. Not only is it more economical to do so, but more importantly, consistency helps the user. You don't want the user to open one manual and find the index in the back; to open another manual and find the index in the front; and to open a third manual and find no index at all. It is important that users become familiar with their manuals and be able to use them with ease. This means that all your manuals should have basically the same type of binder, the same page design, and a similar organizational framework.

Table 3–1 illustrates a simple, effective, and efficient framework that has been chosen for manuals development. You can easily change it around to suit your own preferences or your organization's needs. The important point is to keep a *common* framework for *all* your manuals.

Framework for All Manuals

Unnumbered Documents:	Title Page
	Amendment Record
	Management Endorsement
Numbered Documents:	Table of Contents
	How to Use This Manual
	Subject Index
	Forms Index (if necessary)
	Reports Index (if necessary)
Body of the Manual (Tab 01, 02, etc.)	
Appendix (Tab 99)	

TABLE 3-1
MANUAL FRAMEWORK

TITLE PAGE
◆

Perhaps it is too obvious to state that the title page should be the first item in a manual. Some experts recommend putting the management endorsement or the amendment record first, and some manuals do not even have a title page (it being deemed superfluous since the title will be on the binder spine and cover). However, a title page can serve several purposes other than identification. If it is printed on heavy card stock rather than ordinary bond, it can protect the following pages; the amendment record, which is updated by the user, can be printed on the reverse side of a title page, thereby providing a durable writing surface; and last, but not least, a title page looks attractive and professional.

As far as design is concerned, keep the title page simple and keep the title short. There is no need to print the word "manual" anywhere; it would be redundant. Company name and logo, department name, and the manual title are all that's required. The heaviest type should be used for the title. Keep in mind that you can print your title pages in bulk, thereby saving money and the time and effort of reordering. This will allow flexibility as you identify new manuals in the future. To do this, you would only print the constant data on the page. Variable data may be printed in-house or inserted using a stencil or dry transfer.

Constant Data	Variable Data
Company Name	Department Name
Company Logo	Manual Title

Figure 3–1 is an illustration of a typical title page.

THE AMENDMENT RECORD

The amendment record is required for updating a manual. It is printed on the reverse side of the title page and is used to record each update received. This form can be bulk-printed at the same time as the title page. The amendment record, like any other well-designed form, should always have user instructions, and its design and control should comply with the standards of your forms department. See Figure 3–2 for an example of an amendment record.

MANAGEMENT ENDORSEMENT

Each manual should have a message from someone in a position of authority to the manual holders. This message, or management endorsement, ensures that the policies, standards, and procedures contained in the manual are carried out by the staff. It provides visible evidence that the manual and its contents are backed by management. The signator should be a chairperson, president, or vice-president to provide maximum impact. The management endorsement should state very briefly:

- the aim of the manual
- the basis for the manual (i.e., industry standards, internal standards, company policy, legislation)
- responsibilities
- that unauthorized revisions and copies may not be made
- distribution information.

The management endorsement could be placed on either the organization's letterhead, as in Figure 3–3, or on the manual page. This endorsement should be tailor-made for each manual in the program.

TABLE OF CONTENTS

The first numbered document in the manual should be the table of contents. It lists the Tab, Section, Subject name and location (document number)

74

 Widget
Manufacturing
Company

Finance
Division

Accounts Receivable

FIGURE 3-1   TITLE PAGE

NADIR Inc.   **Amendment Record**

Instructions:
The number in the preprinted column of this Amendment Record corresponds to the Transmittal Number on the Manuals Document Transmittal.
1. Record the date on which each update (Transmittal) is received next to the appropriate number on the Amendment Record.
2. Report any missing updates to the manuals coordinator.

Trans-mittal No.	Date Received	Trans-mittal No.	Date Received	Trans-mittal No.	Date Received	Trans-mittal No.	Date Received
1		26		51		76	
2		27		52		77	
3		28		53		78	
4		29		54		79	
5		30		55		80	
6		31		56		81	
7		32		57		82	
8		33		58		83	
9		34		59		84	
10		35		60		85	
11		36		61		86	
12		37		62		87	
13		38		63		88	
14		39		64		89	
15		40		65		90	
16		41		66		91	
17		42		67		92	
18		43		68		93	
19		44		69		94	
20		45		70		95	
21		46		71		96	
22		47		72		97	
23		48		73		98	
24		49		74		99	
25		50		75		100	

FIGURE 3-2   AMENDMENT RECORD

Widget
Manufacturing
Company

This manual has been written to document the policies and procedures of the Accounts Payable Department of WMC's Finance
Division. Its purposes are to

- provide an easily referenced source of information
- state and clarify policy
- define duties, responsibilities, and authority
- formalize operations
- provide a line of communication between staff and management.

Every document in this manual has been approved by WMC management.
Responsibility for adhering to the policies and procedures in the
manual lies with every staff member. It is the task of supervisors
and managers to ensure that this responsibility is carried out.

Distribution of the manual is on a need-to-know basis. Information
regarding maintenance and distribution of this and other company
manuals may be obtained from the manuals coordinator. Neither this
nor any other company manual may be revised, altered, or copied
without written authorization from the manuals coordinator.

A.B. Cooper

A.B. Cooper
Vice-President, Finance Division

FIGURE 3-3   MANAGEMENT ENDORSEMENT

for each document or Subject in the manual. The Subjects are listed in their order of appearance. The table of contents provides a cover-to-cover review of the contents and the organization of the manual. As the first Subject in the Controls Tab of the manual, the table of contents carries the document number 00–00–01. (Sometimes the Controls Tab is referred to as a Section, since it contains only a few documents.) A page from the table of contents for a data processing manual is illustrated in Figure 3–4.

The table of contents is not intended to serve as a major retrieval device for the manual (the alpha subject index does that). For this reason, it may only be necessary to have a table of contents to the Section level, since anyone wishing to look up a specific Subject should do so in the index rather than in the table of contents. However, during the time between issuing the first documents in the manual and the time the manual is complete, you may not have an index published. So include a table of contents to the Subject level for this period of time. As a general rule you would publish a few documents at a time, rather than wait to publish the whole manual at once, since if you wait until all the material is written before you publish, some of it is bound to be out-of-date when you do so. Not only that, there is a danger that the users will lose interest in the project if results are too long in forthcoming.

If you wish to list all the Subjects (or Sections) you have identified but not yet published in your table of contents, do so, but identify them for your users by putting an asterisk by the location number. Then, at the bottom of the page, put an explanatory note; something like, "No content issued at this time," is appropriate.

All this is not to say that you cannot have both an alphabetic subject index and a table of contents to the subject level—you can. However, a typed (double-spaced) table of contents for a manual can be 10 to 12 pages long. Updating both the index and the table of contents each time you publish a new Subject can present a maintenance problem.

HOW TO USE THIS MANUAL

The document *"How to Use This Manual"* contains a standard set of instructions for manual users. It describes

- the numbering system
- the indices
- how to find a document
- the table of contents
- amendments and updates to the manual.

This is an extremely important document because it transmits the idea that the manual has been written for the user's benefit and reminds the user that his or her input is required to ensure its authenticity. These "How to Use" instructions are located in the Controls Tab at 00–00–02, where they can easily be seen. Figures 3–5 to 3–8 show a "How to Use" Subject for an administration manual.

78

NADIR Inc.

Data Processing

Section
Controls

Subject
TABLE OF CONTENTS

Document Number 00-00-01

*No content issued at this time.

Date
August 19, 19--

Page
3 of 4

FIGURE 3-4   TABLE OF CONTENTS

NADIR Inc. **Administration**	Section Controls	Document Number 00-00-02
	Subject HOW TO USE THIS MANUAL	

SUMMARY

This manual is divided into

TABS — major divisions, physically separated by numbered tab dividers

SECTIONS - divisions within a Tab

SUBJECTS - divisions within a Section.

NUMBERING SYSTEM

Each document (Subject) has a unique 6-digit number. This number is divided into 3 sets of 2 digits which are separated by dashes.

EXAMPLE: 04 - 02 - 03

TAB   SECTION   SUBJECT

INDICES

These are the keys to your manual. They are located in the "Controls" Tab and are separated from all other Control documents by a red divider marked "Indices."

Alpha Subject Index

This index (00-00-03) shows every Subject in the manual in alphabetical order and the document number at which it may be located. To aid retrievability, Subjects are referenced at least 3 ways.

Forms Index

This index lists all forms referenced in the manual in numerical order according to form numbers. When more than one reference is made to a form, the document number for the primary reference is given. Secondary references are indicated as "See also...."

Unnumbered forms, sample letters, and non-Nadir firms are listed separately in alphabetical order according to name.

The Forms Index is located at Document Number 00-00-04.

Date
December 8, 19--

Page 1 of 4

FIGURE 3-5   "HOW TO USE" DOCUMENT—PAGE 1

80

NADIR Inc.

Administration

Section
Controls

Subject
HOW TO USE THIS MANUAL

Document
Number 00-00-02

| LOCATING A DOCUMENT | Document numbers appear in bold print on the upper right corner of each page (see top of this page). To locate a Subject/Form: |

1. Refer to the Indices and locate the Subject/Form you need.

2. Note the Document Number indicated.

   EXAMPLE: 04-02-03

3. Turn to the tab divider marked 04 and within this Tab find Section 02 and Subject 03.

TABLE OF CONTENTS — The table of contents (00-00-01) is intended to give a cover-to-cover overview of the manual contents and organization. It lists contents of a Tab to the Section level. (Subjects are listed in the Alpha Subject Index.)

AMENDMENTS — Registered manual holders are instructed to keep their manuals up-to-date.

All users of manuals are urged to contribute ideas and suggestions for revision to their supervisors.

Manuals Document Transmittal — All new or revised documents are sent to the registered holder of the manual under cover of Manuals Document Transmittal, Form 0192. Transmittals are numbered consecutively. Instructions for use are printed on the form. See illustration on page 3.

Date
December 8, 19--

FIGURE 3-6   "HOW TO USE" DOCUMENT—PAGE 2

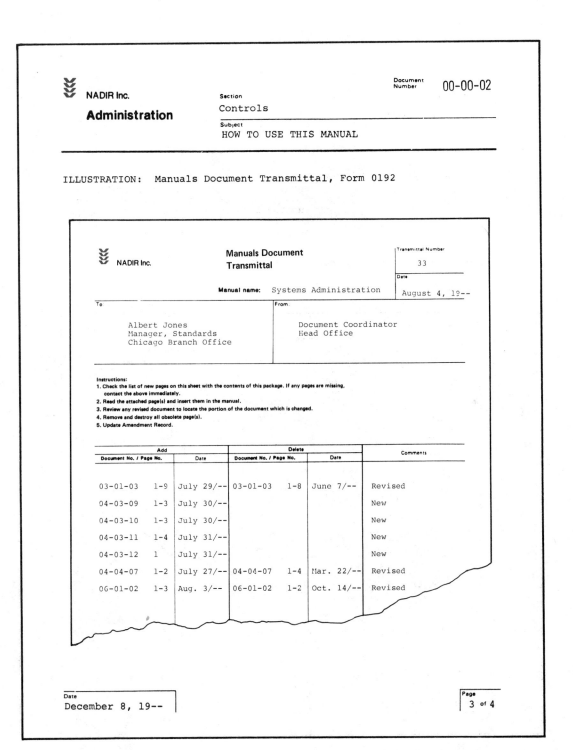

FIGURE 3-7   *"HOW TO USE" DOCUMENT—PAGE 3*

NADIR Inc.		Section	Document Number	00-00-02
Administration		Controls		
		Subject		
		HOW TO USE THIS MANUAL		

Amendment Record

The registered holder of the manual records the receipt of all Manuals Document Transmittals on the Amendment Record. This record and instructions for its use are found on the reverse side of the Manual Title Page (first unnumbered document in this manual).

ILLUSTRATION: Amendment Record, Form 0554

NADIR Inc.   **Amendment Record**

Instructions:
The number in the preprinted column of this Amendment Record corresponds to the Transmittal Number on the Manuals Document Transmittal.
1. Record the date on which each update (Transmittal) is received next to the appropriate number on the Amendment Record.
2. Report any missing updates to the manuals coordinator.

Trans-mittal No.	Date Received	Trans-mittal No.	Date Received	Trans-mittal No.	Date Received	Trans-mittal No.	Date Received
1	Aug 27, 19--	26		51		76	
2	Sept. 4, 19--	27		52		77	
3	Nov. 14, 19--	28		53		78	
4	Feb. 22, 19--	29		54		79	
5	Mar. 17, 19--	30		55		80	
6	June 2, 19--	31		56		81	
7	Aug. 5, 19--	32		57		82	
8	Oct. 22, 19--	33		58		83	
9	Nov. 28, 19--	34		59			
10	Jan. 31, 19--	35					
11	Apr						

Date		Page
December 8, 19--		4 of 4

FIGURE 3-8   "HOW TO USE" DOCUMENT—PAGE 4

SUBJECT INDEX

The alphabetic subject index is the most important retrieval device a manual can have. It provides the manual user with a simply organized and accessible listing of the manual's contents. The subject index lists every Section, every Subject, and important captions within Subjects in alphabetical order. To further aid retrievability, each item is listed three or more ways in the index.

The alphabetic subject index is always located at the front of the manual, in the Controls Tab, due to the frequency of its use. Here it is given the Document Number 00–00–03, and this and the other indices are separated from the other control items (table of contents and "How To Use") by a divider marked "Index" or "Indices." This tab divider is a different color from the other dividers so that it can be easily seen. The construction and set up of a subject index may be seen in Figures 3–9 and 3–10. Note the space left for the addition of new material in Figure 3–10. This space is left so that only one or two pages need to be retyped when new items are put in the index, rather than, in this case, all 26 pages.

The subject index should be organized and written *after* the manual has been completed if you're doing it manually. It is prepared by

1. going through the manual, page by page, and writing the names of the Sections, Subjects, and important captions (especially illustrations), and their locations on index cards
2. cross-referencing each of these items at least three ways (see Figure 3–11 on page 86)
3. arranging the indexed items in alphabetical order.

To do this, put yourself in the shoes of the user and try to think of all the ways the user might look up a particular Subject; make up a card for each.

With word or text processing equipment and software which will alphabetize, it's preferable to index as you go along, issuing a new index with each set of documents.

FORMS INDEX

A forms index is recommended if the text of the manual mentions six or more forms. Even though the forms would be listed in the subject index in alphabetic sequence, they can obviously be found more quickly in the forms index. The forms index is placed immediately after the subject index, at 00–00–04.

A forms index lists all the forms numerically by form number. This list may then be followed by any unnumbered forms in alphabetical order. Unnumbered forms might include items such as form letters and noncompany forms like income tax returns. Unnumbered forms should not include unofficial forms. The manuals writer will come across such forms because employees design forms themselves to make their jobs less complicated and then don't tell the Forms Department about it. But keep in mind that the manuals writer should not condone this practice any more than to allow the proliferation of unofficial manuals.

84

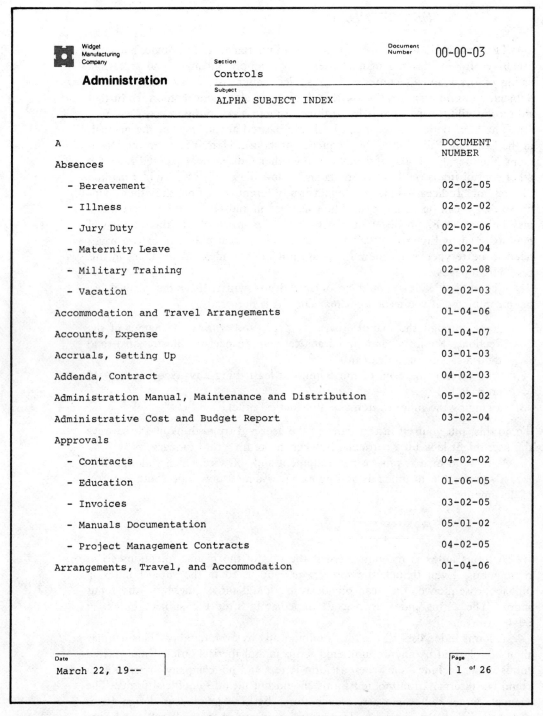

FIGURE 3-9   CONSTRUCTION OF AN ALPHABETIC SUBJECT INDEX—PAGE 1

Widget Manufacturing Company		Document Number	00-00-03

Administration

Section
Controls

Subject
ALPHA SUBJECT INDEX

A (Cont'd)	DOCUMENT NUMBER
Automatic and Manual Sprinkler Systems	06-06-02
Automatic and Manual Halon Systems	06-06-03

B	
Badges, Identification	01-03-03
Bereavement Absence	02-02-05
Budget Analysis, Form 1163	03-03-06
Budget Forecast, Form 1164	03-03-03

Date
March 22, 19--

FIGURE 3-10   CONSTRUCTION OF AN ALPHABETIC SUBJECT INDEX—PAGE 2

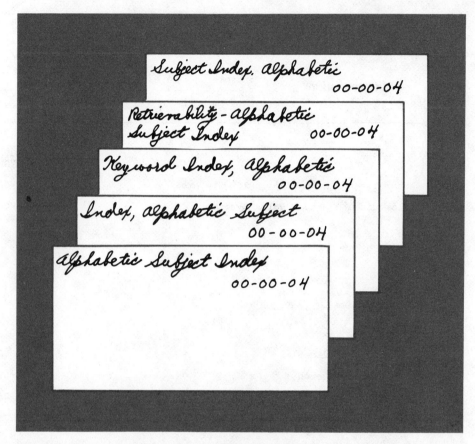

FIGURE 3-11   INDEX CARDS FOR ALPHABETIZING

When the manuals writer does come across unofficial forms, it is necessary to ascertain whether or not the form is really needed. If a new form is required:

- It must be checked for accurate information.
- It must be given a company form number.
- It must be designed according to company standards.
- Printing specifications must be developed.
- Annual usage and reorder points must be established.

If, after analysis, it is discovered that a form is not required, this should be explained to the supervisor or manager concerned.

As with the subject index, it is usually more convenient to leave the preparation of the forms index until the manual is completely written. Figure 3–12 shows an example of a forms index from an administration manual. Note that one of the forms has more than one document number. In this case, the location at which the form is actually described is the primary reference. All other locations are secondary references. Primary references should be set apart from sec-

NADIR Inc.		Document Number	00-00-04
Administration	Section Controls		
	Subject FORMS INDEX		

FORM NUMBER	TITLE	DOCUMENT NUMBER
1823	Performance Review Worksheet (Clerical)	01-05-11
1903	Amendment Record	Reverse Title Pg
1949	Current Year Budget Reforecast	02-02-04
1950	Consolidation Worksheet (Budget)	02-02-05
1951	Current Year Budget Summary	02-02-07
1952	(Annual) Budget Section/Branch Summary	02-02-08
1953	Budget Increase--Cost and Justification (See also 02-02-07, 02-02-08)	02-02-09
1961	Expense Account Voucher	03-05-03

Unnumbered Form Letters/Contracts

	Delegation of Signing Authority (Accounts Payable)	02-04-02
	Letter of Intent (Contract Staff)	05-04-06
	Letter of Intent (Hardware or Software)	04-06-02

Noncompany Forms

	Federal Income Tax Deduction Statement (Individual Employee)	02-06-03

Date May 16, 19--	Page 3 of 3

FIGURE 3-12   FORMS INDEX

ondary references so that the manual user can find them immediately. This can be done in a number of ways by:

- listing the major reference first
- printing the major reference in bold type
- shadow-typing the major reference (overtyping can be accomplished on a typewriter, most word processing equipment, and on a computer printer)
- offsetting the major reference
- stating "See also . . ." for the secondary references
- combining any of the above.

In Figure 3–12, the major reference is listed under the document number and the other references are put in the form of "See also . . .," but the other methods are equally valid. Don't neglect to put a word of explanation at the bottom of the page to point out which is the major reference if it's appropriate. There should also be an explanation in the "How to Use This Manual" document.

It is important to mention the close liaison which must exist between your forms designers/analysts and your manuals writers. It is a good idea to locate these two groups in close proximity to each other. The manuals writers will often need the services of the forms people to issue form numbers, to design forms, to do artwork, to order photomechanical transfers, etc. More will be made of this close liaison in Chapter 8.

REPORTS INDEX AND/OR ILLUSTRATIONS INDEX

The reports index is optional, depending on the number of reports in the manual. A reports index is set up alphabetically by report title. An alternative to the reports index, if you have sufficient illustrations (which are not forms) in your manual, would be a combination reports/illustrations index. Such an index would also be set up alphabetically by report title and illustration title.

THE BODY OF THE MANUAL

Just as the manual itself has a structure, so the subject matter of the manual also has its own structure. It is the Tab/Section/Subject hierarchy which provides the structure for the body of the manual.

Tab 00 in any manual is the Controls Tab and contains the table of contents, the "How to Use," and the various indices. Tabs 01, 02, 03, 04, etc., contain the subject matter of the manual. Tab 01 is the General Tab. Any Section which cannot be grouped into the other Tabs is placed in the General Tab. Each Tab has its own Introduction Section (optional) into which can be placed Subjects which cannot be placed elsewhere, or which introduce later Subjects, or which are of a general nature (but still specific to the Tab in which they are located). The first Subject or document in each Section is the Overview, which acts as a mini table of contents for the Section and gives a short blurb about each of the Subjects to follow. Each Subject in turn has its own Summary.

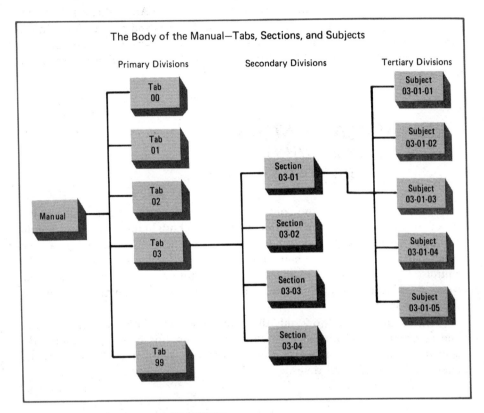

The Body of the Manual—Tabs, Sections, and Subjects

FIGURE 3-13   MANUAL STRUCTURE

APPENDICES

The *appendices* are contained in a separate Tab at the back of the manual, assigned Tab 99. This Tab follows the same format as others; that is, it includes Sections and Subjects. The appendices tab divider should be a different color than the tab dividers in the body of the manual and the same color as the indices tab divider (usually red).

The appendices themselves contain information of a supplementary nature which is not considered appropriate for the other Tabs, such as

- glossary of terms
- abbreviations, acronyms, initials, codes
- reference lists, publication lists
- statistics
- background philosophy and literature
- organization charts, staff lists

- sales brochures, catalogs
- legislation, by-laws.

If there is only a small amount of material to go into the Appendices Tab, it may only be necessary to organize the material into Subjects and not Sections. In this case only a Tab Overview would be required. The Subjects would then be numbered 99–00–01, 99–00–02, 99–00–03, etc., with 99–00–01 being the Overview to the Tab.

3.5
PREASSIGNED NUMBERS AND PRESCRIBED TEXT HEADINGS
▼

Table 3–2 represents the contents of a manual based on the structure described in Section 3.4. The control documents (both numbered and unnumbered) all have prescribed or predetermined text headings and are consistent throughout the manuals program. The other prescribed text headings are the Controls, General, and Appendices Tabs; the Introduction Sections; and the Overview Subjects. All of these items have preassigned document numbers, as can be seen in Table 3–2.

This common framework aids the manuals writers. They can organize and build any manual, no matter what the content, on this one basic framework. Standard assembly also aids the user in becoming familiar with the manuals, thereby reducing retrieval times.

3.6
OVERVIEWS AND SUMMARIES
▼

Each Section in the manual has an *Overview Subject* which briefly describes the contents of that Section. All Subjects, including Overviews, begin with a caption called "Summary," which introduces the Subject content to the user.

OVERVIEWS
◆

Overviews serve several purposes. They offer the user another retrieval device since they are a short-cut to discovering the content of a Section or Subject. Overviews also help the manuals writers to organize the Section content and force them to think clearly about what they have written. Overviews are written after all the other Subjects in the Section have been written because the writer will nearly always have a better idea about how to write the Overview after having written all the other Subjects. It is much easier to summarize something already written than something that has yet to be written.

Tab	Section	Subject	
00 Controls		*Unnumbered Documents*	Title Page Amendment Record Management Endorsement
			01 Table of Contents 02 How to Use 03 Alpha Index
		Optional	04 Forms Index 05 Reports Index
01 General	01 Introduction		01 Overview 02 03
	02		01 Overview 02 03
	03		01 Overview 02
02	01 Introduction		01 Overview 02 03 04
	02		01 Overview
03 etc.	01 Introduction		01 Overview
99 Appendices			

TABLE 3-2
PREASSIGNED NUMBERS
AND PRESCRIBED TEXT
HEADINGS

Following the Summary to the Overview, the titles of each Subject within the Section are captioned in the left margin of the page. A one- or two-sentence precis describing the Subject's content is printed opposite the Subject title. Immediately following these lines and at the right margin is the document number. An Overview from a data processing manual is illustrated in Figure 3–14.

NADIR Inc.

Data Processing

Section
Receiving and Processing Data

Subject
OVERVIEW

SUMMARY

This Section deals with receiving and processing batches of data by Data Processing.

INPUT/OUTPUT
COUNTER

The Data Processing Input/Output Counter serves as a reception area for nonauthorized personnel as well as a distribution point for batches of data. This counter is staffed by Data Processing personnel.   03-01-02

WORK FLOW

This procedure describes in general terms the flow of batches of data in Data Processing, after they have been accepted over the Input/ Output Counter.   03-01-03

PROCESSING
BATCHES

Batches of data sent by users to Data Processing are entered, verified, and saved. The tapes are then forwarded to the computer room for processing and the completed batches are returned to the users.   03-01-04

PROCESSING
RECONCILED
BATCHES

Any batch of data returned to the user as incorrect must be reconciled by the user and returned to Data Processing for keying.
03-01-05

DATA TRANSFER
TO TAPE

Balanced batches of data are transferred to magnetic tape for processing and backup.
03-01-06

Date
July 6, 19--

Page
1 of 1

FIGURE 3-14   OVERVIEW DOCUMENT

Each Subject in a manual should begin with a short, concise Summary of one or two paragraphs in length. *Summaries* are perfect vehicles for policy and responsibility statements, as shown in Figures 3–15 and 3–16.

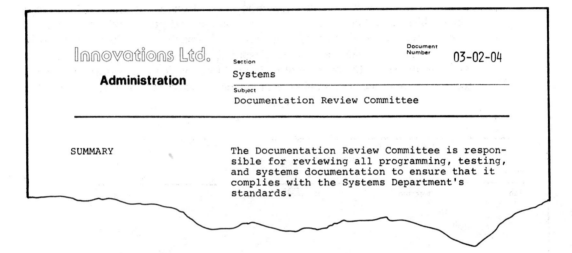

FIGURE 3-15   SUMMARY

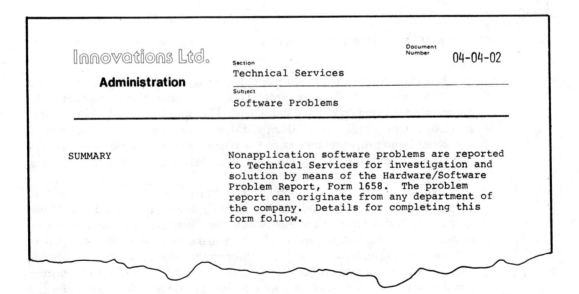

FIGURE 3-16   SUMMARY

3.7
PRELIMINARY
TABLE OF CONTENTS
▼

The *preliminary table of contents* is the first draft of the framework of the manual. To construct it, you must take all the Subjects which you have so far identified and which have been grouped into Tabs and Sections. Add those items which have been described as the controls and prescribed text headings. Then apply the numbering system. This will probably be only the first draft. For this reason, if you do not have word or text processing equipment, it is handy to prepare a blank table of contents format which can be printed or photocopied as required for all manuals produced. This is illustrated in Figure 3–17.

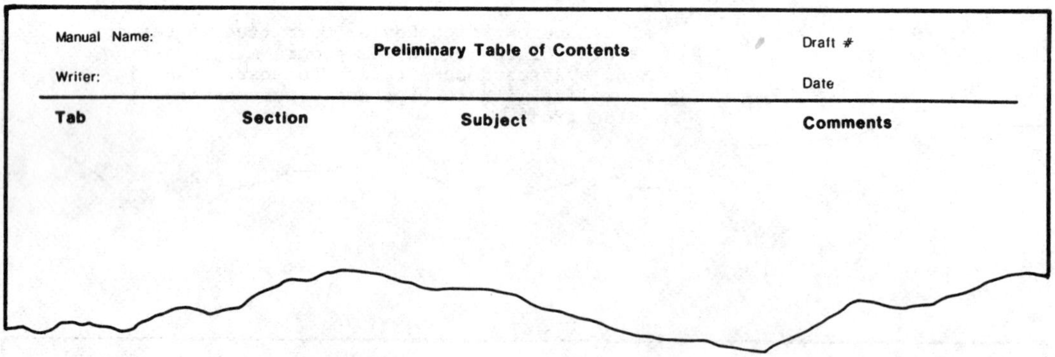

Manual Name:		Preliminary Table of Contents	Draft #
Writer:			Date
Tab	**Section**	**Subject**	**Comments**

FIGURE 3-17 *FORMAT FOR PRELIMINARY TABLE OF CONTENTS TO THE SUBJECT LEVEL*

You may also find it helpful to prepare your preliminary table of contents with the aid of 3″ × 5″ index cards. To do this, each item or Subject to be documented is listed on a single index card. The cards can then be easily sorted into like groups. Cards can be added and deleted, or entire groups can be shuffled about during this preliminary stage. When you have a lot of material, this method is much more convenient than working from written lists of several pages' length.

Your preliminary table of contents should look something like Figure 3–18 which represents page 1 of the preliminary table of contents from the cookbook exercise. It is this table of contents which you distribute to all personnel concerned with the manual, requesting that they make suggestions for the deletion, addition, or reorganization of Subjects. Offering the table of contents for critique not only assists the manual designer in further identification of subject matter, but also serves as a means of educating all concerned with the organization and numbering system of the manual.

Manual Name: Cookbook	**Preliminary Table of Contents**	Draft # 1
Writer: John Milton		Date Sept. 14, 19--

Tab	Section	Subject	Comments
01 General	01 Introduction	01 Overview 02 Meal Planning 03 Emergency Meals 04 Table of Measures 05 Table of Equivalents 06 Table of Substitutions 07 08	
	02 The Well-Stocked Kitchen	01 Overview 02 Staples 03 Flavors 04 Herbs 05 Spices 06 07	
	03 Cooking Methods	01 Overview 02 Roasting 03 Boiling 04 Deep Frying 05 Braising 06 Broiling 07 Steaming 08 09	
	04 Freezing	01 Overview 02 Types of Freezers 03 Unsuitable Foods 04 Preparation 05 Packaging and Wrapping 06 Guide to Freezing Times 07 Thawed Food 08 09	

FIGURE 3-18   *COOKBOOK EXAMPLE OF PRELIMINARY TABLE OF CONTENTS*

WRITING STYLE

4.1   Introduction
4.2   Writer's Rules
4.3   Writing Guidelines
4.4   Measuring Readability
4.5   Methods of Composing

4.1

INTRODUCTION

▼

Writing style is the manner of writing or the method of expressing thought in written form. Writers of prose, poetry, and drama often have a distinctive style. But despite any desire to emulate great writers or to become great literary geniuses, manuals writers must hide their personal style and keep their writing as indistinctive as possible. There are several reasons for this. The most obvious is that manuals are information and reference tools, not fiction or poetry to be read for enjoyment. Manuals, which are constantly changing as the organization changes, seldom have one author. Thus, several distinctive writing styles will give the manual a lack of continuity. The reader may have to take time to adjust to various styles; that is, readability may be hindered. However, writing style may differ from one manual to another, depending on the content and the audience addressed.

There are two elements of style as it affects manuals writing:

1. the *words* themselves, and how the words are put together in *sentences* (including punctuation)
2. the arrangement of the sentences into easily assimilated modules on the page (layout).

These two elements will be discussed in detail—the former in this chapter, the latter in Chapter 5. This chapter's discussion will first focus on grammar, then on the words and sentences manuals writers should use (rules for good manuals writing style). Finally, guidelines to follow in order to achieve consistency of style and optimum readability will be given. In Chapter 5, "Layouts," this will all be put together on the page.

THE WORDS— PARTS OF SPEECH

Words may be divided into eight classes according to their use:

1. Nouns—objects, people, places, ideas, etc.
2. Pronouns—used in place of nouns (her, its, these, any, some, who)
3. Verbs—express action or a state of being
4. Adjectives—describe nouns or pronouns (big, beautiful, green)
5. Adverbs—modify verbs, adjectives, or other adverbs (slowly, furiously, expansively)
6. Prepositions—show the relation between words (to, for, in)
7. Conjunctions—connect words or phrases (and, but)
8. Interjections—used independently to express strong feelings or to draw attention (Hark!)

A brief discussion of nouns and verbs follows.

Nouns. Nouns represent objects or ideas. Classes of nouns are:

1. Common nouns—any one of a group of objects (e.g., city, mountain, artist, etc.)
2. Proper nouns—the name of a single object or group of objects (e.g., Houston, the Alps, Renoir, etc.)
3. Collective nouns—a whole group of objects (e.g., family, bevy, congregation, etc.)

Nouns take on various properties. These properties include:

1. Gender—masculine, feminine, neuter
2. Person—first (I, we); second (you); third (he, she, they)
3. Number—singular, plural
4. Case—nominative, possessive, objective. For example, the nominative case denotes the person or thing about which an assertion is made (e.g., The *girl* dances.). The possessive case denotes ownership (e.g., The *girl's* doll.). And the objective case denotes a person or thing acted upon, or connected to (e.g., I walked to the *lake*. He loves the *girl*.)

Verbs. A verb is a word that expresses action or a state of being. Verbs may take on various properties. These properties show five changes of form: voice, mood, tense, person, and number.

1. Voice—The active voice asserts that the person or thing that is represented by the subject of the sentence does something (e.g., The sun *attracts* the earth.). The passive voice asserts that the subject is acted upon (e.g., The earth is *attracted* by the sun.).

2. Mood—Mood refers to the form of the verb which indicates the manner of doing or being. The three main types of mood are the indicative, the imperative, and the subjunctive. The indicative states or questions a fact (e.g., I *live* here. *Do* you *live* here?). The imperative is a command (e.g., *Go* to bed.) The subjunctive expresses an improbable condition or a wish, command, or desire (e.g., I wish she *were* here.).

3. Tense—Tense indicates action in relation to time. The present tense expresses action in the present (e.g., I *write*). The future and future perfect tenses indicate action in the future (e.g., I *shall write, I shall have written*). The past tense is used to express action in the past (e.g., I *wrote*). The present perfect tense is used to express action beginning in the past and continuing to the present (e.g., I *have written*). The past perfect tense indicates an action completed before another action that also occurred in the past (e.g., I *had written*).

4. Person—The action expressed by a verb may be that of first person—that is, the person speaking; second person—that is, the person spoken to; and third person—that is, the person spoken of.

5. Number—Number refers to either singular or plural agreement. A singular verb expresses the action of one thing (e.g., I *pay*, you *pay*, he *pays*). A plural verb expresses the action of more than one thing (e.g., we *pay*, you *pay*, they *pay*).

THE SENTENCE

A *sentence* is a combination of words that expresses a complete thought. It is composed of two parts—the subject and the predicate. The *subject* is that part of the sentence about which an assertion is made (e.g., *The Egyptians* built pyramids.). The *predicate* is that part of the sentence that makes an assertion about the subject (e.g., The Egyptians *built pyramids.*).

Sentences may be categorized according to their manner of expression. These categories are:

1. Declarative—The sun shines.
2. Interrogative—How are you?
3. Imperative—Move this chair.
4. Exclamatory—Look at this new car!

Manuals writers will primarily be concerned with imperative and declarative sentences.

Sentences may also be categorized according to structure. These categories are:

1. Simple (one subject and one predicate)—Taxes are high.

2. Complex (one or more dependent clauses joined to a simple sentence)—When winter comes, it snows.

3. Compound (two or more simple sentences joined together)—Taxes are high, but rents are low.

4. Compound-complex (one or more dependent clauses joined to a compound sentence)—The man who made the offer is here, but he is too late.

Good manuals writing style differs greatly from good prose or poetry. The goal of the manuals writer is not to impress people with eloquence or erudition. Rather, it is to write clear, concise, simple material. To this end, simple sentences should be used wherever possible. An occasional complex or compound sentence or even a compound-complex one is alright for variety, but these should be kept to a minimum and should under no circumstances be unwieldy.

4.2
WRITER'S RULES
▼

The following rules are important to observe when writing manuals. Many of the rules are general enough to be applied to all writing, while some are specific to manuals writing.

WRITE TO
THE AUDIENCE
◆

This is the single most important rule of all. The message you are trying to convey to the reader must be suited to the reader's needs in terms of content, style, language (level of difficulty), and layout.

ORGANIZE
YOUR MATERIAL
◆

The message you wish to convey must be organized so that readers can follow your meaning. If you haven't planned your message, the chances are great that you will not be able to convey it clearly. The material must be organized into easily digestible bits of information, with plenty of headings or captions, so that the reader does not have to consume large amounts of data to get at a single fact.

REWRITE, REVISE,
AND EDIT YOUR MATERIAL
◆

Don't be afraid to rewrite. Accept criticism with good grace—don't be offended when your drafts come back with many corrections and revisions. It's part of the job. Your aim is to achieve clarity, simplicity, continuity, and brevity.

USE CHARTS AND ILLUSTRATIONS
TO SUPPORT YOUR MESSAGE

It's an old cliché that "A picture is worth a thousand words," but that doesn't make it any less true. Wherever applicable, break up the printed page with graphs, illustrations, tables, matrices, and diagrams. These help your reader visualize your point, and they relieve the eye and brain strain of page after page of written material.

KNOW
YOUR SUBJECT

The first step to knowing your subject is knowing what you are trying to accomplish. You must know what to aim for when you begin a procedure or a manual. If you don't know enough about the subject, then you must learn—through observation, interviews, and even education courses.

USE CLEAR, SHORT,
FAMILIAR WORDS

Your manual users will not be pleased if you use words that are unfamiliar. Some users will read around the word and may therefore misinterpret what you've written. Others will look up the word in a dictionary, but may be aggravated by the inconvenience of having to translate your writing.

Do not use a big word when a short one will do. Large words may be imprecise—if not in reality then in your reader's mind. Avoid jargon, whether it be officialese, legalese, or computerese. No doubt a certain amount of professional jargon will be necessary to your task, but the less used the better.

On occasion everyone falls prey to producing more complicated writing than is necessary. Table 4–1 lists commonly used complicated words and phrases and a simple substitute for each. You can probably think of many more words and phrases needing simplification which are common in the business community.

ELIMINATE
UNNECESSARY WORDS

Overly descriptive, unnecessary words such as adjectives and adverbs are not required in manuals because they obscure meaning. For example, look at the first sentence and then the second sentence presented here.

1. Use the high-speed Xerox 9700 laser printer in the computer room to print the report.
2. Use the Xerox 9700 to print the report.

If you only have one printer, there is no need to describe it at all. Thus, if that is the case, the simplest sentence would be: Print the report.

Words to Avoid	Substitutes
accordingly	so
aforementioned	these
applicable	apply to
assistance	help
attributable	due
be in a position to	can
by means of	by
compensate	pay
consequently	so
considerable	much
correspondence	letter
facilitate	ease
for the reason that	because
foregoing	this
furthermore	also
in as much as	because
indebtedness	debt
in order to	to
in regard to	about
in the amount of	for
in the event that	if
in the near future	soon
on the part of	for
pertaining to	about
prior to	before
provided that	if
purchase	buy
so as to	to
subsequently	after
terminate	end
transmit	send
under separate cover	separately
utilize	use
whether or not	whether
with regard to	about
with the result that	so that

TABLE 4-1
WORDS TO AVOID AND
THEIR SUBSTITUTES

KEEP SENTENCES SHORT AND SIMPLE

Long sentences, like long words, increase resistance between the writer and the reader and impair communication. An appropriate average sentence length for manuals is between 10 and 15 words. Persistent construction of longer sentences risks the possibility of confusing your reader. In addition, as a sentence becomes longer, the chance of making a grammatical error increases dramatically. There aren't many people who can consistently write 40-word compound-complex sentences without making mistakes.

The first sentence below was taken from a real manual. The second sentence is one way in which the first sentence could have been written. Which would you rather read?

1. Printing Department overtime resources will be provided on a request only basis when there is additional work to be printed (from the normal workload) that may result in overtime, depending on volume of material, lead time given (2 days), and date required.
2. The Printing Department will work overtime if necessary. A request indicating volume of printing must be made two days before the date required.

There are two ideas expressed in the second example: (1) The Printing Department will work overtime if the workload is heavier than normal and (2) This overtime must be requested. Besides being too lengthy, there are two basic errors with the first sentence: two ideas have been expressed in the same sentence, and both ideas have been clouded by too many modifiers. There is also some ambiguity about the "request only basis." This is the phrase used in the first sentence which most needs elucidation.

Don't be afraid to use periods rather than commas. If a sentence is too long, try breaking it into two sentences. Then do it again if need be.

USE THE
ACTIVE VOICE

In the active voice, sentences such as the following are natural and straightforward:

1. The girls are playing hopscotch.
2. The engineer built a bridge.
3. The purchasing agent approved the invoice.

If you change the sentences into the passive voice, however, the subject and direct object are switched so that *hopscotch,* *bridge,* and *invoice,* respectively, become the subjects.

1. Hopscotch is being played by the girls.
2. A bridge was built by the engineer.
3. The invoice was approved by the purchasing agent.

The words which were subjects in the active voice are indirect objects of the preposition "by" in the passive voice. Since prepositional phrases are not absolutely necessary to sentence construction, there is a danger that they will be dropped, thereby giving imprecise results such as:

1. Hopscotch is being played.
2. A bridge was built.
3. The invoice was approved.

Now the original subjects have disappeared.

An even greater danger occurs with the use of the passive voice when writing manuals. Contrast these two sentences and determine which action has the better chance of being performed.

1. The inventory file must be updated weekly.
2. You must update the inventory file weekly.

Obviously the second sentence has a better chance of being performed effectively because it is instructive. The first sentence does not make it clear as to who must do the updating.

It is simple to change a passive verb to an active verb. First, you must recognize the passive voice—it always has some form of the verb "to be" in front of the main verb. Second, ask yourself who performs the action. The answer to that question is the subject of your active verb.

USE THE IMPERATIVE MOOD

The imperative mood, used in conjunction with the active voice, is used primarily in the Playscript layout, and sometimes in the Matrix layout. In these layouts it is important to tell the user what steps to perform. In the imperative mood, the second person pronoun "you" is understood and need not be written; e.g., "Open the mail." However, the person who must perform the action is indicated by job title, separately from the instruction. For example:

Clerk 1. Open the mail.
        2. Date stamp the contents.
        3. Deliver to the person addressed.

USE POINT FORM

When you need to list three or more items, consider using point form rather than separating the items by commas or semicolons. In this way, you increase the amount of white space on the page, which reduces eye and brain strain. A good point to remember when putting a list into point form is that numbers or letters should be used for sequential items, and dashes or bullets should be used for nonsequential lists. Illustrations of the use of bullets can be found throughout this text.

USE LANGUAGE, GRAMMAR, AND PUNCTUATION PRAGMATICALLY, NOT LITERALLY

Do not be strictly bound by the rules. They can be bent a little to suit your purpose. If necessary, you may

- begin sentences with *and* or *but*
- end sentences with prepositions
- use the same terms consistently (the reader may be confused if you change words)
- decrease the amount of punctuation which would be grammatically correct.

This does not mean that you can be careless in your choice of words. Remember, your readers are going to take your instructions literally. Figure 4–1 shows what happens when this occurs.

FIGURE 4-1

USE A CONVERSATIONAL STYLE

Use of conversational style does not mean that you should use slang, just that you should be informal rather than formal. Most people communicate better when they are speaking than when they are writing. One reason for this is the instant feedback available to them when they speak with another person, but another reason is the tendency to write to impress rather than to express. Everyone falls prey to this tendency at some time. One way around this is to pretend you're talking to another person when you're writing. Put yourself in the speaking mode, rather than in the writing mode. This, of course, does not relieve you of the responsibility of being more precise when you write than when you speak. The lack of instant feedback means that this is a necessity.

KEEP CONSTRUCTION PARALLEL

Parallel construction means that parts of a sentence that are parallel in meaning should be parallel in structure. Look at the following example of nonparallel construction.

The duties and responsibilities of the senior data entry operators are

- verifying the accuracy of other operators' entries
- key sensitive data such as payroll
- making error corrections and balancing out-of-balance batches
- to key format and conversion coding sheets
- to key test data
- train other data entry operators.

Now see the following example of parallel construction.

The duties and responsibilities of the senior data entry operators are to

- verify the accuracy of other operators' entries
- key sensitive data such as payroll
- make error corrections and balance out-of-balance batches
- key format and conversion coding sheets
- key test data
- train other data entry operators.

Note that in the parallel construction, either the infinitive (to key) or the present participle (keying) form of the verbs can be used. However, one form must be chosen and used throughout. Thus, in the latter example, the infinitive is used consistently.

The following examples illustrate the same point.

1. The stranger was sinister and mustachioed, and rode a black stallion.
2. The stranger was sinister, mustachioed, and rode a black stallion.

In Sentence 1 the verb "was" is understood to take both the objects "sinister" and "mustachioed" by use of the conjunction "and"; that is, the sentence could read "was sinister and was mustachioed." But in the nonparallel construction (Sentence 2), the conjunction "and" has been left out and has been replaced by a comma. As a result, the verb "was" no longer takes the object "mustachioed," but incorrectly takes the phrase, "and rode a black stallion" as an object. Thus, it is important that when you express ideas which are parallel in meaning, the grammatical form must also be parallel.

One way to test for parallel construction is to bullet the pertinent phrases or clauses. Thus, the foregoing example would become:

Parallel   The stranger

- was sinister and mustachioed
- rode a black stallion.

Nonparallel   The stranger   The stranger was

- was sinister   - sinister
- mustachioed   *or*   - mustachioed
- rode a black stallion.   - rode a black stallion.

ALLOW MEANING TO DETERMINE WHETHER COLLECTIVE NOUNS ARE PLURAL OR SINGULAR

A singular collective noun is illustrated in the following example:

The Board is pleased to announce the election of Fred Smith as chairperson.

Here, the Board is acting together as a single unit, and the singular form "is" is used. A plural collective noun is illustrated in this example:

The Board were split in their views of the new company manual.

Here, the subject "Board" refers to its separate members; thus, the plural form of the verb is used.

USE POSITIVE WORDS
RATHER THAN NEGATIVE WORDS

◆

Some words, simply by their presence, can supply either a positive or negative connotation, or can provoke either a positive or a negative response. Some examples are presented in Table 4–2.

Look at the following way of phrasing the same sentence in both the positive and the negative.

1. Lock the door when you leave.
2. Don't neglect to lock the door when you leave.

Positive Words	Negative Words
admirable	disagreement
benefit	failure
distinction	fault
effective	fear
glad	if
good	neglect
happy	never
loyal	no
right	not
useful	suspicion
willing	weak
yes	wrong

TABLE 4-2
POSITIVE WORDS AND
NEGATIVE WORDS

USE TRANSITIONAL WORDS
TO SMOOTH RELATIONSHIPS BETWEEN
IDEAS, SENTENCES, AND PARAGRAPHS

◆

Avoid abrupt changes when you shift from one topic to another or from one paragraph to another. This can be done by adopting the following transitional words:

accordingly	meanwhile
although	nevertheless
because	presumably
consequently	that is
conversely	therefore
however	thus
in addition	since
later	so

Many pairs of words in any language, particularly in English, have similar meanings. A good writer is aware of these words and tries to use the best word possible. Some of these words and their proper usage are listed in Table 4–3.

Words	Correct Usage
Fewer—refers to number:	There are *fewer* accidents on the roads this year.
Less—modifies a singular noun:	There is *less* carnage on the highways this year.
Anxious—worried:	We are *anxious* about our missing child.
Eager—desirous:	The waiter is *eager* to serve you.
Between—used when there are two objects:	There was a disagreement *between* Bill and me.
Among—used when there are more than two objects:	There was fighting *among* Bill's three children.
Disinterested—without self-interest:	The judge must be *disinterested*.
Uninterested—not interested:	I am *uninterested* in opera.
Almost—nearly:	*Almost* all major league baseball players make a good living.
Most—superlative form of much:	That is the *most* expensive dress in the store.
Numerous—refers to an exact number, although the quantity is unknown:	The stars are *numerous*.
Many—a large, indefinite number:	*Many* parking lot attendants dent fenders.

TABLE 4-3
PAIRS OF WORDS AND
THEIR CORRECT USAGE

ENSURE SUBJECT
AND VERB AGREEMENT

Remember, words linked to the subject and the verb do not always affect the number of the verb. For example:

Sally, as well as her sister and her brothers, *was* a good student.

It is incorrect to say:

Sally, as well as her sister and her brothers, *were* good students.

Some singular nouns which may cause confusion are: each, everybody, everyone, anyone, no one, nobody, anybody, etc.

IDIOT-PROOF YOUR WRITING

It's sometimes a good idea to have a fellow writer "idiot-proof" your written work before you distribute it to the critique committee. This will ensure that you have clearly expressed what you wish to say, especially if your fellow writer knows nothing about the subject matter.

4.3
WRITING GUIDELINES

A guideline differs from a rule or standard in that it is merely a suggested way of doing something, whereas a rule or standard is more stringent—it must be followed. In the previous section, rules to improve your manuals writing skills were discussed. For example, everyone would agree that, "write to your audience," is sensible advice which should be followed to write good manuals. In this section, each of the guidelines presented deals with a specific area of concern—such as the use of notes in text—and presents a logical way of handling it. These guidelines have been adopted by many organizations and have thus become industry standards. Whether or not you adopt these guidelines as your standards or develop your own standards, they must be documented.

THE USE OF NOTES

Notes are used to highlight points or to reference other information that is relevant to the text. The word NOTE is printed in uppercase and is followed by a colon. Then the note itself appears. The word NOTE is aligned with the left-most character of the text to be noted. Notes are offset by leaving white space between them and the rest of the text. The following examples illustrate a single note and show how to set up more than one note.

ID Badges	In accordance with company policy, it is the responsibility of all Systems staff and visitors to wear identification badges while on company premises.
	NOTE: Refer to the Administration manual for details.

Hockey Records	Wayne Gretzky of the Edmonton Oilers broke all the goal-scoring records in the National Hockey League in the 1981/1982 season.
	NOTE: 1. The previous record for most goals in a single season had been held by Phil Esposito, with the Boston Bruins.
	2. The previous record for average goals per game had been held by Maurice (Rocket) Richard of the Montreal Canadiens.

Footnotes and chapter notes should not be used in manuals. They waste the reader's time with unnecessary cross-referencing. If it's not important enough to merit a place in the text, eliminate it.

ACRONYMS
AND ABBREVIATIONS

An *acronym* is a word formed from the first letter or letters of each of the successive parts of a compound element. For example:

- Snafu—situation normal, all fouled up
- Radar—radio detecting and ranging
- Scuba—self-contained underwater breathing apparatus

Some things, especially agencies, have abbreviations which are acronyms as well. Often these acronyms are in uppercase form. To save time and effort, commonly used acronyms should be written without periods or spaces between the letters.

- NASA—National Aeronautics and Space Administration
- NATO—North Atlantic Treaty Organization
- UNESCO—United Nations Educational, Scientific, and Cultural Organization
- NOW—National Organization of Women

An *abbreviation* is a shortened form of a word or phrase used in place of the word or phrase. For example:

- amt.—amount
- i.e.—*id est,* that is
- dept.—department
- Sask.—Saskatchewan

Here, however, the periods should be retained.

Acronyms and abbreviations can be used if they aid readability. However, they should either be commonplace and understood by everyone, or they should be explained. In technical manuals, where acronyms and abbreviations are common, include a "Glossary of Terms" Subject in the appendix, and refer to it in the "How to Use" Subject as well as in the index.

UNDERLINING

Underlining for emphasis should not be done in manuals. If you use the layouts described in this text, there will be little, if any, need for it. Once someone starts underlining, it tends to be overdone. However, if you feel you absolutely must underline, keep it to a minimum (once or twice a page).

CAPITALIZATION

A certain amount of capitalization is necessary in manuals. However, you should not use it for emphasis because once you start there is a tendency to overdo it. The following is a list of situations calling for capitalization in manuals:

- First word of a sentence.
- Proper nouns.
- Titles.
- Terms used to show divisions of a manual (i.e., Tab, Section, Subject) when reference is made to them formally. They are not capitalized, however, when informal reference is made to them.
- Primary captions—these are typed entirely in uppercase.
- The first letter of most words in secondary captions. (Use the same rule used for capitalizing titles.)
- The first letter of words in tertiary captions.
- Words such as EXAMPLE, NOTE, ILLUSTRATION, when used as titles, are typed entirely in uppercase.

NUMBERING HIERARCHY

Use Arabic numerals, then lowercase letters, to show a sequence within a sequence. For example,

1.
2.
   a.
   b.
3.
4.
   a.
   b.
   c.

If there are more than two hierarchical levels in which sequence must be shown, look at your subject again. The steps listed may be too complicated.

Avoid the use of Roman numerals as they take up too much room and not everyone understands them.

EXPRESSING NUMBERS IN TEXT

You should express numbers as numerals whenever possible. The use of a number in text indicates that the item is important, otherwise, the writer would have used a word such as "some," "many," or "a few." Numbers expressed as numerals stand out in the printed text and are therefore more likely to be noticed and remembered by the reader.

The only exception to the standard of expressing numbers as numerals is when the number occurs at the beginning of a sentence; e.g., Thirty people attended the meeting.

Many grammar books say that in the following cases numbers should be spelled out:

- numbers under ten
- approximate or indefinite numbers; e.g., about four hundred people, over a thousand dollars
- very large numbers; e.g., $6.8 billion, 50 million stars
- ordinals; e.g., third, twentieth
- centuries and decades; e.g., the twenties, the nineteenth century

In manuals, however, use numerals rather than words in these cases.

LISTS

To show hierarchy in lists, use bullets for primary topics and dashes for secondary topics. For example,

- flowering shrubs
  —rose
  —forsythia
  —mock orange
- flowering trees
  —magnolia
  —chestnut
  —cherry
  —apple

REFERENCE TO FORMS

Forms are identified by name and number. For example: Request for Technical Services, Form 1802; Purchase Order, Form 0077; etc. There are two basic reasons for doing this. First, by mentioning both the title and the number, you reduce the chance of error. Second, if the form is known by its title rather than by its number, or if the title of the form was established before a number was assigned to it, many users will continue to refer to the form by its title only.

In a procedure, all forms are identified by name and by number at first reference; subsequent references within that procedure use only the form number. Again, the reasons for this are simple: The form number takes up less room, there is less monotony and repetition, and use of the number aids readability and retrievability.

EXPRESSING BOTH SINGULAR AND PLURAL NOUNS AND VERBS

When you need to show a noun as both singular and plural (this should be avoided if at all possible), use parentheses for the added pluralization. For example: department(s), class(es), child(ren), ox(en). If the noun form changes, use a virgule (/) to separate the two words: mouse/mice, die/dice, company/companies. Separate singular and plural verbs with a virgule as well: is/are, was/were, go/goes, etc.

USE OF
PRONOUN GENDER
◆

When writing manuals, try to avoid the use of male/female pronouns or the once commonly used male form of pronouns when referring to general persons. The alternative, the modern male/female, his/her, he/she approach to writing is annoying to write and to read, but trying to avoid these pronouns is very difficult. However, with a little extra effort you can rephrase sentences to get around this pronoun problem. Study the following pairs of sentences to see how pronoun gender can be avoided.

1. Notify the employee on the first day of his/her 6-month probationary term.
2. Notify the employee on the first day of the 6-month probationary term.

1. A meeting will be arranged with the employee, his/her manager, and a union representative.
2. A meeting will be arranged with the employee, the employee's manager, and a union representative.

When it is absolutely necessary to use third-person pronouns, use both the masculine and feminine genders separated by a virgule (i.e., he/she, his/her, etc.).

MISCELLANEOUS
PUNCTUATION GUIDELINES
◆

Avoid the use of semicolons as much as possible by using point form and by using bullets and dashes for lists. Italics are sometimes used to indicate foreign words or phrases; avoid them whenever possible. Parentheses, brackets, and dashes in sentences should be used sparingly. Write new sentences to avoid using these forms of punctuation, and for other rules of punctuation refer to a dictionary or a basic grammar book. These reference items are invaluable tools for writers.

4.4

MEASURING
READABILITY
▼

The previous sections of this chapter should convince you, if you didn't already know, that it is as difficult to write a good manual as it is to write good prose. However, when writing prose, you can adopt whatever writing style suits you; the same is not true when writing manuals. When writing manuals, you must make your writing style clear, concise, and consistent no matter who your audience is; and you need to be flexible enough to write to different audience levels. In order to ensure that your writing is at the required level, you can test and measure its readability.

There are many methods of measuring readability. The first of these is based on a method developed by Rudolph Flesch. Other well-known readability tests are: the Lensear Write Formula; The Fog Index, developed by Robert Gunning; and Fry's Readability Graph, which has similarities to both Flesch's and Gunning's readability tests. Finally, there is the Clear River test, which uses the metaphor of a piece of writing floating down the river of comprehension. Each of these readability tests will be discussed here.

THE FLESCH READABILITY TEST

The following test, developed by Rudolph Flesch, measures readability on a scale of 0 to 100. The higher the score, the greater the reading ease. The following steps make up the test:

1. Choose a sample of text that is 100 to 200 words long. Count the words.
2. Count the number of syllables in the sample. To save time, you could underline all syllables but the first as you count the words. Count the syllables the way you pronounce the word; e.g., asked—1, tested—2, 1960—4, $—2, etc.
3. Count the number of sentences in the sample. A colon, a semicolon, or a dash can be considered as a period if there is a complete sentence on both sides of it.
4. Calculate the average sentence length. Divide the number of sentences into the number of words to obtain this average.
5. Calculate the word length by dividing the number of syllables by the number of words. Then multiply this number by 100.

$$\text{Word Length} = \frac{\text{Number of Syllables}}{\text{Number of Words}} \times 100$$

6. Using Figure 4–2, connect the number you calculated for average sentence length on the left-hand scale with the number you calculated for word length on the right-hand scale. The spot where this line intersects the reading-ease scale gives the Flesch Readability score.

THE LENSEAR WRITE FORMULA

The Lensear Write Formula yields a percentagelike number: the higher the score, the simpler the material is to read. Study the following steps for carrying out this readability test.

1. Count the total number of words in your chosen sample (a 100–200 word excerpt is representative of a given piece of text).
2. Count the one-syllable words except *the, is, are, was,* and *were.* (Note: Numbers in digit form are considered to be one-syllable words.)
3. Count the number of sentences. Colons, semicolons, and dashes may be

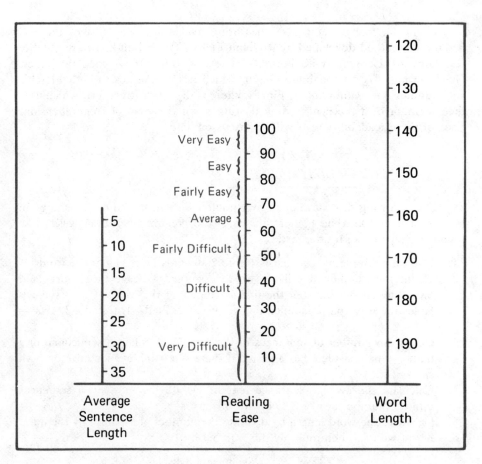

FIGURE 4-2   FLESCH READABILITY SCALE

considered as periods if there is a full sentence on either side of them. Bulleted phrases and clauses may be counted as complete sentences.

4. Use the following formula to determine the readability value:

$$\text{Lensear Score} = \frac{\text{One-Syllable Words} + (3 \times \text{Sentences})}{\text{Total Number of Words}} \times 100$$

A Lensear score of roughly 70 to 80 points is ideal for manuals. Lower than 70 points means the text may be too complicated for easy comprehension by manual users. Higher than 80 points means the sample may be too elementary.

THE
FOG INDEX
◆

The Fog Index, developed by Robert Gunning, expresses readability as the number of years of schooling required to read the text with ease. The following steps are taken when applying this readability test.

1. Count the number of words in your chosen sample of text.
2. Count the number of sentences.
3. Count the number of hard words in the passage. Hard words are defined as those of three or more syllables in length with the exception of (1) words that are capitalized; (2) combinations of short, easy words such as book-keeper, grasshopper, butterfly; and (3) verb forms made into three syllables by adding "ed" or "es." However, count as hard words those where "ly" or "ing" is added.
4. Determine the average sentence length. Divide the number of sentences into the number of words.
5. Determine the percentage of hard words in the sample:

$$\text{Percentage of Hard Words} = \frac{\text{Number of Hard Words}}{\text{Number of Words}} \times 100$$

6. Use the following formula to calculate the Fog Index:

Fog Index = (Average Sentence Length + Percentage of Hard Words) × 0.4

FRY'S READABILITY GRAPH

Fry's readability graph, first published in *The Reading Teacher* (March, 1969) and *The Journal of Reading* (April, 1968), has similarities to both Flesch's and Gunning's methods. Like Flesch, Fry uses coordinates plotted on a graph to find the reading level, but he then expresses the result as the grade level of schooling needed to understand the text, similar to the Fog Index. Study the following steps to apply this readability test.

1. Select three 100-word samples (Stop on the 100th word.).
2. Count the sentences per sample (Count the last partial sentence as complete.).
3. Count the syllables in the sample (It is easier to count if the syllables are marked first.).
4. Compute the average number of sentences per 100 words and the average number of syllables per 100 words from the three samples.
5. Plot the position of the text on the readability graph in Figure 4–3 by using the computed averages.

CLEAR RIVER TEST

As mentioned earlier, the Clear River Test uses the metaphor of a piece of writing floating down the river of comprehension. There are four docks jutting out into the river. The more complicated the writing, the further out the docks jut, thereby impeding the progress of the text on its way to comprehension. The standards to attain in order not to block-readability for this test are:

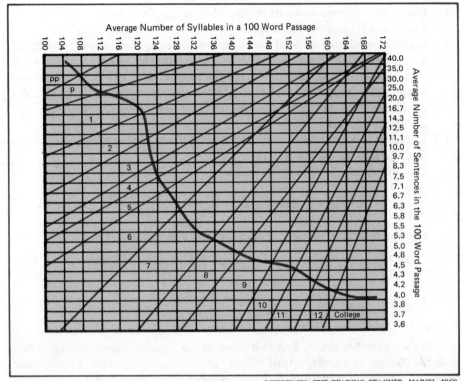

Average Number of Syllables in a 100 Word Passage

REFERENCES: THE READING TEACHER, *MARCH, 1969*
JOURNAL OF READING, *APRIL, 1968*

FIGURE 4-3   FRY'S READABILITY GRAPH GRID

- 25 words or less per sentence
- 12 words or less per punctuated pause
- 75 words or less per paragraph
- 150 syllables or less per 100 words.

If a piece of writing can meet all four of these standards, there is no obstacle to reader understanding (thus, the clear river metaphor). The more docks (obstacles) that jut out into the river, however, the more difficult it is to pass unhindered.

SUMMARY
AND CONCLUSIONS

All five of the formulae for measuring readability basically gauge the degree of difficulty of narrative text. These methods of readability are not exact, so don't be too concerned if you're a few points off either way. When you use any of these methods to measure the readability level of your material, don't just do it for a single passage of text. Take a few samples to obtain a representative reading and calculate each one. That way you won't be misled if one sample is atypical.

It's not necessary to test your writing daily or even weekly—it just won't change that much from day to day; three or four times a year should suffice. However, if you have a tendency to be verbose, you should test samples of your writing more often to make sure you aren't slipping into any bad habits.

Remember, too, that all five formulae ignore the fact that a 4½- to 5-inch reading line is best for readability and that layout plays a big role in aiding readability.

4.5

METHODS OF COMPOSING
▼

The days of a writer composing subject matter with pen and paper are fast disappearing. The invention of the ballpoint pen and the typewriter were technological advances in the past. But today's advances such as word processors and computer-assisted text-editing systems may well make the pen and the typewriter obsolete in the not-too-distant future. For instance, today's newspaper reporters and best-selling novelists no longer bang away at the old Underwoods; they use computer terminals and word processing equipment to write their stories.

Most computer manufacturers offer some form of text-editing software. Printers and photocopiers are also becoming so good that you can't tell the difference between an original and a copy.

To date, most of the advances in office automation have been in the implementation of systems to support clerical functions. A prime example is the word processor. However, the focus is now shifting toward increasing the productivity of professionals. For example, Bell Laboratories has developed a program called Writer's Workbench, which cleans up bad technical writing by substituting simpler words, by changing verbs from the passive to the active voice, by simplifying sentence structure, and by correcting spelling, punctuation, and grammar. IBM is also developing a document composition system called Janus which, using a dual display, helps authors and editors to visualize the results of their efforts in final form while working on their documents. One display is for the entry, editing, and manipulation of data; the second display shows the text as it will look in final form.

Modern technology has provided faster, less costly, more precise methods of composing. Take advantage of these if you can. These methods of composing will be tied in with production methods in Chapter 6.

LAYOUTS

5

5.1
GENERAL PRINCIPLES
▼

Layout is the term used to describe the manner in which text or subject matter is presented or "laid out" on the page. Much thought must be given to the layout of each and every Subject so that the information presented to the user is done so logically, simply, and aesthetically.

The user must be considered at all times. A solid page of narrative discourages a reader, while short paragraphs surrounded by white space are more likely to hold the reader's interest. As mentioned earlier, the length of the reading line is also of primary concern. Studies show that the most desirable reading line is 4½" in length. Based on these studies, the page format and the layouts used to present text (particularly Caption and Playscript) should be designed to accommodate this length of reading line.

There are eight types of layout which can be used in manuals:

1. Narrative
2. Headline
3. Caption
4. Matrix
5. Flowchart
6. Playscript
7. Data Flow Diagram
8. Illustration

Of these eight layouts, the first two (Narrative and Headline) should be used very seldom, and others (especially Caption and Playscript) should be used very often. The choice of layout will depend upon the subject matter to be presented and the users of the manual.

GENERAL GUIDELINES FOR LAYOUTS

The following general guidelines should be applied no matter what layout is used.

Every Subject Has a Summary. A *Summary* introduces the Subject to the reader and outlines the scope and objectives of the document. It may present policy and/or background information such as why a procedure is to be carried out and who is responsible for carrying it out. A Summary provides management with a synopsis of the details which follow. Consider the confusion that might exist if a user of a manual suddenly came upon a matrix, illustration, or flowchart which had no explanation and which seemed to have no relationship to Subjects before or after it. A Summary can provide this transition from Subject to Subject.

Although a Summary appears first in every document, it should be written last; that is, after the writer becomes completely familiar with the subject matter.

Use Short Paragraphs. Remember the advice in Chapter 4—keep your words and sentences short and simple, as well as your paragraphs.

Keep Subjects Short. In Chapter 3, it was demonstrated that the primary (Tab), secondary (Section), and tertiary (Subject) breakdown of material allows the author to write short, concise Subjects. For example, if you were writing a Section on handling mail, you could write several short Subjects about individual functions such as "Sorting Incoming Mail," "Delivery and Pick-up," "Inter-Office Mail," etc. The breakdown of subject matter in this manner allows the writer to describe only those details necessary to perform each activity.

Write Only to the Audience Concerned. A very important concept to remember in order to keep Subjects short is that no Subject should cross the boundaries of the manual. In other words, write only to the audience who is reading the manual. Describe only the duties that are performed by the users of the manual. Figure 5–1 illustrates this concept.

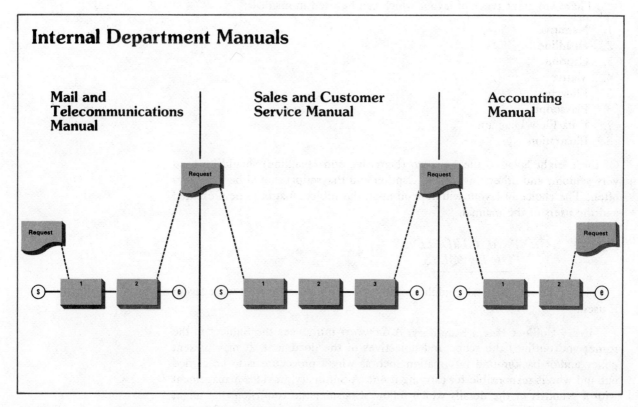

Internal Department Manuals

FIGURE 5-1 *WRITE ONLY FOR THE AUDIENCE CONCERNED*

     In Figure 5–1, the term Internal Department Manuals is used to differentiate between the manuals which are used within an organization to carry out day-to-day procedures and public manuals (or external manuals) such as those which might be written by a government agency for the users of its services. In either case, you write only for the user of the manual. Examples of procedures which might be in public manuals are "How to Apply for Injury Compensation" or "Application for Veteran's Allowances." Such manuals would also outline the criteria for making an application, the benefits accorded by legislation, etc. Public or external manuals would not need to describe all the processes which have to be performed to deliver the services to the public user. Internal department manuals would fulfill this function. However, each department manual would only describe those processes which are relevant to the individual department. Thus, in Figure 5–1, there is a Request (for services) entering an organization. The first department through which the request will be processed is the mail room and those procedures are described in the appropriate "Mail and Telecommunications" manual. The request continues on its journey through the organization—to the sales department and the accounting department, etc. Employees of each of these departments are provided with their respective manuals which only describe (but in detail) how to carry out their activities to process the customer's request. The manuals do not cross department boundaries even though the request does.

Cross-Reference Only When Necessary. Cross-referencing between manuals, Tabs, Sections, or Subjects should be done only when required since cross-referencing must be maintained.

Include Detail. The inclusion of detail does not contradict what has been said here about keeping Subjects short. One of the problems most often encountered is the tendency to leave out detail, particularly when documents are written by employees who perform the activities. This is a result of the writer being too close to the Subject; that is, of knowing the Subject too well. However, the inclusion of detail is essential if Subjects are to be thoroughly understood and if procedures are to be followed accurately.

5.2
NARRATIVE
▼

As the name suggests, the *Narrative layout* is freestyle writing. It presents information to the user in paragraph format. However, this layout is not recommended for use in manuals because it hinders readability and retrievability. Manuals are information tools, and the information must be presented so that it can be extracted easily and quickly. The Narrative layout does not present the user with highlighted captions, text headings, or procedure steps. What is presented is straight paragraphs of text, all of which the user may have to peruse in order to find one specific fact.

Another problem is that although the recommended reading line of 4½″ can be applied to the Narrative layout, it makes the page look off balance and gives the impression of incompleteness. So, in Figure 5–2, which illustrates the Narrative layout, a longer reading line has been used. To assist the user, the text has been double-spaced.

If you find it is necessary to use this layout, do so sparingly and only for short policy statements, company philosophy, or historical background. The only Subject for which the Narrative layout is recommended is the Management Endorsement (Chapter 2), which is most often published on an organization's letterhead. Compare retrievability and readability in this layout with those that follow.

5.3
HEADLINE
▼

A *Headline* is a title line placed above the text. It is usually printed in boldface type and briefly summarizes or suggests the content of the text which follows (as in newspapers).

122

Widget
Manufacturing
Company

Administration

Section
Forms Design Guidelines

Subject
FORM TITLES

Document Number 03-02-03

All forms will be assigned a descriptive title. For aesthetic reasons, the title will not appear on such forms as letterhead,
envelopes, and checks. All other forms will carry a title, preferably
in the top right quadrant using a flush-right format.

Functional requirements may necessitate alternative positions, in
which case the title can be moved to the left, towards the graphic
signature, or to the bottom left or right quadrants.

When positioned at the top, the minimum grid distance between the
signature and title is equal to the space between the logo and the
company name. Multiples of the distance may be used between the
signature and title only, but the actual distance should be determined by what is most aesthetic. Where space on a form is at a
premium, the minimum grid distance will generally be used.

In all applications, the top of the title will touch the same plane
as the company name. The actual title length and available space
will determine the number of lines required.

Multiple line titles will align with the top and bottom of the
company name. To keep the space between title lines (leading) to an
acceptable minimum, double line titles should be set in 14 pt. Helvetica Medium when using the standard 10 pt. logo type. Single line
titles should not be set smaller than 12 pt. nor larger than 18 pt.

Titles of more than one line will have a flush-left vertical alignment. When positioned in the usually top right quadrant of a form,
the longest line will touch the right-hand margin.

Date
September 10, 19--

Page
1 of 3

FIGURE 5-2   NARRATIVE LAYOUT

The *Headline layout* is similar to the Narrative and Caption layouts in terms of writing style. However, the Headline layout is superior to the Narrative layout in that the text is divided into organized blocks which are highlighted for the reader. The Headline layout is functionally inferior to the Caption layout described in 5.4. To verify this statement, examine some headline applications: textbooks, magazines, and newspapers. The text of these publications is meant to be read from beginning to end. The primary headline (which may be the only one) introduces the Subject and the secondary headlines (if they exist) offer alternative lines of thought. Headlines are primarily used as thought-directors or eye-catchers, not as retrieval devices. By being placed over the text or imbedded in the text, headlines are less visible than captions.

Another point to consider is the effort and expense required to produce headlines if a hierarchy is needed. There are very few businesses outside of the publishing and printing industries that have the resources to produce the typefaces and sizes required to make headlines stand out properly. Most people are lucky if two or three type fonts are available. Without these resources, problems regarding headline hierarchy occur and the result can be a chaos of special effects, such as using all caps in one place, uppercase and lowercase in another, numbering headlines, underlining, etc. None of these techniques aids retrievability or readability. Figure 5–3 illustrates the Headline layout. Compare it with the Caption layout which follows.

5.4
CAPTION
▼

Captions are keywords which appear in the left margin of the page and which highlight or describe the blocks of text opposite them. *Caption layout* is the most commonly used and the most versatile of the eight layouts mentioned. In Chapter 3, "Organization," the breakdown of subject matter into primary, secondary, and tertiary divisions was discussed. Captions offer a further breakdown of text.

ADVANTAGES
◆

Caption layout has the following advantages:

- The Caption layout is simple and attractive. It allows ample use of white space which makes the text easier to read. See Figure 5-4.
- This layout is also perfect for applying the 4½″ reading line.
- Captions, because of their high visibility, save retrieval time and reading time.
- The Caption layout can be used for almost any type of subject matter.
- Caption layout can easily be mixed with the other layouts. For example, it is a simple matter to include illustrations, decision tables, flowcharts, or data flow diagrams to support the text.

Widget
Manufacturing
Company

Administration

Section

Forms Design Guidelines

Subject

FORM HEADINGS, CAPTIONS, AND INSTRUCTIONS

Document
Number 03-02-04

HEADINGS

Headings may be positioned in a number of ways, depending on the
application. As a heading to major sections, the flush-left format
is most effective, particularly when set in a heavier face than the
remaining headings. There is a more pleasing appearance if the
heading is centered vertically and horizontally when used as column
headings, or encompassing reserved fill-in areas.

The standard for system page identification is the centered columnar heading, with the word abbreviations as shown in the illustration on page 2.

Date headings will follow the columnar heading format. The words
or abbreviations used will be subject to the system's requirement.

CAPTIONS

The standard format is upper box captions. The caption is set in
6- or 7-point and positioned in the upper left corner (subject to
the standards governing "column numbers").

Exception: Captions will be set below the entry space on vertical
            file cards.

INSTRUCTIONS

General instructions should always be located at the top of the
form, in order that they are read before the form is filled in.
Detailed instructions are better understood if located at the
beginning of the appropriate section. Instructions needed to

Date
September 10, 19--

Page
1 of 2

FIGURE 5-3   HEADLINE LAYOUT

Widget
Manufacturing
Company

**Systems
Administration**

Section
Software Facilities

Subject
DCF (Document Composition Facility)

Document
Number 05-02-07

SUMMARY

DCF is an IBM text processing system which
uses computers to prepare printed materials.
Text processing consists of

- text entry

- text editing

- word processing

- manuscript preparation

- document markup

- page makeup and composition

- printing.

AT WMC

DCF operates in WMC's TSO environment, using
computer terminals for keying and display.
It utilizes a text processing program called
Script/VS to print on impact printers located
in the Branch offices and the laser printer
in the Head Office.

HOW DCF WORKS

DCF reads the input data file, then formats
the data according to the simple program
codes inserted by the operator.

e.g.   .pa = new page

            .sk = skip a line

The formatted data is routed by DCF to the
output device requested by the operator. It
is then printed.

DCF input consists of text, symbols, control
words, and macro instructions.

Date
August 15, 19--

Page
1 of 4

FIGURE 5-4   CAPTION LAYOUT

- This layout lends itself to the use of bulleted lists and phrases. Bulleting separates and therefore highlights individual pieces of information.

DISADVANTAGES

Conversely, the following disadvantages can result from the use of Caption layout:

- Because this layout is so simple to use, writers tend to overuse it even though the subject matter may lend itself to another, more suitable layout.
- This layout should not be used for describing sequenced actions, time sequences, or situations in which there are many variables. It is ineffective for these applications.
- Caption layout does not take into account the relative importance of material; therefore, it is sometimes difficult to organize captions into a meaningful order.

WHEN TO USE

The Caption layout is best used for descriptive text that answers all the questions: who, what, when, why, and where. Examples of subject matter which may be written in the Caption layout are:

- policy statements
- responsibility statements
- descriptions of forms, reports, equipment, etc.

Also, the Caption layout is particularly useful for Overviews, which are described in 3.6.

HOW TO USE

First, apply all the general principles for layouts discussed at the beginning of this chapter. Then, study the example of Caption layout in Figure 5–4 and the text explaining the captions. Note that the Section title is descriptive yet simple. The entire Section is about Software Facilities. The same is true of the Subject title, DCF. Notice that the abbreviation has been introduced and the meaning for it given in the Subject title so that when you get into the text of the Subject it can be referred to as simply DCF.

The Summary, always the first caption no matter what the layout, introduces and explains the Subject to the reader in general terms.

All captions must be simple and short (one or two words) and they must be relevant to the text they highlight. Captions can be excerpts from the text or they can describe the text. Try not to repeat any words which are in the Section or Subject title (unless it aids the user). In Figure 5–4, the second caption is entitled "AT WMC," rather than "DCF AT WMC." But now look at the caption entitled "HOW DCF WORKS." The rule of not repeating the Subject title has been broken because it would have looked strange to have a caption read "HOW IT WORKS."

As you can see, captions give the reader a means of locating specific information on a page simply by scanning the margins until the data is found. If that data is what is required, it is not necessary to read the Summary of a Subject or any other captioned text of that Subject—one reads only what is needed. For this reason, care must be taken so that the text of each Caption, when read in isolation, makes sense. For example, consider Figure 5–5, which illustrates this self-sufficiency.

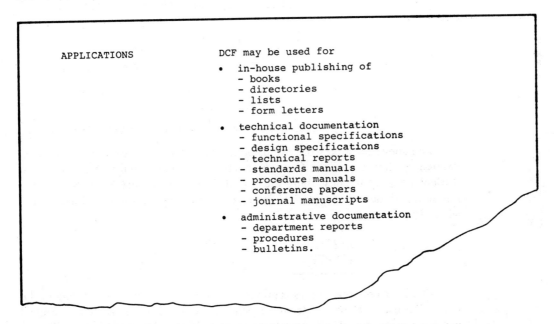

APPLICATIONS

```
DCF may be used for
  • in-house publishing of
    - books
    - directories
    - lists
    - form letters
  • technical documentation
    - functional specifications
    - design specifications
    - technical reports
    - standards manuals
    - procedure manuals
    - conference papers
    - journal manuscripts
  • administrative documentation
    - department reports
    - procedures
    - bulletins.
```

FIGURE 5-5   CAPTIONS AND THEIR TEXT SHOULD BE SELF-SUFFICIENT

Here, again, DCF is not repeated in the caption. However, in the text it is necessary to start with the words "DCF may be used for . . ." rather than "It may be used for . . ." to ensure that the reader is properly oriented and able to read this piece of text by itself. Repetition in cases like this is necessary so that the time gained by using captions is not lost due to the inability to comprehend the text.

The text in Figure 5–5 is also a good example of how to show unsequenced lists. Hierarchy is indicated by using bullets for primary applications and dashes for secondary applications. Presentation of data in this manner not only aids the user in retrieving the information but also in remembering it.

There is a use for secondary as well as primary captions. Secondary captions help the user by breaking down the Subject to a more specific level. They also assist retrievability. However, secondary captions should not be overused. To differentiate between the two, primary captions are typed in uppercase at the extreme left margin, whereas secondary captions are typed in upper- and lower-case and are indented three to five spaces from that margin. The exact spacing depends on the page design.

```
HIRING
RESPONSIBILITIES

    Systems    The supervisor is responsible for

               •  recommending a candidate

               •  obtaining approval to hire from the
                  manager

               •  notifying Personnel.

    Personnel  The personnel officer is responsible for

               •  making the job offer, in accordance
                  with company policy

               •  induction and orientation interviews.
```

The above illustrates the use of primary and secondary captions. Earlier, in discussing when to use the Caption layout, it was mentioned that this layout is particularly good for describing the use of forms (see Figure 5–6). Notice that the Summary describes the form, indicates when, how, and who will use it, and where it is illustrated.

INDEXING CAPTIONS

The keywords selected as captions may well be the words that spring to the mind of a user who wants to find a Subject in a manual. It is therefore good practice to consider placing important captions in the alphabetic index. Thus, a Subject on Caption layout, for instance, might be indexed in the following ways:

- Caption Layout
- Layouts—Caption
- Indexing Captions
- Primary Captions
- Secondary Captions

5.5
MATRIX
▼

Matrices have become an integral part of everyday life—they are found in newspapers, magazines, TV guides, and travel schedules. Although a matrix may

Widget
Manufacturing
Company

Administration

Section
Budget

Document
Number 02-02-02

Subject
CURRENT YEAR BUDGET REFORECAST, Form 0002

SUMMARY

Form 0002 is completed by branch managers
during the first week of July. The purpose
of the form is to

- compare actual expenses incurred during
  the first half of the fiscal year to the
  approved budget

- show variances between actual expenses
  and approved budget

- assist management in the re-allocation of
  funds for the second half of the year

- identify budgeting omissions and errors
  for future years.

Form 0002 must be typed in duplicate. Part 1
must be submitted to the comptroller by mid-
July. Part 2 is kept in the branch budget
files. All applicable fields on the form
must be completed accurately. A detailed
description of each column follows. An
example of a completed form is illustrated on
page 3.

COLUMN 1

Insert account codes against which expenses
have been incurred.

COLUMN 2

Insert account descriptions.

NOTE: Account codes and descriptions may
be found in the chart of accounts
at 02-01-03.

COLUMN 3

Show total actual expenses incurred during
the current year (January 1 to June 30)
for each account.

COLUMN 4

This column is completed for you. It is
the "Approved Budget" for the branch.

Date
January 18, 19--

Page
1 of 4

FIGURE 5-6   *USING CAPTION LAYOUT TO DESCRIBE FORMS*

take you as much time and effort to prepare as it takes to produce several pages of text, the matrix may also take the place of those pages. The time and effort are rewarding to the user as well as to the writer.

A *matrix* is a chart which lists related constants and variables (or independent and dependent variables) on horizontal and vertical axes. At the intersection of lines drawn from each axis (in the body of the matrix) may be found such information as

- relationships between constants and variables
- actions to be performed depending on variables or conditions
- answers.

An example of each of these is illustrated in Figures 5–7, 5–8, and 5–9.

ADVANTAGES

The following advantages accrue from the use of matrices:

- Data is presented graphically in a simple and logical order.
- Repetitive information is eliminated.
- A one-page matrix may replace many pages of text.
- Retrieval time and reading time are saved.

| Player | Team | | | |
	New York Yankees	Montreal Canadiens	San Diego Chargers	Los Angeles Dodgers
Berra, Yogi	Coach/ Catcher			
Fouts, Dan			Quarterback	
Gilliam, Jim				Coach/ Second Base
Koufax, Sandy				Pitcher
Mantle, Mickey	Center Field			
Richard, Rocket		Right Wing		

FIGURE 5-7   MATRIX (RELATIONSHIPS)

Time	Entrance/Exit
6:30 a.m. to 6:00 p.m.	Enter/exit at Lincoln Street.
6:00 p.m. to 9:30 p.m.	Enter/Exit at Washington Street.
9:30 p.m. to 6:30 a.m.	1. Enter/exit at Washington Street. 2. Sign in/out at security desk.

FIGURE 5-8   *MATRIX (ACTIONS)*

Multiplicand	Multiplier						
	1	2	3	4	5	6	7
1	1	2	3	4	5	6	7
2	2	4	6	8	10	12	14
3	3	6	9	12	15	18	21
4	4	8	12	16	20	24	28
5	5	10	15	20	25	30	35
6	6	12	18	24	30	36	42
7	7	14	21	28	35	42	49

FIGURE 5-9   *MATRIX (ANSWERS)*

It is best to use a matrix when *if-then* situations occur or when *actions depend on variables*.

It is not always easy to recognize whether the subject matter which is being dealt with is right for a matrix. Look for the conditions which earmark the matrix and then follow these tips and techniques.

1. Remove all repetitious or redundant information. This redundant information may be a result of describing similar situations and/or related activities.
2. Indicate each if-then type of situation.
3. Format your matrix. Keep the user in mind—make it simple. List the constants (or independent variables) on the vertical axis. List the variables (dependent variables) on the horizontal axis. List variables or constants according to hierarchy or, when none exists, list them alphabetically or numerically.
4. Add only that information which is required to make the matrix understandable. Accent special conditions with asterisks or numerals and explain them at the foot of the matrix as notes.
5. Prepare the artwork. Use different typefaces or sizes to differentiate between the data in the body of the matrix and the variables and constants on the axes.
6. Write a Summary to introduce the matrix to the reader.

Consider Figure 5–10, which is fairly simply written text.

The only information which really stands out in Figure 5–10 is the list of courses and their titles. There are also a number of if-then type situations (*if* you take certain courses *then* you will be eligible for a certain certificate). However, from a retrieval and readability point of view, the user may have to read all three pieces of text describing the certificates to find the one desired. Information is also repeated throughout each description. How, then, can you present the information in the text so that it stands out simply and clearly? Follow along with the application of the six steps previously described.

1. The original document has 157 words. Removal of all repetitious information leaves the following skeleton of 91 words:

```
The Records Management Program at Gotham College offers
seven courses:

RM 900        Introduction to Records Management
RM 901        Advanced Records Management
RM 902        Forms Management
RM 903        Manuals Design and Development
MICRO 900     Microfilm for Your Business
FORM 900      Procedural Analysis
FORM 901      Forms Design
```

NADIR Inc.

Administration

Section
Education

Subject
RECORDS MANAGEMENT COURSES

Document
Number 02-02-04

The Records Management Program at Gotham College offers seven
courses:

- RM 900   Introduction to Records Management
- RM 901   Advanced Records Management
- RM 902   Forms Management
- RM 903   Manuals Design and Development
- MICRO 900   Microfilm for Your Business
- FORM 900   Procedural Analysis
- FORM 901   Forms Design

Three certificates are offered. The details and requirements of
each are listed below.

PAPERWORK SIMPLIFICATION CERTIFICATE--AABFM
This certificate is offered by the American Association for
Business Forms Management (AABFM). Students are required to
take three of the seven courses in order to receive this certificate. They are RM 902, FORM 900, and FORM 901.

RECORDS MANAGEMENT CERTIFICATE--ARMA
The Association of Records Managers and Administrators (APMA)
offers their certificate to students who take four of the seven
courses offered. RM 900 and RM 901 are mandatory. Any two others
may be taken.

RECORDS MANAGEMENT CERTIFICATE--Gotham College
The College offers a certificate to students if they complete six
of the seven courses. RM 900 and RM 901 are mandatory. Any four
others may be taken.

Date
June 18, 19--

Page
1 of 1

FIGURE 5-10   *NARRATIVE TEXT BEFORE MATRIX*

Three certificates are offered:

- PAPERWORK SIMPLIFICATION CERTIFICATE—AABFM (American Association for Business Forms Management), three mandatory (RM 902, FORM 900, FORM 901)

- RECORDS MANAGEMENT CERTIFICATE—ARMA (The Association of Records Managers and Administrators), two mandatory (RM 900, RM 901), two optional (of those remaining)

- RECORDS MANAGEMENT CERTIFICATE—GOTHAM COLLEGE—two mandatory (RM 900, RM 901), four optional (of those remaining)

2. The if-then situations are then identified.
   —if AABFM certificate is desired, take RM 902, FORM 900, FORM 901
   —if ARMA certificate is desired, take RM 900, RM 901, two others
   —if GC certificate is desired, take RM 900, RM 901, four others

3. Formatting the data is done by listing the certificates (independent variables) on the vertical axis and the courses (dependent variables) on the horizontal axis.

COURSES

CERTIFICATES	RM900	RM901	RM902	RM903	MICRO900	FORM900	FORM901
AABFM							
ARMA							
GC							

There are two types of courses in relationship to the certificates: mandatory and optional. These are denoted with an "M" and an "O" respectively. The result looks like this.

COURSES

CERTIFICATES	RM900	RM901	RM902	RM903	MICRO900	FORM900	FORM901
AABFM			M			M	M
ARMA	M	M	O	O	O	O	O
GC	M	M	O	O	O	O	O

4. The matrix still needs to indicate how many courses are required for each certificate. To do this, a column is added on the far right entitled, "Number of Courses Required." A note explaining the certificate abbreviations is added to the foot of the matrix (Figure 5–11).

5. The lettering for the matrix artwork can be done on 8½″ × 11″ paper using a Kroytype lettering machine. Then it is reduced on a photocopy machine to fit the manual page.

NADIR Inc.

Administration

Section
Education

Subject
RECORDS MANAGEMENT COURSES

Document
Number   02-02-04

SUMMARY

The Records Management Program at Gotham
College offers seven courses:

RM 900   Introduction to Records Management
RM 901   Advanced Records Management
RM 902   Forms Management
RM 903   Manuals Design and Development
MICRO 900   Microfilm for Your Business
FORM 900   Procedural Analysis
FORM 901   Forms Design

Three certificates are offered. Mandatory
(M), optional (O), and total requirements
for each certificate are outlined in the
following matrix.

CERTIFICATE
REQUIREMENTS

| Certificates | Courses | | | | | | | No. of courses required |
	RM 900	RM 901	RM 902	RM 903	Micro 900	Form 900	Form 901	
AABFM[1]			M			M	M	3
ARMA[2]	M	M	O	O	O	O	O	4
GC[3]	M	M	O	O	O	O	O	6

NOTE: 1. Paperwork Simplification-American Association of
          Business Forms Management
       2. Records Management-Association of Records Managers
          and Administrators
       3. Records Management-Gotham College

Date
June 18, 19--

Page
1 of 1

FIGURE 5-11   TEXT CONVERTED TO MATRIX LAYOUT

6.   The last step is to write the Summary, which contains the remaining information necessary for the user to understand the matrix.

The final result, which is simple and attractive, is illustrated in Figure 5–11.

SPECIAL KINDS
OF MATRICES

Decision tables and *decision trees* are special kinds of matrices. They also document procedures where many if-then conditions exist. They are especially useful for programming applications, but they are perhaps too formalized for presentation as actual procedure layouts. However, they can certainly be useful in developing your matrices. An extensive exposition on decision tables and decision trees will not be given here, since there are books written on the subject. Now it will suffice to show a very simple decision table which could result from the same procedure as the Entrance/Exit matrix (Figure 5–8).

The decision table has three parts (see Figure 5–12):

1.   The condition stub—represented by the various times
2.   The action stub—has the enter/exit and sign-in/sign-out instructions
3.   The rules—consisting of a series of columns

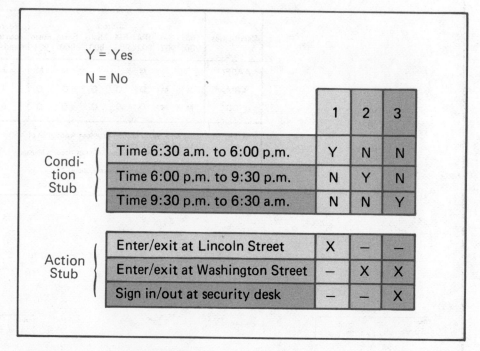

Y = Yes N = No		1	2	3
Condition Stub	Time 6:30 a.m. to 6:00 p.m.	Y	N	N
	Time 6:00 p.m. to 9:30 p.m.	N	Y	N
	Time 9:30 p.m. to 6:30 a.m.	N	N	Y
Action Stub	Enter/exit at Lincoln Street	X	—	—
	Enter/exit at Washington Street	—	X	X
	Sign in/out at security desk	—	—	X

FIGURE 5-12   DECISION TABLE

Note that if there are three conditions, there are theoretically $2^3 = 8$ columns or rules available. For the example in Figure 5–12, these would be:

1	2	3	4	5	6	7	8
Y	Y	Y	N	Y	N	N	N
Y	Y	N	Y	N	Y	N	N
Y	N	Y	Y	N	N	Y	N

In this example, however, because of the nature of the conditions, only three rules (Columns 5, 6, and 7) are possible. For example, the first rule of all Y's (yesses) is ridiculous, since all three times cannot occur at once. Working out all the theoretical rules (and then eliminating the impossible or impractical) serves as a thorough check for your decision tables.

Decision trees are less widely used. The yes/no variables are represented by a structure resembling a tree rather than by a table. This is shown in Figure 5–13, which is the same entrance/exit procedure as Figures 5–8 and 5–12.

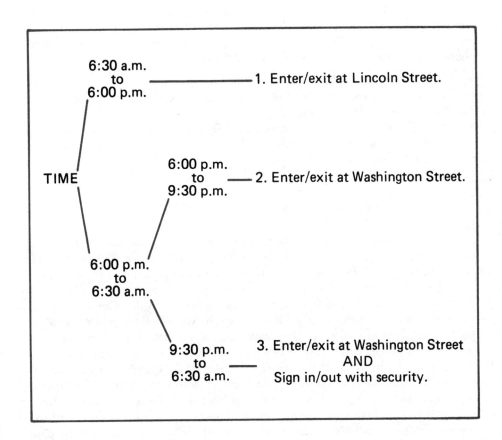

FIGURE 5-13   DECISION TREE

Decision tables and decision trees are sometimes a little difficult for the uninitiated to understand; for this reason, it is recommended that you try to compose as simple a matrix as possible for your manuals.

5.6

FLOWCHART
▼

Flowcharts are graphic diagrams in which symbols are used to depict persons, places, actions, functions, and equipment, and to illustrate the step-by-step progression of an activity. The flowchart is perhaps the most useful organizational and analytical tool manuals writers can use. It can be the graphic framework upon which a procedure is developed or it can stand alone.

WHEN TO USE FLOWCHARTS
◆

Some specialists say that flowcharts are an organizational or analytical tool only, and that they should only be used in technical or systems manuals. But many people enjoy reading simple flowcharts and in some cases they understand them better than the written word. Simple flowcharts should be used

- for analysis and organization
- to present users (particularly in the first stages of writing procedures) with an overview of the activities
- if users are familiar with the symbols (it is a simple matter to include a legend on a flowchart)
- as supplements to other layouts
- for systems manuals.

PREPARATION
◆

A rough draft of the flowchart may be drawn during the investigation and analysis stage; i.e., while you are interviewing and gathering all information about the activity or after all the information has been accumulated.

Flowcharts may be drawn on rolls of inexpensive paper such as Telex or Kraft wrapping paper. The faint lines on this paper aid in the alignment of the symbols. However, flowcharts are more often drawn on rolls of paper which are produced just for this purpose. One manufacturer, for instance, makes flowcharting paper in 350-foot rolls and in two sizes: 11″ deep and 15″ deep. The paper is perforated every 8″ so that segments can be easily detached, added on, or inserted. The paper is available in 40M bond or translucent tissue. The paper is preprinted with ½″ squares which act as drawing guides. Once the chart has been drawn, it can be folded accordian-fashion. The 11″ paper can be fanfolded (on the perforation, every 8″) for insertion in manuals. The charts may also be photoreduced to fit the pages of a manual.

Using a bit of imagination, one might say that the use of flowcharts goes as far back as our cave-dwelling ancestors who carefully recorded their daily activities on the walls of their homes. Most races of people (particularly the Egyptians, the Aztecs, and the Mayans) left "texts" describing their social and commercial procedures on plates, walls, stone pillars, lintels, panels, etc.

Symbols have therefore always been important in the lives of people. Some have been (and will continue to be) used throughout the centuries. Many symbols have been standardized and universally recognized. Symbols with which everyone is familiar are: $, %, #, @, ¢, =, −, etc. Many scientific symbols, however, are not so easily recognized, except by those persons directly involved in the sciences. Some of these scientific symbols are presented in Figure 5–14. In all cases, however, symbols are simple, meaningful time-savers, and so it is with those used in flowcharting.

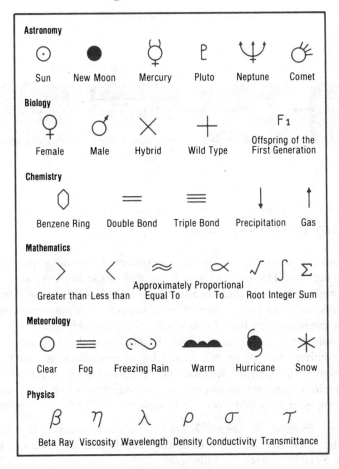

FIGURE 5-14   RECOGNIZED SCIENTIFIC SYMBOLS

Although the first drafts of a flowchart may be roughed out, templates are usually used to draw the symbols for the finished product. There are many types of templates available, varying according to the type of chart required and in some cases the systems development methodology prescribed within the organization. You may purchase templates with as many as 20-odd symbols on them. However, it is possible to flowchart any manual procedure (or system) with just the four symbols and connectors discussed here. These are internationally recognized.

Process or Activity Symbol. The *rectangle* is used to depict any manual process or administrative activity performed by individuals (not machines). For example, see Figure 5–15 which illustrates the following procedure:

> Upon receipt of mail, the clerk must open the envelopes and staple them to the contents. The contents must be date-stamped, sorted according to department, and forwarded.

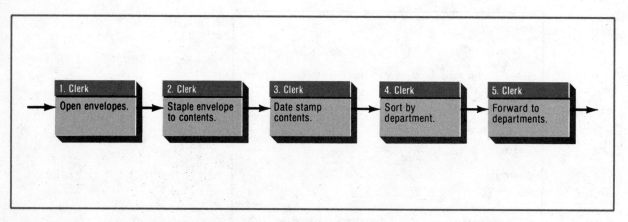

FIGURE 5-15 *THE PROCESS OR ACTIVITY SYMBOL IN A FLOWCHART*

The process or activity box is usually numbered to show sequential progression of the activity. The number may be placed inside the box, as shown, or, if there is not enough room, directly above it. The title of the actor who performs the activity is indicated in the top portion of the box. It is not necessary to repeat the title in every activity box if it is always the same. However, when there is more than one actor, it is essential that the flowchart clearly indicate who does what. The activity statements within the boxes must be short, each beginning with an action verb: open, staple, sort, etc. If special notes need to be added to further explain a step, put an asterisk or note number in the box and place the corresponding note directly below the process box at the foot of the page.

Decision Symbol. A *diamond* is used to indicate situations in which a decision must be made between two (or more) variable courses of action. For example, Figure 5–16 illustrates the following:

The supervisor must review the forms. If they are completed correctly they must be sent to the manager. If they are incorrect they must be returned to the originator.

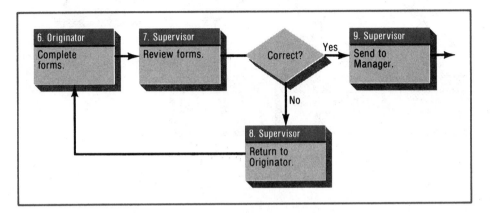

FIGURE 5-16   THE DECISION SYMBOL IN THE FLOWCHART

In Figure 5–16, the supervisor reviews the forms. The question to be asked is: "Are the forms correct?" If the answer is yes, the activity proceeds. If the answer is no, an alternative activity takes place. Once a decision symbol has been introduced you must make sure that the process boxes are numbered correctly. Numbering remains sequential but negative processes are numbered before positive processes. The result is that there will be more steps to perform if something goes wrong and fewer steps to perform if everything proceeds normally. In Figure 5–16, Step 9 is performed if the forms are correct, whereas Step 8 must be performed if the forms are incorrect. Steps 6 and 7 must then be repeated to correct the error.

The examples in Figures 5–17 and 5–18 show two ways to indicate actions to be taken when there are more than two variables. The following text is illustrated:

When mail is opened the contents must be date-stamped and forwarded to the appropriate department. Invoices are sent to Accounts Payable; checks are forwarded to Accounts Receivable; purchase orders go to Sales; and general correspondence is sent to the manager of administration.

Document Symbol. This symbol, which looks like *a page that has been cut off,* is used to illustrate any type of paper such as letters, computer printouts,

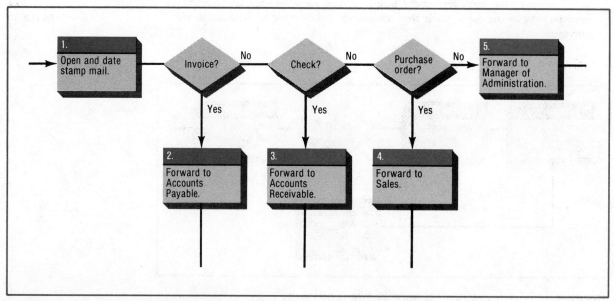

FIGURE 5-17   MULTIPLE DECISIONS (METHOD 1)

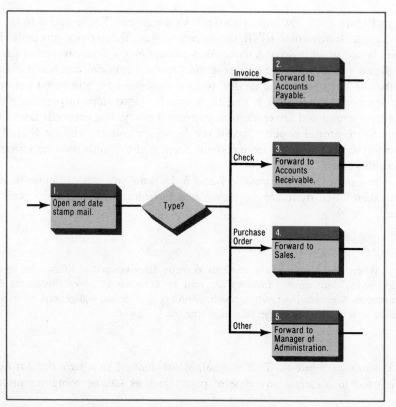

FIGURE 5-18   MULTIPLE DECISIONS (METHOD 2)

forms, etc., connected with the procedure. For example, Figure 5–19 illustrates the following:

> Form 001 is a three-part form. The supervisor, upon receipt, retains Parts 1 and 2. Part 3 is sent to the manager.

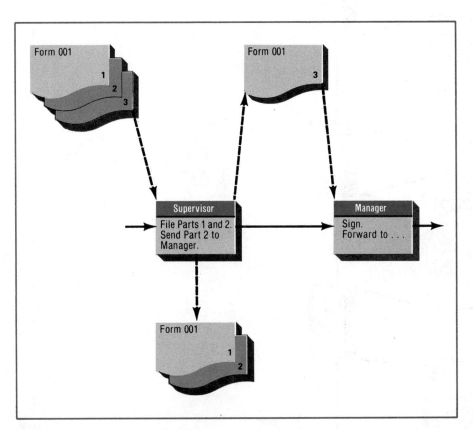

FIGURE 5-19   DOCUMENT SYMBOL IN A FLOWCHART

The title of the document is printed on the upper left corner of the document symbol. If it is a form, the form number should be indicated, and the part of the form is shown in the bottom right corner. Note that reference is made to parts of forms, not original and copies. The document symbol is positioned above the process boxes so that the reader can see all the parts as they are dispersed throughout the procedure. Documents are connected only to process (activity) boxes and to files.

If there are different documents or forms, they are introduced at the appropriate places in the flowchart. Each is always indicated separately, but brackets may be used to show when two or more different documents progress together through the processes. This is illustrated in Figure 5–20.

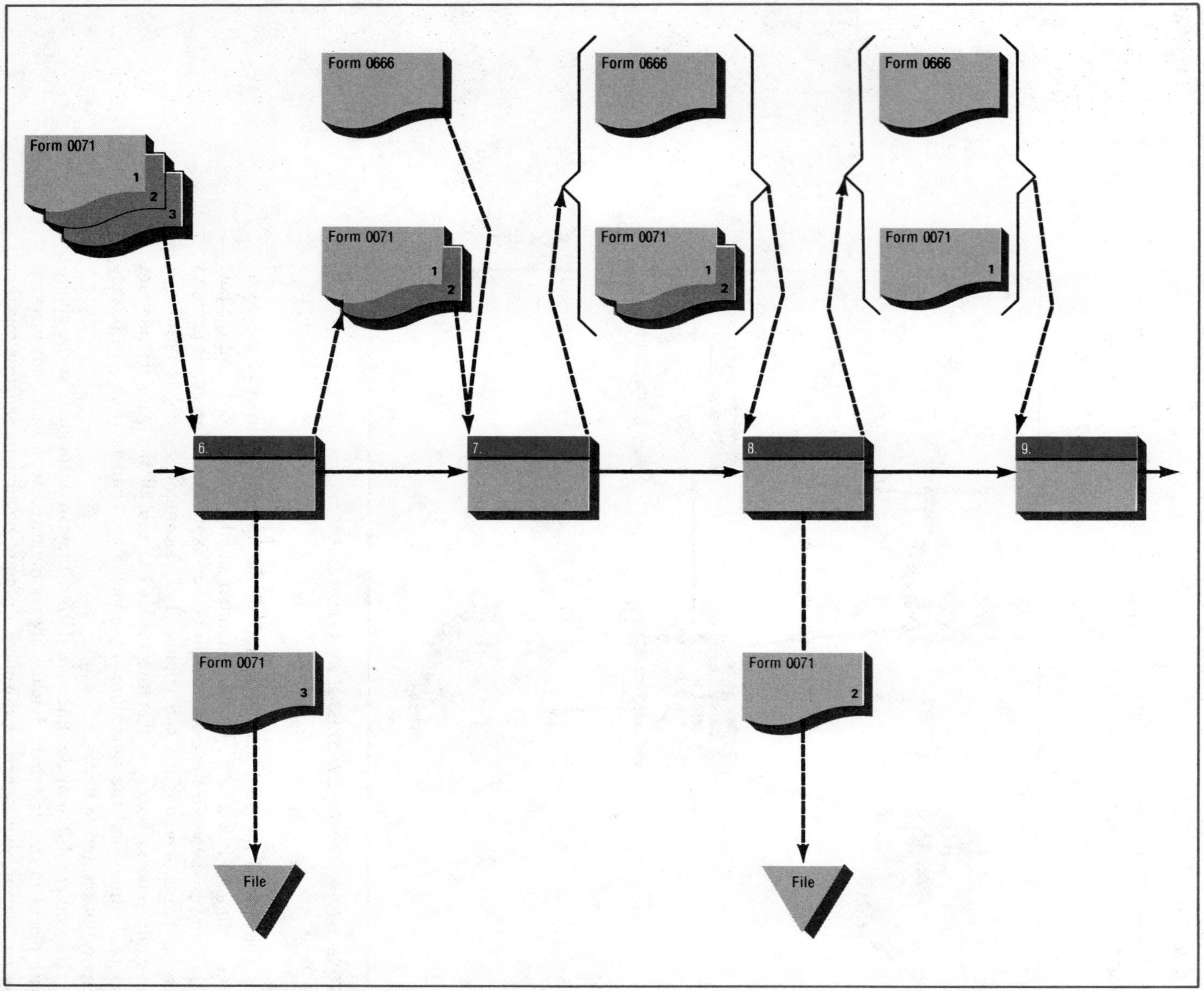

FIGURE 5-20   MULTIPLE DOCUMENTS

Manual File Symbol. The inverted *triangle* is used to symbolize a manual file or paper file (as opposed to a computer file). If the file has a name such as "Invoice File" it should be printed on the symbol. Figure 5–21 illustrates the following text:

> Form 002 is a two-part form. Upon receipt, the supervisor must file Part 1 in the invoice file and forward Part 2 to the costing clerk.

In this example, a two-part form is shown coming to a supervisor. Part 2 of the form is forwarded to a cost clerk and Part 1 is shown going into a file.

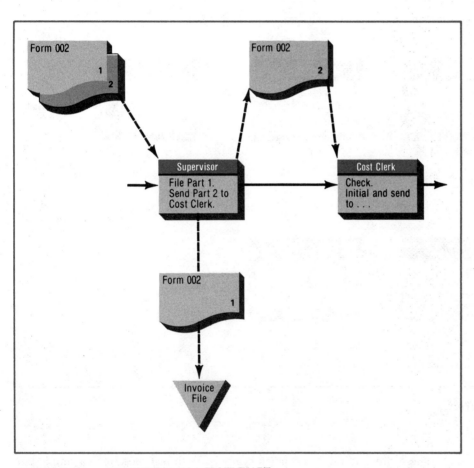

FIGURE 5-21   FILE SYMBOL IN A FLOWCHART

Connector Symbols. Connectors are used to join the symbols in the flow-chart when the flow is interrupted by the end of a line or page. Only the simplest connectors need to be used.

Start: A *small circle with the letter "S"* is used to indicate the beginning of the procedure.

End: A *small circle* (of the same size as the start circle) is used *with the letter* "E" to indicate the end of the procedure.

Continued: When a flowchart must be partitioned because of its length, *sequentially numbered circles* are used to indicate to the reader where to go next. These circles can be used as either on-page or off-page connectors (see Figure 5–22).

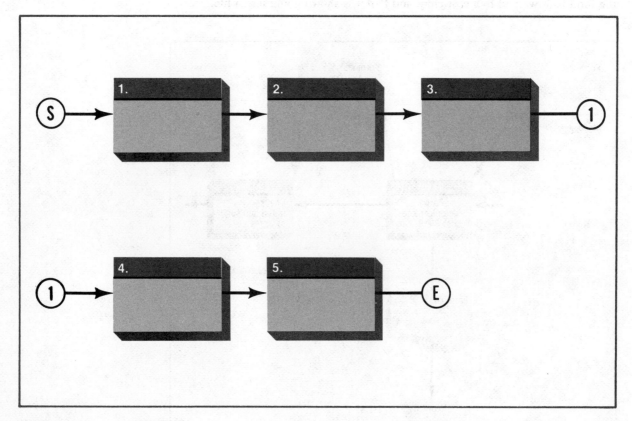

FIGURE 5-22   CONNECTORS

These then are the best known symbols. With just these few, a simple but extremely effective flowchart can be devised. A few of the lesser known symbols, but ones which are extensively used in systems flowcharts, are illustrated in Figure 5–23.

Choose your symbols carefully. Do not use symbols which you do not know how to use. Use only those symbols which you know your audience will recognize, and include a legend at the beginning of the flowchart if you think it might help.

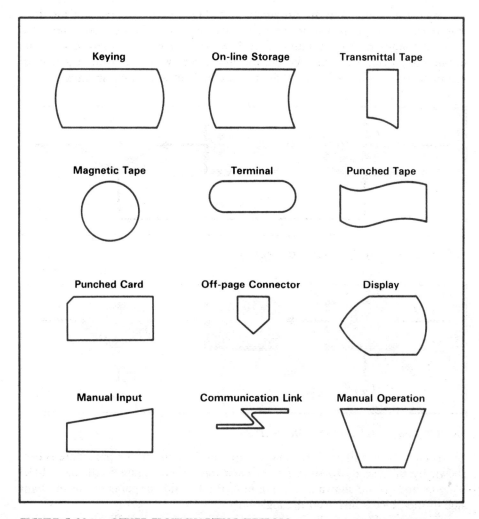

FIGURE 5-23   OTHER FLOWCHARTING SYMBOLS

The Logic Line. The Logic Line is the central process and/or decision-making line of the flowchart. It is a *solid line*. Arrows indicate the direction to take.

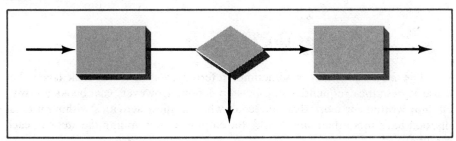

FIGURE 5-24   THE LOGIC LINE

Iterations. Iterations are *procedure loops*. They occur as a result of the decision process. The steps within the procedure loops must be iterated or repeated until all conditions for continuing have been met. If it is awkward to show the entire loop, a connector may be used to indicate to which step the reader must return. Figures 5–25 and 5–26 show two methods of illustrating iterations.

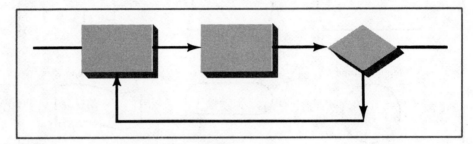

FIGURE 5-25   ITERATIONS (METHOD 1)

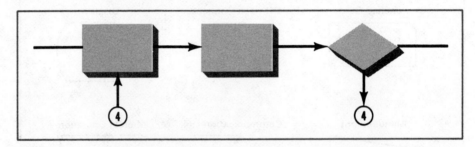

FIGURE 5-26   ITERATIONS (METHOD 2)

Input/Output Flow. The flow of paper or documents in a procedure is best shown by the use of *hyphenated or nonsolid lines*. (See Figure 5–20, page 144.) The documents are shown as coming in to the left side or going out of the right side of the process boxes on the logic line.

Figures 5–27 and 5–28 illustrate a flowchart of a typical office routine. Note the logic line, how the input/output documents feed into it, and how the connectors have been used. Steps 4 to 8 make up an example of an iteration or procedure loop.

5.7
PLAYSCRIPT
▼

The *Playscript layout* is sometimes referred to as the cookbook layout because it describes sequential step-by-step action. However, cookbooks are usually not written for more than one cook whereas most activities within an organization have more than one "cook" (or employee) performing the steps in each activity.

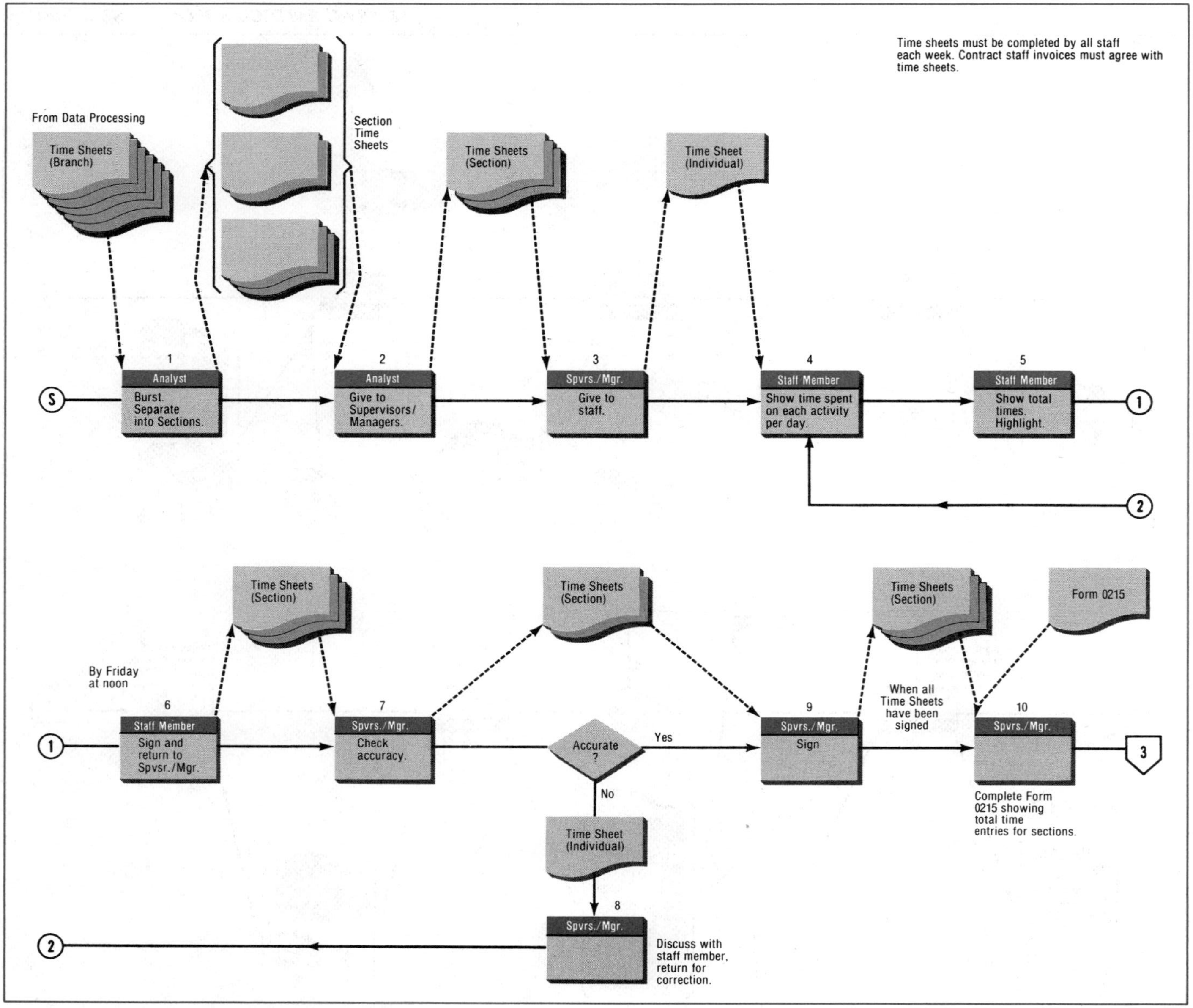

FIGURE 5-27   OFFICE ROUTINE (PART 1)

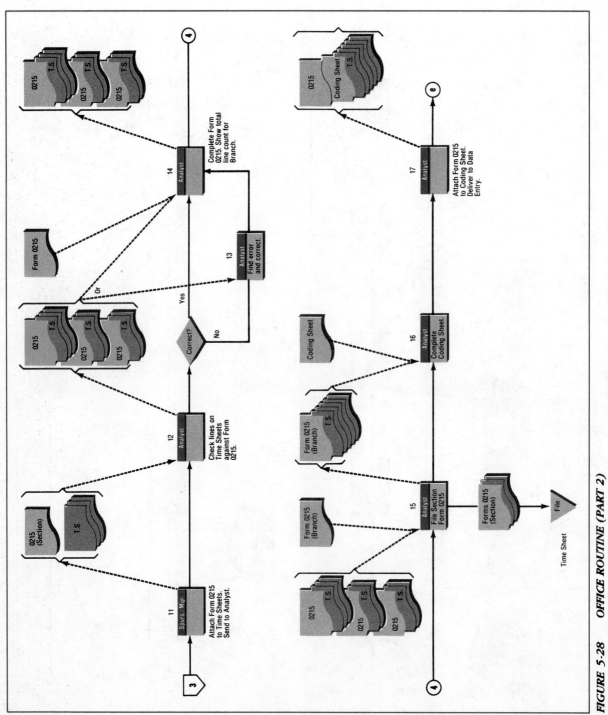

FIGURE 5-28 OFFICE ROUTINE (PART 2)

Playscript may also be considered to be a literal translation of the linear flowchart. However, *Playscript* is the most commonly used name because the information is presented to the reader in the same form as a play. The actors (i.e., employees) are identified in the left margin and the parts (i.e., functions) they perform are described to the right of the actors' names. Each function or step is then shown in the sequence in which it is to be performed.

This section will help you understand how and when to use the Playscript layout effectively.

ADVANTAGES

Some of the advantages of the Playscript layout are:

- It identifies *who* does *what, when.*
  Who—Each employee involved in the procedure is identified.
  What—Each step in the procedure is described in detail.
  When—The sequence in which the steps are to be performed is identified by sequentially numbering the steps.
- Information in a Playscript layout is easy to find; just scan the page and find the job title and the steps desired.
- The Playscript layout is easily understood by all. Language is simple and sentences are short and to the point.

WHEN AND HOW TO USE

The Playscript layout should be used for any activity in which step-by-step routines are performed sequentially by one person or a number of persons.

Before you actually start to write the Playscript, you must gather any written documentation (including forms) that already exist and interview the employees involved in the procedure you are describing. Start with the supervisor or manager who is in charge in order to get an overview of the activity. It is this interview which sets the stage for the "play." You learn who the actors are, what props they use, and what the proper timing is. When this is done, you can begin to trace the activity with the individuals who know it best: the staff who carry out the activity.

Once you've gathered all the information required and have identified and interviewed all the employees involved in the procedure, you can begin to write or, if you prefer, flowchart (remember, a Playscript layout is a literal translation of a linear flowchart). Once the first draft of the procedure is done, check it with everyone you've interviewed. Then translate it to the Playscript layout, which consists of these three parts:

1. Summary
2. Set-Up
3. Procedure

THE SUMMARY

As mentioned at the beginning of this chapter, every Subject must have a Summary. The Summary is particularly important when using the Playscript layout because it is the only place where policy statements can be made or background information can be supplied. The Set-Up and Procedure steps are not the place for descriptive narrative. The following is an example of a typical Summary.

SUMMARY   The Forms Administration Department uses exter-
            nal suppliers for art and filmwork required by
            the company. It is the responsibility of the
            Forms Administration staff to ensure that

            ● invoices received from suppliers are correct

            ● approvals for payment of invoices are ob-
              tained from the appropriate department head
              on the Invoice Approval Voucher, Form 0987

            ● all appropriate documentation is forwarded
              to the Accounting Department.

THE SET-UP

The Set-Up is that portion of the Playscript layout which lists the forms and/or other tools required by the user to carry out the procedure. If the individual who performs an activity is prepared in advance of the actual performance, time and effort will be saved. This follows the "cookbook" method of gathering all necessary ingredients and implements prior to the preparation of food. Setting up includes gathering paperwork (forms), reference works (texts, manuals, etc.), and special tools (date stamps, templates, etc.).

Forms are listed by their titles and their form numbers in the order in which they are used in the procedure. Having given both the name and the number of each form in the Set-Up, it is not necessary to use the name again in the procedure steps. Only the form number is used, thereby saving space and eliminating unnecessary repetition. The following is an example of a typical Set-Up. Note that the form number of the supplier's invoice is not given because it is another organization's form.

SET-UP   ● Supplier's Invoice (2 copies)
          ● Date Stamp
          ● Invoice Approval Voucher, Form 0987

THE PROCEDURE

When documenting a step-by-step procedure, remember the general rule that no procedure should overlap the boundaries of another manual. That is, if procedures interact between two departments and each department has its own manual, describe in each manual only that department's part of the procedure.

For example, suppose Form 1000 originates in the Systems Department and is then forwarded to the Accounting Department where it is processed and filed. The Systems manual should only describe the procedure for originating and forwarding the form. The Accounting manual should describe the procedure beginning with receipt of the form and continuing through the last step performed in that department. Some other rules and standards to assist you in writing the procedure section of Playscript follow.

Job Titles. Always use the proper job title in the actor captions just as it is listed in the job specification; e.g., Forms Analyst, Administration and Support Services, etc. These captions should always be placed at the left margin, and they should be in upper- and lowercase so as to distinguish them from the captions Summary, Set-Up, and Procedure, which are typed in uppercase only. Do not use personal names because employees may leave the organization, necessitating costly revisions in the manual.

Some manuals writers always use the plural of job titles; e.g., managers, file clerks, etc. However, this is unnecessary, even when more than one person performs the activity, because you are addressing only the person reading the manual at that time.

Time Statements. Either at the outset of a procedure or during the procedure, it may be necessary to indicate when a step is to be performed. Such a statement may be general in nature (for instance, indicating that a step must be performed upon the receipt of a certain form), or it may be very specific (such as stating that a step must be done at a certain time of day). The following illustration shows the difference between general and specific time statements.

```
UPON RECEIPT OF FORM 0123     EVERY MORNING AT 9 A.M.

1. Date stamp the form.        1. Unlock cash drawer.

2. . . . .                     2. . . . .
```

Time statements are not procedure steps. Thus, they are not numbered. They stand alone and should be printed entirely in uppercase. Extra space should be left between these time statements and the procedure steps.

Variable Directions. There is seldom a procedure which does not have a conditional if-then situation. The reader must be made aware that the variable conditions exist and must be told what to do in every instance. If three or more variables exist in a given procedure and each of these variables causes steps that are extremely diverse, stop and reconsider the Subject, as it may be that more than one Subject is required, or that the Matrix layout is more appropriate than a Playscript. The following is an example of variable directions in a Playscript.

```
10. Verify data on time sheets

DATA CORRECT—Proceed to Step 13.

DATA INCORRECT—Continue.

11. . . . .
```

When documenting variable steps, remember to direct the user around the steps which are the exceptions just as you would in a linear flowchart. In the previous example, if the data is incorrect, several extra steps must be taken to correct the information; but if correct, the procedure progresses to Step 13. Again, more space should be left before and after variable statements so that they stand out from the procedure steps.

Sequential Numbering. Each step in the procedure must be numbered. The numbers are sequential, starting at the first step and continuing right through to the last, no matter how many different individuals take part. The following example shows the consecutive numbering of steps in a Playscript layout.

```
Operations      1. . . . .
Technician
                2. . . . .

                3. . . . .

Operations      4. . . . .
Supervisor
                5. . . . .

Clerk           6. . . . .
```

Action Verbs. Start each step of the Procedure with an action verb, like *start, discuss, correct, arrange, review,* etc.

Short, Simple Steps. The most critical thing to remember when writing a Playscript is to keep the steps short and simple. There is no point in using this layout if each step is five or six lines long. Here are some hints for keeping steps short:

- Eliminate unnecessary adjectives and adverbs.
- Do not describe more than one major function in any step. To do this, get rid of compound and complex sentences by eliminating the conjunctions "and" and "but," colons, and semicolons. However, it would be a waste of space not to join short or very minor steps. For example, "Sign and date form," "Sign Form 1004 and forward to supervisor," "Open envelopes and date stamp contents."
- Use only form numbers, not form titles, in the steps of the procedure. Form titles are too lengthy. The user can refer to the Set-Up to get the form title if need be.
- Eliminate articles such as "the" whenever possible. For example, say "Point out discrepancies," instead of "Point out the discrepancies." However, you must be careful not to change the meaning of the instruction by this elimination. If you think it's necessary to use articles, do so. If in doubt, leave the article in.
- If the job titles are very long, do not use full titles in the procedure steps. For example, if a procedure is written just for one department, it is not

necessary to use the full title of the manager in the step, particularly if the position is unique. However, show the full title in the margin, as in the following example.

```
Systems          9. . . . .
Analyst
                10. Sign Form 1002 and forward
                    to manager.

Manager,        11. Review . . . .
Systems
Services
```

Notes. Notes may be inserted between the steps of a procedure either to highlight a step or to refer the user to additional information. The note to a specific step is indented so that the word *NOTE* aligns with the text. Runover lines are indented so that the word *NOTE* stands alone. If there is more than one note in a sequence, number each of the notes consecutively and do not repeat the word *NOTE*, as illustrated in the following example.

```
 3. Complete Form 1002; show actual time spent on each
    activity.


    NOTE:  1. Show time to one decimal position.
           2. A detailed explanation of how to com-
              plete Form 1002 can be found . . .
```

A note that is common to all preceding steps is typed starting at the same tab stop as the step numbers, as shown in the following example.

```
 1. Add each line across to find total . . .
 2. Add each column down to find . . .


    NOTE: The sum of the line totals must equal the sum
          of the column totals.
```

PUTTING THE PLAYSCRIPT TOGETHER

Figures 5–29 and 5–30 represent a procedure before its conversion to Playscript. Figures 5–31, 5–32, and 5–33 represent the same procedure after its conversion. Note how much easier it is to retrieve and read information from the Playscript version. Many of the writing faults seen in the document before conversion have been eliminated as a result of using the Playscript layout.

Widget
Manufacturing
Company

Administration

Section
Corporate Services

Subject
REQUESTING BINDERS (ARTWORK SPECIFICATIONS)

Document
Number 02-03-02

Manual binders must meet the design standards and specifications
determined by WM Company. To ensure this, all departments
requesting manual binders must submit requests for same to the
Standards Group. All departments must use Form 1208 for this
purpose. It is a snap set and consists of three parts. Its title
is "Requisition for Supplies."

The Standards Group is responsible for preparing a draft of the
binder artwork for the covers and the spines on behalf of the
requesting department, and they are also responsible for obtaining artwork of the covers and spines from a supplier. They must
also submit the proofs of the artwork to the requesting department
and prepare production specifications for the binders. Basically
they act as a liaison between Purchasing and the supplier and
the requesting division.

The following is the procedure which should be followed by the
department requesting binders. The procedure that the Standards
Group uses to process the requests is located in the Standards
Group manual. The procedure that the Purchasing Department uses
is in the purchasing manual. Binder Construction Specifications
follow this Subject.

The first thing that the originator of the request must do is to
complete Form 1208, Requisition for Supplies. Then the originator
must sign the field captioned "Originator." He/She forwards all
the parts of the form to his/her department manager who must then
sign the form in the field captioned "Approved by" and then return
it to the originator who forwards it to the Standards Group. However,
Part 2 is taken off. It should be noted that approximately seven
working days later, the Standards Group will forward the artwork
proofs. When they come they should be reviewed carefully to make

Date
July 19, 19--

Page
1 of 2

FIGURE 5-29   TEXT BEFORE PLAYSCRIPT (PAGE 1)

157

Widget
Manufacturing
Company

Administration

Corporate Services

Subject
REQUESTING BINDERS (ARTWORK SPECIFICATIONS)

Document
Number 02-03-02

sure that there are no mistakes, or revisions to be made. If there
are mistakes, or revisions to be made, these should be marked on the
proof in red. If there are no mistakes, or revisions to be made,
the originator just signs and dates the proofs and returns them to
the Standards Group.

It should be noted that the Standards Group will forward the
correct and approved artwork and the binder construction
specifications to the purchasing people. This will be done
under the cover of the Form 1208 (one of the parts). Secondly,
Purchasing will tender the job and issue a purchase order. This
is Form 0305 and they will send only Part 4 of it to the originator.

When the originator receives Part 4 it should be filed with the
Form 1208, Part 2.

Binders will be delivered to the originator about six to eight weeks
after the purchase order has been sent out.

		Requisition for Supplies/Services 43980
Date July 8, 19-- Department Accounts Receivable	Expense Code 08-30-01	6 538-8721
Quantity ordered 100	Binders - 1½" capacity, red, super-combi	

Originator's signature *Frank Hamilton* Approved by *Gloria Medina*

Date
July 19, 19--

Page
2 of 2

FIGURE 5-30   TEXT BEFORE PLAYSCRIPT (PAGE 2)

158

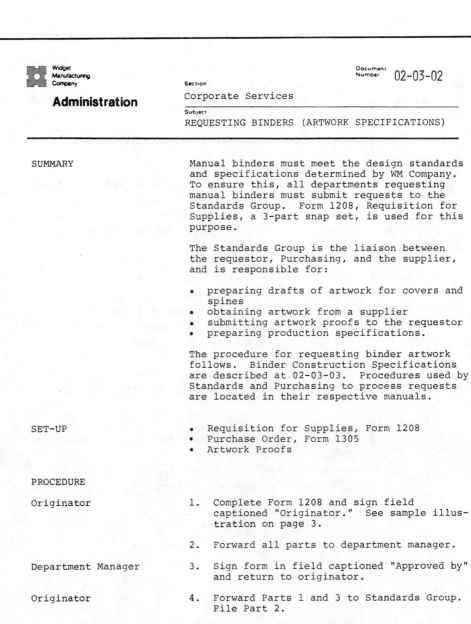

<table>
<tr><td>Widget
Manufacturing
Company

Administration</td><td>Section
Corporate Services</td><td>Document
Number 02-03-02</td></tr>
</table>

	Subject
	REQUESTING BINDERS (ARTWORK SPECIFICATIONS)

SUMMARY

Manual binders must meet the design standards and specifications determined by WM Company. To ensure this, all departments requesting manual binders must submit requests to the Standards Group. Form 1208, Requisition for Supplies, a 3-part snap set, is used for this purpose.

The Standards Group is the liaison between the requestor, Purchasing, and the supplier, and is responsible for:

- preparing drafts of artwork for covers and spines
- obtaining artwork from a supplier
- submitting artwork proofs to the requestor
- preparing production specifications.

The procedure for requesting binder artwork follows. Binder Construction Specifications are described at 02-03-03. Procedures used by Standards and Purchasing to process requests are located in their respective manuals.

SET-UP

- Requisition for Supplies, Form 1208
- Purchase Order, Form 1305
- Artwork Proofs

PROCEDURE

Originator

1. Complete Form 1208 and sign field captioned "Originator." See sample illustration on page 3.

2. Forward all parts to department manager.

Department Manager

3. Sign form in field captioned "Approved by" and return to originator.

Originator

4. Forward Parts 1 and 3 to Standards Group. File Part 2.

NOTE: Standards will order artwork. Turnaround time is approximately 7 working days.

Date
July 19, 19--

Page
1 of 3

FIGURE 5-31   TEXT CONVERTED TO PLAYSCRIPT (PAGE 1)

Widget
Manufacturing
Company

Administration

Section
Corporate Services

Subject
REQUESTING BINDERS (ARTWORK SPECIFICATIONS)

Document
Number   02-03-02

Originator

UPON RECEIPT OF ARTWORK PROOFS

5. Review carefully.

IF PROOFS ARE CORRECT--Steps 7 and 8

IF PROOFS ARE INCORRECT--Steps 6 and 7:
Repeat Steps 5, 6, and 7 until correct.

6. Indicate revisions or corrections to be
    made in red.

7. Sign, date, and return proofs to Standards
    Group.

NOTE: 1. Standards will have artwork revised.
           It will be returned to originator
           for review.

       2. Standards Group will forward
           correct and approved artwork, along
           with binder construction specif-
           ications, under cover of the Form
           1208, to Purchasing.

       3. Purchasing will tender the job and
           issue Purchase Order, Form 1305.
           Part 4 of Form 1305 will be sent
           to originator.

UPON RECEIPT OF FORM 1305, PART 4

8. File with Form 1208, Part 2.

NOTE: Binders will be delivered to originator
       approximately 6 to 8 weeks after
       Purchase Order has been sent out.

Date
July 19, 19--

Page
2 of 3

FIGURE 5-32   TEXT CONVERTED TO PLAYSCRIPT (PAGE 2)

Widget Manufacturing Company		Section	Document Number 02-03-02

Administration

Section
Corporate Services

Subject
REQUESTING BINDERS (ARTWORK SPECIFICATIONS)

ILLUSTRATION: Form 1208

Widget Manufacturing Company	Retain part 2 for your records. Send remainder of set to ☐ Purchasing ☐ Stores	**Requisition for Supplies/Services** 43980

Date July 8, 19--	Department Accounts Receivable	Expense Code 08-30-01	Floor no 6	Telephone number 538-8721

Quantity ordered	Complete description of Item or Service (show form number, supplier part numbers and recommended supplier)	Price	Quantity issued	Quantity on back order
100	Binders - 1½" capacity, red, super-combi			

Originator's signature *Frank Hamilton*   Approved by *Gloria Medina*   Purchasing approval

Purchasing Use
Name of Vendor | To attention of

Delivery date | Purchase Order number | Terms | Mechanics Lien ☐ Yes ☐ No | U.L. ☐ Yes ☐ No

Federal Tax ☐ exempt ☐ extra ☐ included | State Tax ☐ exempt ☐ extra | Ship Via | F.O.B.

Date
July 19, 19--

Page
3 of 3

FIGURE 5-33   TEXT CONVERTED TO PLAYSCRIPT (PAGE 3)

5.8
DATA FLOW DIAGRAM

▼

Data flow diagrams were developed as tools of structured analysis, but can be used as tools of procedure analysis as well. Like flowcharts, data flow diagrams (also called DFD's or bubble charts) can be used as a type of layout. However, whereas flowcharts show a flow of control, data flow diagrams show a flow of data. Thus, the major difference between the two is that the flowchart portrays a situation from the point of view of the people acting upon it or controlling it, while the data flow diagram shows the same situation from the point of view of the data.

One of the advantages of using data flow diagrams as opposed to flowcharts is that it is relatively easy to portray nonsimultaneous, as well as simultaneous, actions on the DFD—something which can be confusing on a flowchart. The four elements or symbols used in data flow diagrams are described in Figure 5–34.

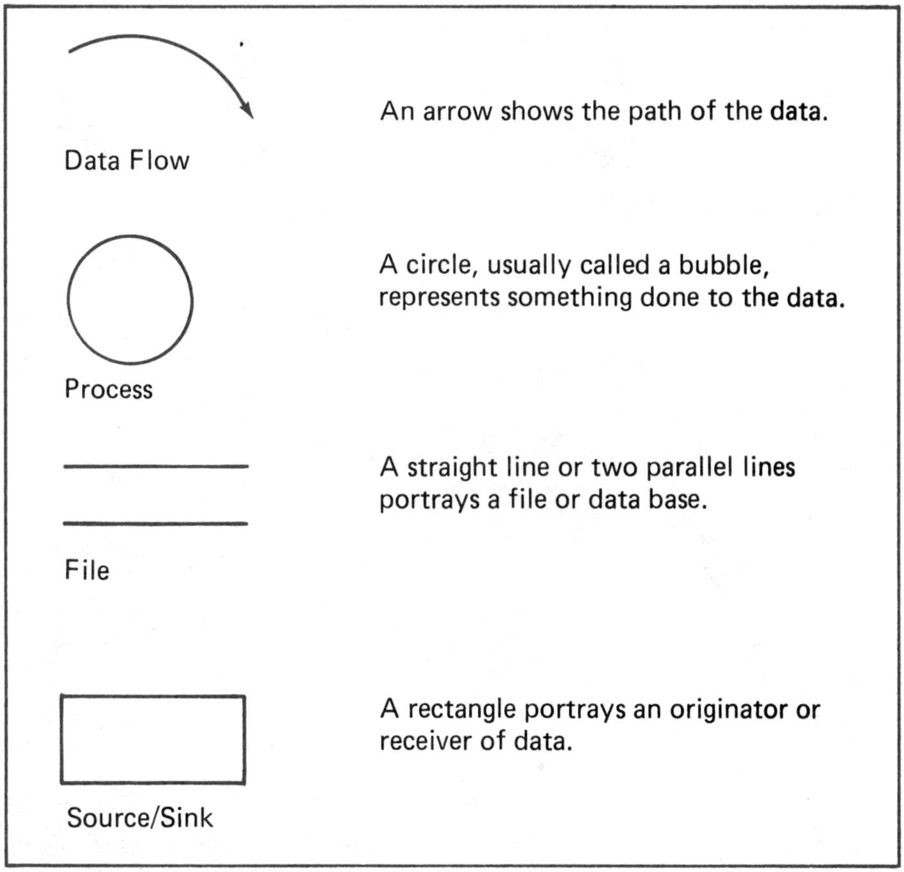

Data Flow — An arrow shows the path of the data.

Process — A circle, usually called a bubble, represents something done to the data.

File — A straight line or two parallel lines portrays a file or data base.

Source/Sink — A rectangle portrays an originator or receiver of data.

FIGURE 5-34   SYMBOLS USED IN DATA FLOW DIAGRAMS

Figure 5–35 portrays a simplified data flow diagram of the manuals development cycle. It is called a Level 0 diagram because the five processes or bubbles represent an overview of the manuals development cycle. Each one of these

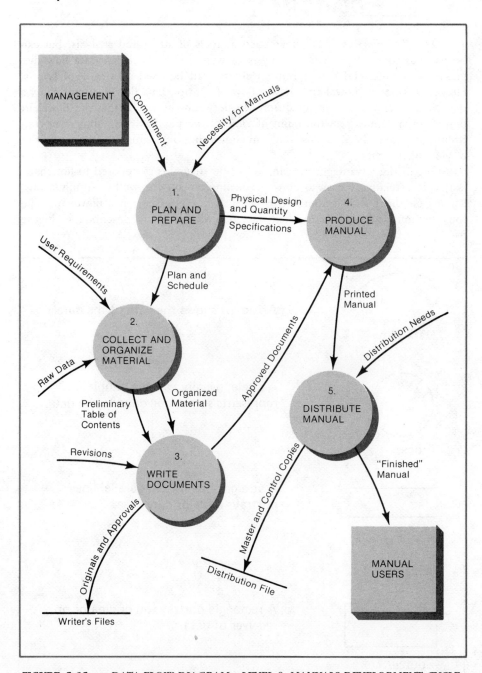

FIGURE 5-35 *DATA FLOW DIAGRAM—LEVEL 0, MANUALS DEVELOPMENT CYCLE*

major processes can be expanded to show greater detail, if necessary. For example, the Produce Manual bubble (Number 4) in Figure 5–35 consists of a number of sub-activities. These could be shown on a separate data flow diagram called Level 4 (Figure 5–36). Note that the bubble numbers in the Level 4

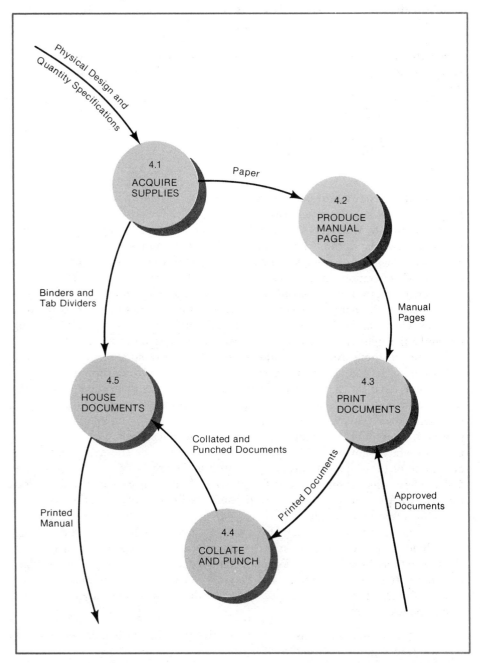

FIGURE 5-36   DATA FLOW DIAGRAM—LEVEL 4, MANUALS DEVELOPMENT CYCLE

diagram (Figure 5–36) are 4.1, 4.2, 4.3, etc., indicating that these are secondary activities of Process 4 on the Level 0 diagram.

Data flow diagrams may be broken down into as many levels as required. The first bubble from Level 4, for instance, could be broken down on another data flow diagram called Level 4.1. The processes on that diagram would then be numbered as 4.1.1, 4.1.2, 4.1.3, etc.

Data flow diagrams are seldom used in manuals because referencing between the various levels of data flow diagrams can be confusing to the user. However, they are worthwhile as an analysis tool used prior to writing procedures.

5.9
ILLUSTRATION
▼

The *Illustration layout* has a special relationship to the other layouts already mentioned. In addition to being used as a layout on its own, it is also the most frequently used supplemental layout.

According to Webster's Dictionary, *to illustrate* means "to make clear, intelligible, or obvious; to throw light on something by examples, comparisons . . . ; a picture or diagram that helps make something clear or attractive." The primary purpose of illustrations in manuals is to do just that—to make clear. *Illustration*, however, is referred to as a layout when the illustration(s) can stand alone, with a Summary. Although you may not be aware at the moment of Subjects in your manuals which can be illustrated without text, you should be constantly ready to recognize the right circumstances or Subjects for this layout.

Some excellent examples of illustrations that can stand alone may be found in instructional booklets for office machines, and sometimes even on the office equipment itself, such as the diagrams often found on photocopier machines which show how to change toner, paper, etc. Other excellent uses of illustrations that stand alone may be found in first-aid booklets, safety pamphlets, and highway and other public warning signs. One of the finest examples is an airline guide to safety—how to use life jackets, oxygen masks, escape exits, seat belts, etc. Some of these illustrations are presented in Figures 5–37, 5–38, 5–39, and 5–40. These illustrations successfully illustrate important concepts without the use of text. After all, illustrations are the universal means of translation.

How often you use illustrations in your manuals will depend to a great extent on how much time you have for creative thinking. Schedules and deadlines often hinder the creative process. It is essential to recognize, too, that most of the illustrations used in manuals do not stand alone. They usually support other layouts (particularly the Caption and Playscript layouts) and they most often illustrate forms. However, here are some situations where illustrations can and should be used in manuals.

- Equipment—photographs or representative sketches to familiarize or show use (see Figures 5–41 and 5–42).

PERMISSION FROM INTERACTION RESEARCH CORP.

FIGURE 5-37   ILLUSTRATION—OXYGEN MASK PROCEDURE

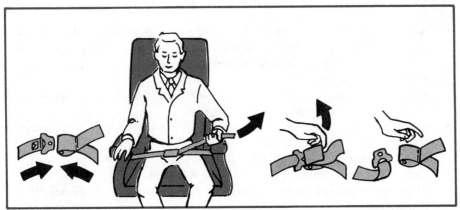

PERMISSION FROM INTERACTION RESEARCH CORP.

FIGURE 5-38   ILLUSTRATION—SEAT BELT PROCEDURE

PERMISSION FROM INTERACTION RESEARCH CORP.

FIGURE 5-39   ILLUSTRATION—TAKEOFF AND LANDING PREPARATION

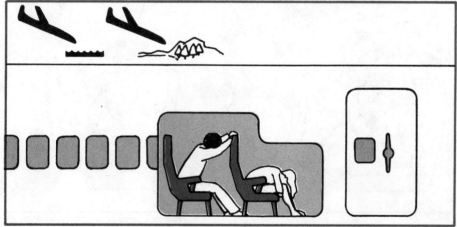

PERMISSION FROM INTERACTION RESEARCH CORP.

FIGURE 5-40   ILLUSTRATION—FORCED LANDING PREPARATION

- Safety/Health/Security—simple line sketches to demonstrate the right way or the wrong way of doing tasks such as the following: lifting and/or carrying, wearing safety equipment, sitting for lengthy periods of time at equipment, using ladders, etc.
- Form letters, memos, reports—samples of actual forms to relay information or to show correct preparation of these forms.
- Computer terminal screens—illustrations of messages within screen-shaped frames to show terminal queries, responses, etc.
- Symbols—representative sketches or templates to illustrate use.
- Patterns—line sketches of patterns to be followed.
- Maps—geographical representations to show regional or divisional offices, markets, etc.
- Floor plans—line drawings or blueprints of offices to show placement of equipment, furniture, exits, entrances, fire escapes, extinguishers, etc.

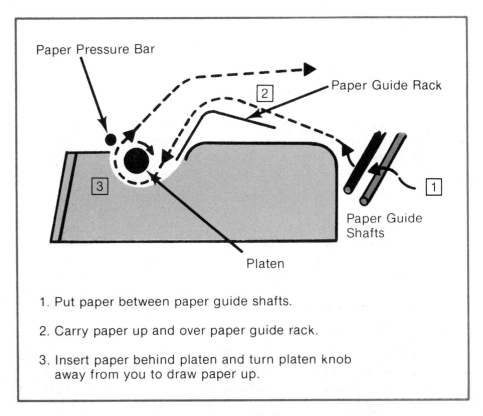

Paper Pressure Bar

Paper Guide Rack

2

3

Paper Guide Shafts

1

Platen

1. Put paper between paper guide shafts.

2. Carry paper up and over paper guide rack.

3. Insert paper behind platen and turn platen knob away from you to draw paper up.

FIGURE 5-41   EQUIPMENT ILLUSTRATION WITH TEXT—PAPER FEED

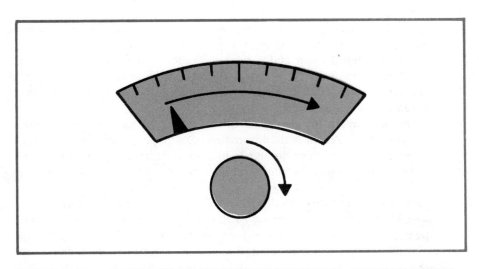

FIGURE 5-42   EQUIPMENT ILLUSTRATION WITHOUT TEXT—RHEOSTAT SETTING

- Organization charts—line drawings to show hierarchical company structure and direct and indirect reporting relationships.
- Bar/line/pie graphs—illustrations that represent variations or comparisons.

PREPARATION GUIDELINES
AND STANDARDS

Although the skills of a graphic artist or printer may be required for the more technical artwork, the manuals writer can often produce professional-looking illustrations with common office tools. Here are some guidelines to help with the preparation of illustrations.

- Each illustration should be presented neatly on the manual page, not on a blank page.
- Each illustration should have a caption to identify it. However, the illustrations in manuals should not be numbered because frequent revisions may occur which may, in turn, change your illustration sequence. Furthermore, illustration numbers are redundant since illustrations are placed on manual pages and are an integral part of the Subject which already has been assigned a document number. A typical illustration caption could then be:

ILLUSTRATION: Organization Chart, Accounts Division

- Use a blue pencil (lightly) and blue-lined paper such as a form-spacing chart to draft freehand artwork. The blue-lined paper acts as a guide and eliminates the need for a lot of measuring. The color blue does not reproduce when photocopied. Thus, when the sketch or outline is completed to your satisfaction, you can ink in the illustration with a fine felt-tip pen.
- Obtain good photocopies of your original artwork to paste onto the pages. Retain your originals on file in case revisions are required in the future.
- When necessary, photoreduce your illustration to fit neatly within the margins of the manual page. However, do not reduce the illustration so much that the user cannot read the print.
- Use a black felt-tip pen and a ruler to border your illustrations. Borders should not be too heavy or they will detract from the illustration.
- Trim your illustrations with a ruler and an art knife. Scissors tend to produce uneven cuts and are more cumbersome.
- Use rubber cement for gluing the illustration to the manual page because even after several months the illustrations can be peeled off the page. Furthermore, rubber cement doesn't bubble or curl the paper and the excess can be easily removed by gently rubbing the illustration after the glue has dried.
- If you would like to use an illustration you have found in a magazine for a manual but the illustration is too small or too large, you can carefully measure and draw a grid, of say 1/2″ squares, on the original. Then using a larger (or smaller) piece of paper, draw the same grid but twice as large (or half the size) and then lightly, using a blue pencil, copy what you see in each

square on the original onto the larger (or smaller) grid. You can leave out
unessential parts of the illustration thereby simplifying the diagram, if necessary. When you get the essential drawing done to your satisfaction, ink in
the lines you want with a fine tip pen and then erase all the unwanted lines
on the drawing and the grid lines. When your new drawing is photocopied,
you will be surprised how good it looks. This technique works very well on
equipment illustrations. An example of this technique is illustrated in Figure 5–43.

The standards recommended for the illustration of forms are relatively
simple.

- Present the illustration on the manual page.
- Complete all the fields on the form which you wish your users to fill in.
- Complete all fields exactly as the users should; that is, print, write, or type
  as necessary.
- Reproduce forms at full size whenever possible; otherwise, reduce them
  sufficiently to fit on the page.
- If a form is being illustrated solely for information purposes, illustrate only
  as much as is necessary for recognition.
- The original wording or design of forms should not be altered.
- Place illustrations as close to their text references as possible.
- Long or complicated forms can be illustrated in portions. Place each portion
  directly after the text which describes it.

5.10
CHOOSING
THE BEST LAYOUT

Regardless of what kind of manual you are writing, most of the material
(i.e., policies, procedures, standards, etc.) can be put into one of the following categories: sequenced action, unsequenced action, or action depending on variables.

SEQUENCED ACTION

Sequenced action encompasses any process which should be described step-
by-step. The preferred layout for sequenced action is Playscript, which can be
supported by illustrations of the forms and equipment required to perform the
steps. Then, policy statements and the descriptive background can be covered
in the Summary.

UNSEQUENCED ACTION

In *unsequenced action,* general information is given—not step-by-step procedures. Thus, the preferred layout for unsequenced action is Caption, supported
by illustrations if necessary. These illustrations can also take the form of matri-

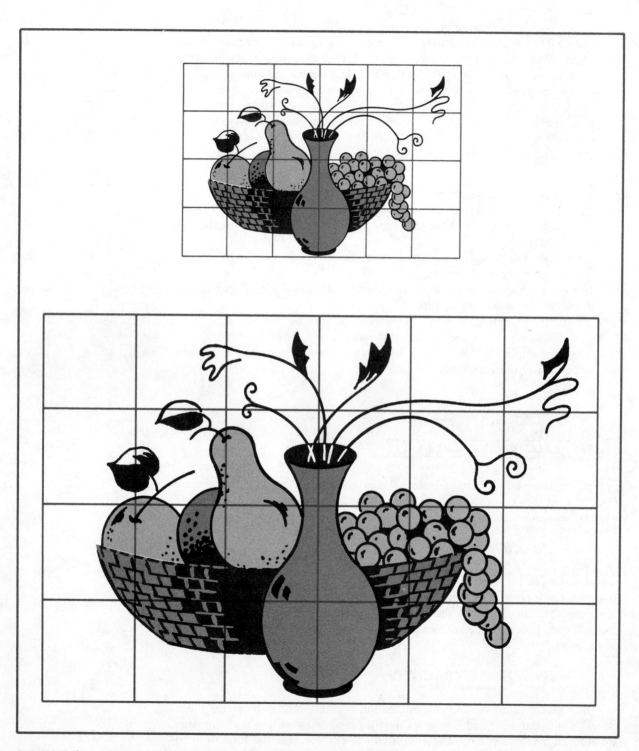

FIGURE 5-43   USING A GRID TO ENLARGE OR REDUCE AN ILLUSTRATION

ces, data flow diagrams, or flowcharts, as well as illustrations of forms, equipment, charts, graphs, etc.

ACTION DEPENDING
ON VARIABLES

Action that depends on variables is usually best presented by the use of matrices. General information which is too detailed to be included in a matrix or in the footnotes to a matrix can be included as captions after the Summary or following the matrix. The matrix can then be used to support what has now become Caption layout.

A matrix for choosing the correct layout is presented in Table 5–1.

	Preferred Layout	Supported by	Other Choices
Sequenced Action	Playscript	Illustration	Flowchart DFD
Unsequenced Action	Caption	Illustration	Headline Narrative
Action Depending on Variables	Matrix	Caption	Caption Headline

TABLE 5-1
CHOOSING THE BEST
LAYOUT

Another point to keep in mind is that reading a manual that is written entirely in one layout can be boring. Variety of layout enhances both the interest value and the appearance of manuals. It makes the reading less monotonous for the user, and makes the writing more exciting for the manuals writer.

MIXING
LAYOUTS

On the whole, mixing layouts within a Subject is not recommended. This does not mean, however, that layouts can never be mixed, for in certain situations it can be done very effectively. Illustrations, in particular, function well with other layouts, especially with the Caption and Playscript layouts. Flowcharts and data flow diagrams also function well with the Caption layout. Before mixing layouts, however, consider your users and your alternatives. Remember, it is essential that standards be maintained. One of the greatest problems of mixing layouts is the difficulty of maintaining standards—particularly typing standards.

Any deterioration of standards will be detrimental to the overall appearance and effectiveness of your manuals.

Chapter 5 presents eight layouts. These eight layouts can be divided into two groups: written layouts and graphic layouts. *Written layouts* are Caption, Playscript, Headline, and Narrative. *Graphic layouts* are Matrix, Flowchart, Data Flow Diagram, and Illustration. The following guidelines, employing these two groupings, should be considered:

- Any of the eight layouts can stand alone with a Summary.
- If a written layout is chosen as the major layout for a Subject, do not mix other written layouts with it.
- Support written layouts with illustrations whenever possible.
- If a graphic layout is chosen as the major layout for a Subject, do not mix it with other graphic layouts.
- The only other layout which should be mixed with Playscript is Illustration.

The three layouts which should be used most often in the production of manuals are Caption, Playscript, and Matrix. Use flowcharts and data flow diagrams primarily as analysis tools and only occasionally as true layouts. Try to avoid using the Narrative and Headline layouts altogether. Use Illustration wherever appropriate, and especially as an adjunct to other layouts.

PRODUCTION

6

6.1

PREPARATION METHODS

▼

In Chapter 4, composing methods and writing tools such as pen and paper, keyboards, tape recorders, etc., were discussed briefly. In this chapter, the discussion will be expanded to include a nontechnical description of word processing and text processing, and a comparison of these two methods.

There are many technological variables for production of text. Your hand-written or typewritten document can be read by a character recognition scanner or by an optical recognition device (ORD). The data can then be translated to a printer, or simply stored on any of the various electronic media (computers or word processors). This data can be displayed on a visual display unit (VDU), edited and/or reformatted by the operator, stored, and printed when required. And, in the not-too-distant future, you will be able to dictate your procedures and have them translated to the written word via an audio recognition device.

Creating text electronically is much less expensive than creating your documentation on a typewriter. However, cost figures made available by manufacturers are based on optimum use of equipment; that is, using the equipment for repetitive work. Producing manuals documentation is one of the most practical applications, since each document usually goes through a number of drafts before it can be published. Even then, the document must be stored so that if a policy or procedure requires revision in the months or years to come, it can be done with minimal cost and effort.

The big question is what type of electronic equipment to use to automate your manuals program. To make such a decision, learn all you can about the equipment available on the market and the differences among the various types, and be aware of the fact that the state of the art today will be history tomorrow. It is essential that your strategic planning for the future ensures that each piece of equipment be compatible with every other. Manufacturers' sales representatives will be happy to help you in this endeavor. Or, if you have the money to spare, have an independent feasibility study done before you talk to the manufacturers. The study could be done by your own staff if they have the time to do the research, or you could hire a consultant to lay out all the facts and make a qualified recommendation. Technological changes are being made every day and no organization can keep up without an effort. However, good research and strategic planning can keep you in the running and can ensure a return on your equipment investment for many years.

WORD PROCESSING
SYSTEMS

Word processing systems were created to process text. They are "user friendly," reliable, and extremely sophisticated.

In the 1950's the first memory typewriters (descendants of the older flexowriters) were introduced. They were new and expensive, so the business community waited for proof of their worthiness. Then came IBM's Mag Card Selectric Typewriter and shortly thereafter the Mag Tape Selectric Typewriter, an electric typewriter with a magnetic tape on which reams of typed documents could be stored and later typed at high speed by the typewriter over and over again. This proved to be a great boon to business, for with this machine organizations could make all their correspondence look like originals. Form letters, standard contracts, etc., could be memorized on tape and printed when required. The typists would merely insert the variable information such as names, addresses, and special clauses to make them individualized. The problem with this type of equipment, however, was that large revisions to the memorized text were not made easily. The typist could not see what was being keyed onto the tape. Only after the text was printed out could the typist actually see what the document looked like or what revisions were required. So, some manufacturers came along with similar equipment that had small display panels which allowed the typist to see the line of type just keyed, so that adjustments could be made on the spot. But still, the typist was unable to view the entire formatted document.

It didn't take long for manufacturers to realize that a lot of improvements still needed to be made. In the 1970's the industry took off. Today, the word processor has a visual display unit which, like a television screen, allows the operator to see an entire page of text as it is being keyed in. The word processor allows the operator to shift words, lines of text, paragraphs, and entire pages. Insertion of simple codes causes the text to be formatted, justified left or right, indented, wrapped, etc. By using special programs and a few simple codes and/ or function keys, figures typed randomly can be put into column format. Such repetitive functions as line drawings for flowcharts and organization charts can also be produced automatically. Some programs even produce alphabetized indices and correct poor grammar and misspellings.

A typical stand-alone word processing unit, illustrated in Figure 6-1, consists of a terminal (a keyboard and a display screen) with the processing power of a microcomputer, some type of data storage medium, and a printer. With such a stand-alone unit, the operator can key, format and save (memorize), recall the text at a later date, edit and save, and then print as many times as necessary.

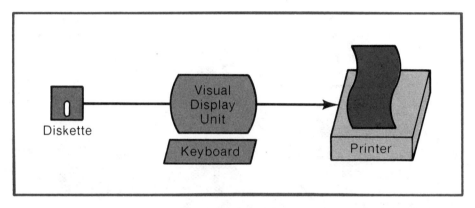

FIGURE 6-1   STAND-ALONE WORD PROCESSING UNIT

This word processor could just be the start. If you choose your base equipment carefully, you will be able to add modules or individual pieces of hardware as your organization or manuals program grows. Eventually, a shared resource network similar to that illustrated in Figure 6-2 can be established. In Figure 6-2 there is a host terminal (keyboard and screen) with extensive processing power supplied by a central processing unit (CPU), and some form of storage, linked up to dumb terminals (i.e., terminals that have no processing power of their own). The dumb terminals share the processing power and storage of the host, and they are much less expensive than the host terminal. In addition to shared processing and storage, extra printers can also be added and shared by two or more terminals. Another configuration, and one which may be more practical, is a number of stand-alone systems hooked up to a CPU. In such a configuration each unit would retain its independence of operation and application. Modular systems will always be less expensive for organizations with applications other than the manuals program.

One of the most important matters you must plan for is storage. Some word processors use diskettes that are very similar to 45 rpm records. These diskettes are inserted into the word processor and are "played" while the operator inputs, views, or edits the data. When the job is complete, the diskette is removed from

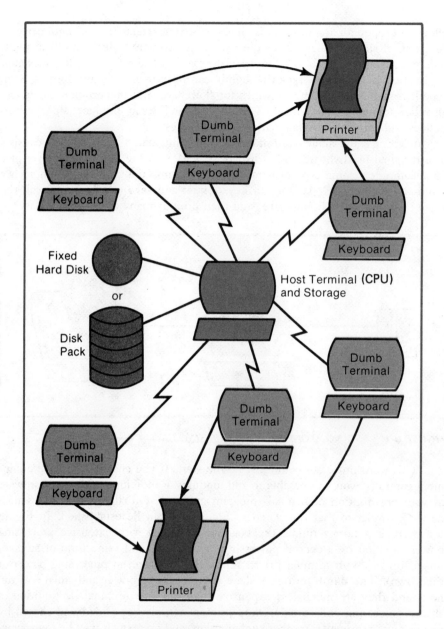

FIGURE 6-2   *SHARED RESOURCE WORD PROCESSING NETWORK*

the word processor and is stored. These diskettes can hold up to 500 pages of text, which would be suitable for one good-sized manual. So, for a manuals program, you would probably require one diskette for each manual and extras for backup and for the program's administrative documentation such as distribution lists, reports, schedules, transmittal notices, etc. This, then, would require the installation and maintenance of a well-organized manual file system and index for the diskettes.

For a small but growing program, particularly if your word processor will be used for other applications, you may be better off with starter equipment which can give greater storage flexibility, such as equipment with rigid (fixed) disks. Rigid disks usually have a capacity of approximately 3,000 (8½" x 11") pages. For the large program there are disk packs or cartridges which can store up to 20,000 pages of text. Although this may seem to be a tremendous amount of storage space, it is infinitesimal in comparison to the millions of pages of storage capacity of mainframe computers.

TEXT PROCESSING
SYSTEMS

Text processing is simply a time-sharing function that can be performed at a computer terminal using text processing software and the computer for processing power and storage. (The reference here is to the traditional large computer and not to the newer personal computers.) Only by accident was it discovered that some of the components of time-sharing systems could be utilized with special tools to perform text processing functions.

Unfortunately, these text processing systems have not been particularly user friendly with nontechnical operators, since the systems tend to be fairly technical and often require extensive training. Furthermore, hands-on courses are difficult to find. You must also learn to use the product manuals, which are difficult to follow even for the technical operator. A further drawback is that the computer terminal is nothing more than an electronic keyboard and screen to communicate with the computer. In word processing language, it's a dumb terminal. This means that you can key text in at the terminal but as soon as you attempt to do line insertions, line or block moves, memorize what you have keyed, or transmit to a printer, you must use the computer's power. This, in itself, is not a time-consuming activity if you are the sole user of the computer, but when you are time-sharing (many users sharing the system concurrently) the machine has to divide its time among many, and you and every other user will receive a smaller amount of that computing time. As the number of users increases, the system responds to the individual user more slowly.

Text processing systems (the software) also slow down the operator because thus far they tend not to be interactive. In other words, you key your text unformatted, surrounding it with a markup language (codes) which will format the text. Once this is done you then transmit the text to the CPU where the codes are translated and the text is formatted accordingly. When this has been done, the operator can then view the text, page-by-page, as it will appear in print. If, however, the operator decides the format is not good enough, or if a word is changed, the formatting (or scripting) process must be done all over again. When the document finally looks satisfactory, it may then be electronically transmitted to a printer.

The main advantages of text processing in a large computing environment are the vast amounts of storage space available, and the hardware (VDU's) already in place, which allow for on-line distribution of manuals to terminal users.

COMPARING
WORD PROCESSING AND
TEXT PROCESSING

With the stand-alone word processor, which is dedicated to the individual user, there is very little of the slowdown which can occur with the text processing systems. The user also does not need to deal with any intermediate component, nor wait to see the translated results of the intermediary on the screen. Because the interplay between keying and formatting on the word processor is so fast as to be almost imperceptible, the operator can concentrate entirely on authoring, keying, editing, or formatting the text right on the screen. However, it should be noted that the response time on a shared word processing network will also be affected by the number of users, but never to the degree that it is affected on a large computer network. There are very few large computer installations that can promise the same instantaneous response time as a stand-alone word processor or even a shared word processing network.

A comparison of the attributes of word processing systems and text processing systems is presented in Table 6-1.

Word Processing	Text Processing
• Each terminal may have its own computing system to control its functions.	• The terminal has no computing power of its own; it must use and share the power of a computer.
• The total system is designed to perform autonomously.	• The system is an addition to a computer and consists of a number of independent programs which are part of the general purpose time-sharing system; not autonomous.
• The components are tailored to support only the word processing functions.	• Only a few components of the computer are specifically designed to process text.
• It is user friendly.	• It is not as user friendly as word processing.
• Most systems have the ability to continually show on the screen the document in a formatted view, similar or identical to its final form on paper.	• Text processing requires the operator to code and key and then process separately. The operator does not see the formatted view at all times (although it is on the way).
• On-line storage is limited.	• On-line storage is much greater.

TABLE 6-1
COMPARISON OF WORD PROCESSING AND TEXT PROCESSING

You can link up a stand-alone word processor or a shared resource word processing network to a computer, as illustrated in Figure 6-3. The link, or *modem*, acts as a relay allowing communication between the two different electronic systems. Here, your operators have the ability to key, edit, format, and save independently of the computer, and also to transfer data back and forth from one system to the other.

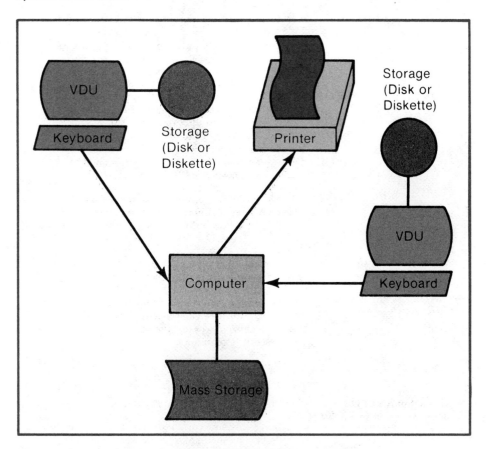

FIGURE 6-3   *WORD PROCESSORS ON LINE WITH A COMPUTER*

Best use is made of this configuration when you have a large and growing manuals program (30 or more manuals of 350 pages or more). With this much material changing at a rate of 30 percent per year, you will have 10,500 pages of current documentation, and at the end of five years an archives file of 15,750 pages. So, storage may be the deciding factor as to whether you choose to hook up your word processing units to the computer. If the current records retention (archival) legislation in your jurisdiction or company policy requires you to retain every document for a number of years, then you might as well use the existing storage of your computer, rather than buy peripheral storage for your word processors.

If you intend to use the word processor to key, edit, and format current documents, and to use the computer for storage, you should decide upon some text transfer and storage guidelines, such as those shown in Table 6-2. This will allow optimum utilization of the attributes of each system.

At the Word Processor:	1. Key in the new draft document and save it on disk, diskette, etc. The draft document should remain on the word processing medium during the draft stages.
Once Approvals Have Been Received to Publish:	2. Print the approved document. This is the printing master to which illustrations will be pasted and which will be sent for mass printing. This is kept in the printing master file during the life cycle of the document so that copies can be made as required. (See Chapter 9 for a full explanation of the printing master and the printing master file.)
	3. Move (do not copy) the document from the word processing medium to computer storage. This frees up the word processing medium for new draft documents.
When Revision to the Document is Required:	4. Copy (do not move) the document back from computer storage to the word processing medium. You now have two of the original document. The one in computer storage remains intact as it was when first approved and is kept for archival purposes; the one on the word processing medium can be revised.
	5. Revise and reformat the document on the word processor.
When Approvals Have Been Received to Publish:	6. Print the newly revised document.
	7. Move this new current document from the word processing medium to computer storage. You now have two versions of the document in computer storage: the current published document and the obsolete or archival document.

TABLE 6-2   TRANSFER AND STORAGE GUIDELINES WHEN USING WORD PROCESSORS LINKED TO A COMPUTER

The steps in Table 6-2 are constantly repeated as new documents are added and current documents are revised. Obsolete documents (archives) should be transferred from the computer's on-line storage to off-line storage at regular intervals.

DESIRABLE FEATURES
OF ANY WORD OR
TEXT PROCESSING SYSTEM

Whichever system you decide upon, there are certain capabilities which are enormously helpful for producing manuals. Not every system has all of these features, but you should look for one which has as many as possible. The most useful features for manuals are:

- repaginate—automatic page numbering and renumbering
- automatic indexing—creates a keyword index or cross-reference list
- revision indicators—reduce proofreading time of revised documents
- line drawing—allows fast preparation and professional presentation of charts and forms
- list/merge—combines things like form letters with address lists for repetitive jobs
- search and replace—locates and replaces a word or phrase (character string) with a different character string throughout the document
- glossary—allows for storage and recall of frequently used character strings
- dictionary—checks spelling of standard words and words you specify and input.

If you are going to use text processing, look for a simple system with as little markup language as possible.

Once the text has been processed electronically, there is also the capability of transmitting the text to internal devices such as printers and to external devices such as phototypesetters. This is accomplished with a modem, which acts as the link between your word processor and/or text processing system and the telephone system. Your documentation can thus be relayed over telephone lines to any other office with a receiver, where it can subsequently be printed. This obviates postage and shipping charges. And if your printers have graphics capabilities you can also transmit documents with illustrations.

Regardless of which electronic system (hardware and software) you use to input your documentation, you must still choose the output medium you want to distribute to your users. Paper is the standard, but there are others such as microfilm, microfiche, videocassettes, and computer output microfilm, all of which require display equipment for the user. Or, you can distribute your procedures to the user on-line by allowing the user to log on at a terminal and access the appropriate documents. Some computer hardware and software companies have even taken to giving their customers computer tapes of their user manuals rather than the hard copies. Their customers then mount the tapes, and the users view the manuals on-line.

In addition to choosing an output medium, you must also consider which methods of backup to use. You should always have backup copies of all your current documentation off-site to ensure against disaster. The medium for your backup could be paper, tape, disk, diskette, fiche, or film, but paper should never be the sole backup. Backup should be on a medium which can be reproduced effectively on paper, thereby ensuring that the data need never be keyed again.

If you've decided upon paper as your output medium, high quality print (letter quality) should be an important specification of your system. There are many reliable printers in a wide range of prices to choose from on the market. They vary from small matrix printers used by people who want only the facts rather than good type quality, to laser printers which give terrific resolution and have a host of automatically interchangeable type fonts and graphics capabilities.

For most manuals programs, one or more good quality impact printers will suffice. These printers come with interchangeable print wheels offering a wide range of typefaces. The one disadvantage is that you cannot change the typeface during the printing of a page. But you can overprint lines (that is, print twice) to make them bolder.

6.2
THE DRAFT PROCESS
▼

As a technical writer, you must be prepared to write and rewrite your material over and over again if necessary and not be offended by your critique committee's criticism. If you have prepared the material properly and have analyzed it thoroughly, you should not need any more than two preliminary drafts to produce your final product. In fact, many organizations make the two draft process a standard.

The *draft process* basically ensures that what you are writing is accurate. It may be as formal or informal as your organization requires it to be. Usually, the greater the number of employees involved, the more formal the draft process will be.

Regardless of how complex and formal your draft process is, or how many drafts you need to produce to reach the final document (the printing master), there are certain guidelines which should be followed in draft preparation.

LAYOUT
◆

Produce the draft in the same layout in which the Subject is to be published and use the appropriate typing standards. This ensures that your critique committee knows what the document will look like in final form.

PAPER
◆

Typewritten documents should be produced on the appropriate procedure paper. This will reduce your workload if the draft is approved as is, or if only minor revisions are required for approval.

Documents produced by word processors or computers can be printed on blank paper, thus saving your more expensive preprinted manual pages for approved documents. However, if it is absolutely necessary that the draft be printed on the preprinted manual page, a single sheet feeder is required. If you do not have a single sheet feeder, the draft could be produced on continuous paper and then overprinted on the pre-cut procedure pages. This can be done by putting the blank procedure pages into a photocopier and copying the draft onto the pages.

Laser printers also offer two other possibilities. The first is *forms flash,* a method which uses a negative on an acetate to print the background image while at the same time printing the text. The second possibility is *programmed printing,* a method where the constant data for a form, such as the manuals page, is pre-programmed and is printed at the same time as the variable text. In either case, blank paper is used in the printer.

FORMS

Documents in which forms are illustrated must have the illustrations of the forms placed as physically close to their reference as possible. This avoids the time-consuming and often irritating need to turn back and forth between the pages when forms illustrations are far removed from their reference. Occasionally you will have to say "see the illustration on page 3" on page 2, for example, but do it only when there isn't room for the illustration on page 2. Never present the forms as exhibits at the end of the document in what amounts to an appendix to the document; and never have a whole Section or Tab for forms.

You should notify your forms department of the need for any new or revised forms as early as possible in the draft process. This will enable a properly designed form that conforms to company design standards and resembles the final version of the form to be included in the draft procedure. It also enables you to obtain form numbers before the form is designed, if the form is to be referenced only, and not illustrated in the procedure. The form should not be sent out for final printing until the draft/critique process is complete. Providing the forms analyst with all relevant documentation (draft procedures, flowcharts, analysis notes, etc.) will result in the best quality form in the shortest time.

PRINTING/PHOTOCOPYING

Critique copies should be printed or photocopied one side only for several reasons. One-sided printing is simpler and less time-consuming since you eliminate the necessity of marking up the pages (left and right) for the printer or putting the document through the photocopier twice. From the point of view of the reviewer, one-sided printing allows lots of blank space (all left-hand pages) for writing comments which might otherwise be crammed into the margins. For the writer/editor, critique notes are much easier to read if they appear on the pages opposite the printed text.

RELATED DOCUMENTS

Write related Subjects, such as all those in a Section, at one time. It is much simpler for the critique committee to review half a dozen procedures on data processing security at one time, than it is to review one this week, two next week, etc. Time your writing process so that these similar Subjects are ready for review at the same time, ensuring that no material is reviewed out of context. This applies to all related documents, even those for different manuals.

DATE STAMPING

The first page of every copy of all Subjects submitted for review should be stamped in the bottom left-hand corner with the word "DRAFT" and the date of issue (see Figure 6-4). Subsequent draft versions must show the new date to avoid confusion.

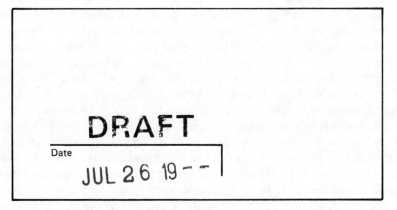

FIGURE 6-4   DRAFT AND DATE STAMP

DISTRIBUTING DRAFTS

The drafts should be sent to the critique group with a covering memo. The purposes of this memo are to:

- identify the analyst to whom comments should be returned
- state the subject matter covered
- identify the manual(s) in which the document(s) will be published
- state the date by which comments must be received
- indicate how the critique should be carried out. (See the Critique section in this chapter.)

Include a distribution list at the foot of the memo so that anyone concerned can readily see who is reviewing the draft.

6.3
GENERAL SPACING AND TYPING STANDARDS
▼

The use of a standard page format, designed so that its preprinted elements create an alignment grid for margins and tab stops, allows common typing standards to be used for all manuals (as discussed in Chapter 2). A well-designed page eliminates guesswork and annoyance for the manuals writer, the manuals reader, and the typist, and results in a page that is attractive and balanced. The typing standards outlined here can be applied to any method of production: typing, word processing, or text processing.

TYPING ELEMENT
◆

The Courier 72 or a similar typing element is recommended for all manuals. This element is a 10-pitch serif typeface. (*Pitch* is the number of characters per inch of type; *serifs* are the little strokes at the top and bottom of the characters.) This typeface is ideal because the characters are a good size for reading, unlike 12-pitch, which is smaller in height as well as width. Also, the serifs let the eye follow the reading line better than Gothic typefaces and yet allow a greater density of text than sans serif typefaces.

PAGE MARGINS
◆

As illustrated in Figure 6-5, the left margin for typing is directly aligned with

- the left side of the company logo (or name, if there is no logo)
- the left edge of the dividing line between the masthead and the body of the page
- the date box at the foot of the page.

The right margin for typing is aligned with

- the right edge of the dividing line between the masthead and the body of the page
- the right edge of the page number field.

The text should not be right justified, for right justified text is not as readable as text with a ragged edge. This is because extra spaces have to be inserted between words and letters to make the last character of the last word on each line align at the right margin.

In order to allow for hole punching, nothing should be typed in the margins. In Figure 6-5, 7/10" margins are used (seven character spaces on a 10-pitch

186

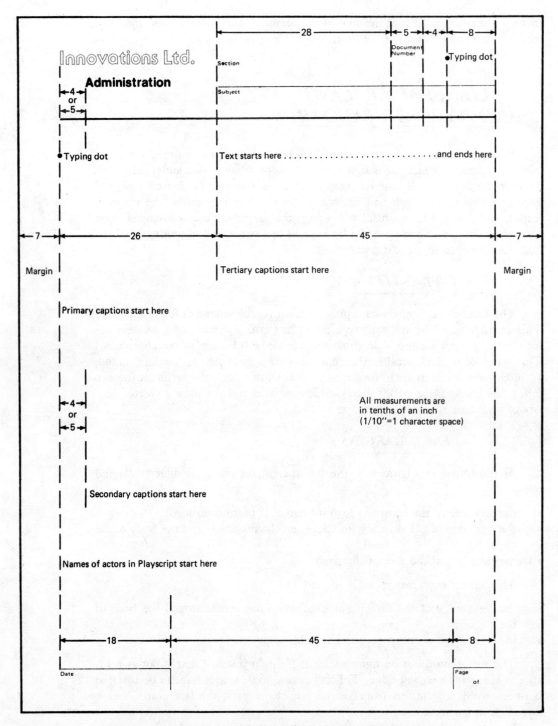

FIGURE 6-5   *PAGE MEASUREMENTS (IN CHARACTER SPACES) FOR TYPING*

alignment grid). Character spaces and tenths of inches will be referred to interchangeably from now on.

MASTHEAD

As mentioned previously, the preprinted logo or name is aligned with the line separating the masthead from the body of the page, seven character spaces from the paper's edge. The manual title is indented another four spaces. The department name (if required) could be placed beside or beneath the company name.

The caption "Document Number" begins 54 character spaces from the left margin (or 28 spaces from the beginning of the Section caption). The Document Number caption takes 5 spaces and the document number itself is positioned another 4 spaces to the right of the caption, indicated by a typing dot. To emphasize this entry, an Orator or other boldface typing element may be used. If you do not have the ability to change typing elements within a document, you can *shadow print*—type the number twice to make it darker—or you can enter the document numbers after the document has been printed by using dry transfer.

The section title is typed in upper- and lowercase. The typing line is aligned directly under the preprinted section title caption. A tab stop should be set at this position for typing. This area can accommodate a line of 45 characters. The subject title is also aligned directly under its preprinted caption. However, it is typed entirely in uppercase, one of the rare cases where caps are used for emphasis. A line 45 characters in length can also be accommodated here. However, if you have the ability to use bold type, i.e., variable fonts or typesetting, then caps shouldn't be used.

FOOT OF THE PAGE

The date is always typed in full to avoid any confusion that may arise from the use of numeric dates, especially if date standards have not been established for your organization. For example, September 10, 1983, expressed as a six-character numeric in the United States, would be 09-10-83, the digits placed in the same order as the written date. In many other countries, however, it would be noted as 10-09-83. And for some applications such as data processing, this date would be written as 83-09-10 or its Julian equivalent of 83-253. Thus, it is safest to type September 10, 1983. Since the longest date, including blank spaces, is 18 characters long, this is the length used here for the open-ended date box. The date box also starts at the left margin, 7/10" from the edge of the page. This is where typing of the date should be started.

In the lower right-hand corner of the page is another open-ended box for the page number. The left edge of this box is 45 spaces from the right edge of the date box and the box is eight spaces in length. It extends to the right margin, 7/10" from the edge of the page. The page number is typed on the same line as the date.

VERTICAL MEASUREMENTS
ON THE MANUAL PAGE

◆

Due to the vicissitudes of printing or photocopying, it is sometimes a little difficult to ensure that the vertical measurements on the manual page remain constant. (The same is true of horizontal spacing but the horizontal alignment is not as critical.) Vertical spacing is measured in twelfths and sixths of an inch rather than tenths, since there are six lines to an inch. (These sixths will be referred to from here on as lines.)

As for typing standards, the only ones you need to know are that the typing dot for the document number is 4/6" from the top of the page, the typing dot for the body of text is 2⅙" (¹³⁄₆'s) from the top of the page, and you should leave about half an inch between the bottom of your typed text and the date and page boxes (see Figure 6-6).

TYPING STANDARDS
COMMON TO ALL LAYOUTS

◆

The following typing standards should be used regardless of what layout you choose for your document.

Page Body. A typing dot indicates the first typing line. The left margin is aligned with the left edge of the line dividing the masthead from the rest of the page. The right margin is aligned with the right edge of the line dividing the masthead from the rest of the page. There should be about ½" of white space between the last typing line and the date box.

Notes. Begin notes within the text at the same tab stops as the text itself. For example:

```
text text text text text text
text text.


NOTE: Note note note note.
```

Leave two blank lines between the text and the note following, and between the note and the text following, to make the note stand out. Type the word "NOTE" in uppercase letters. Leave two character spaces between the colon after the word "NOTE" and the note itself.

Multiple Notes. Leave one line between each note. Number each note consecutively and don't repeat the word "NOTE." For example:

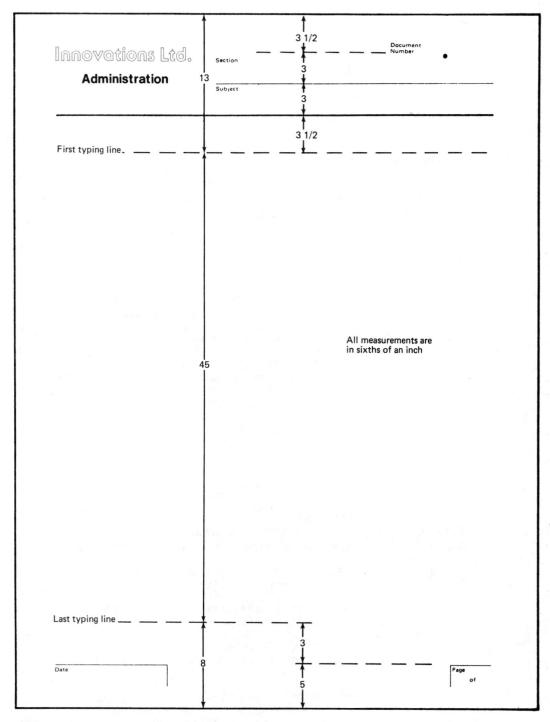

FIGURE 6-6   VERTICAL MEASUREMENTS ON THE MANUAL PAGE

```
text text text text text text
text text.
```

```
NOTE:   1. Note note note.

        2. Note note note.

        3. Note note.
```

```
Text text text text text text.
```

Bullets. Type bullets beginning at the same tab stop as the text being bulleted. Leave two character spaces between the bullet and the text of the bullet. The spacing between text and bullets depends on the length of the text and personal preference. For instance, if you were bulleting a list of cities, you might leave only one line between the text, and single-space the cities, as shown in the following example.

```
International     The Atlanta head office of
Sales Offices     Widget Manufacturing Company
                  serves all of the United States,
                  Canada, and Mexico. Overseas
                  offices are located in

                  •   Sydney, Australia
                  •   London, England
                  •   Osaka, Japan
                  •   Canton, China
                  •   Paris, France
                  •   Oslo, Norway
                  •   Cairo, Egypt.


                  NOTE: The Beirut, Lebanon, office
                        was moved to Cairo in
                        June, 1982.
```

If, on the other hand, each bulleted item consists of a sentence or two, or is a few lines in length, then leave a line between each one, as shown here.

```
Functions     The functions of the senior data
              entry operator are to

              •   perform data entry tasks to aid
                  the production coordinator

              •   enter WMC data into machine
                  recognizable format via the key
                  to disk system

              •   report regularly to the data
                  processing shift supervisor on
                  scheduling, workflow, and
                  technical difficulties.
```

Notice, too, in the previous example that the second (and each succeeding) line of text is aligned with the first character of the first line; not with the bullet. Also, since the whole piece of text could be read as one sentence, the first word in each bullet has not been capitalized. If the text consists of one or more complete sentences within each bullet, capitalize the first letter. If you are bulleting a list which is not part of a sentence, caps are optional.

No punctuation (for example, commas or semicolons) is necessary after each bullet because the bullet itself serves as a punctuation mark. However, if you are bulleting complete sentences or paragraphs, they should be punctuated as they would normally be. Also, if the last bullet completes a phrase, clause, or sentence, end it with a comma, semicolon, or period, as appropriate.

Dashes. Dashes are used to indicate secondary hierarchy in lists, and bullets are used to indicate primary hierarchy, as mentioned in Chapter 4. The same rules of usage that apply to bullets can also be used for dashes. You should be extremely cautious about going beyond these two levels of hierarchy for two reasons. First, the typing line is cut down further with each new level of hierarchy. Second, a confusion factor sets in with your reader when you go beyond two levels. With too much subdividing, the reader loses track of the first and most important level.

Typing Standards for Specific Layouts

▼

So far, the discussion has centered on typing standards which should be applied to all layouts. However, there are typing standards which apply only to specific layouts, as described in this section.

Typing Standards for the Narrative Layout

♦

In Chapter 5, it was determined that the Narrative and Headline layouts should not be used in manuals except for the Management Endorsement. Nevertheless, if you must use the Narrative layout, double-space the text (leave one blank line) and triple-space (leave two lines) between each paragraph. A small amount of underlining is permissible, since this may be the only way the reader can locate specific facts.

When you have a consistent, integrated set of standards, they all seem to work hand-in-hand. Conversely, when one standard is violated, this sometimes produces a domino effect on other standards as well. Narrative layout is a case in point. The ideal reading line (4 ½") looks awkward on the manual page when Narrative layout is used. So, a longer reading line is usually used in Narrative layout, and a longer reading line raises the question of where to set the margins. Another problem with Narrative is that you may find yourself underlining to

191

PRODUCTION

improve readability and to emphasize points, violating the guideline of avoiding underlining discussed in Chapter 4. Again, this illustrates the point that violation of one standard often leads to violation of others.

TYPING STANDARDS FOR THE HEADLINE LAYOUT

The same erosion of standards occurs when using Headline layout. Nevertheless, here are the basics.

Hierarchy. You will need a hierarchy to your headlines, such as,

- primary—uppercase and underlined
- secondary—uppercase
- tertiary—upper/lowercase.

Spacing. Single-space the text (leave no blank lines) and double-space between paragraphs within the same headline. Leave either one or two lines between the headline and the text which follows it (but be consistent), and leave three lines between the end of one headline and the beginning of the next one.

Reading Line. Weigh the factors of readability, aesthetics, and practicality in making your decision. Keep in mind that the closer you approach 7" (from the ideal of 4½"), the less readable the text becomes. Aesthetically speaking, a reading line of 7" makes the page look crowded, while one of 4½" without captions makes it seem sparse. A 6" line could be a reasonable compromise. Practicality of the Headline layout is questionable because regardless of which reading line you adopt, it will be difficult to achieve consistency with the margins.

TYPING STANDARDS FOR THE CAPTION LAYOUT

By definition, *captions* are keywords taken from the text, and are placed to the left of the text where they can easily be seen. Typing standards for this layout follow, except for standards for notes, bullets, right margins, and the last typing line, which have already been discussed in Section 6.3.

Summary. This caption is typed in uppercase at the left margin. The tab stop for the text of the Summary is aligned with the preprinted Subject and Section fields. The text is single-spaced, in upper- and lowercase. Use standard spacing for paragraphs, bullets, and notes within the Summary.

Primary Captions. Primary captions are started at the left margin and are typed entirely in uppercase.

Secondary Captions. These captions are indented 4 or 5 spaces from the left margin and are typed in upper- and lowercase. However, whether you choose to indent 4 or 5 spaces does not matter, as long as you are consistent in your application of the standard.

Tertiary Captions. Try to avoid third-level captions, but when they are absolutely necessary, use headlines for them and type them in upper- and lowercase. Then leave one line between the headline and the text.

Text Spacing. Single-space within paragraphs. Align the tab stop for the body of the text with the preprinted Subject and Section fields. Leave one line between paragraphs within a primary caption and one line between a primary caption and all secondary captions. Leave two lines between the text of a primary caption and the beginning of another primary caption.

TYPING STANDARDS FOR THE PLAYSCRIPT LAYOUT

The Playscript layout presents the text of the subject in the same form as a play in which the actors are identified and the actions they take are detailed. A Playscript procedure normally consists of three parts, each designated by a primary caption: "SUMMARY," "SET-UP," "PROCEDURE."

Summary. The typing standards for the Summary in the Playscript layout are the same as those for the Caption layout. Leave three blank lines between the text of the Summary and the next caption, "SET-UP." Not every procedure will require a Set-Up. If there is none, leave three blank lines before the next caption, "PROCEDURE."

Set-Up. The Set-Up lists the forms and other unusual items used in the procedure. For example, it may seem obvious, but tools such as pencils, pens, etc., would not be mentioned in the Set-Up, whereas something like a draft stamp would be.
The caption "SET-UP" is typed in uppercase at the left margin. Each item listed in the Set-Up is preceded by a bullet (provided there are two or more items). The bullets line up with the preprinted Section and Subject fields in the masthead. Items are listed in chronological order using the standards in Section 6.3 for typing bullets. Leave three lines between the Set-Up and Procedure.

Procedure. The Caption "PROCEDURE" is typed in uppercase at the left margin. Leave a blank line between the caption "PROCEDURE" and the first job title (actor). Type all job titles in upper- and lowercase beginning at the left margin. As secondary captions, job titles would normally be indented 4 or 5 spaces from the left margin; however, because of the length of some job titles, it is more convenient to have all the space available.
Each procedure step is numbered consecutively. Type the number at the same tab stop as the text in the Summary and the bullets in the Set-Up. But if the procedure is to have more than nine steps, indent Steps 1 through 9 by one space so that they can be properly aligned with Steps 10 and beyond, as shown here:

RIGHT	WRONG
7.	7.
8.	8.
9.	9.
10.	10.

Leave 2 spaces between the period after the numeral and the procedure step. Type the procedure steps in upper- and lowercase.

Notes. The standards for notes described in Section 6.3 apply to the Playscript layout as well. However, there is one variation unique to Playscript. That is, a note which is concerned with *all preceding steps* (to the procedure as a whole) is typed starting at the same tab stop as the step numbers, as shown below:

7. Text text text text text.

8. Text text text.

NOTE: Note note note.

Notes which relate to *one specific step only* are indented so that the word "Note" is started at the same place as the text, as shown below:

7. Text text text text text.

8. Text text text.

    NOTE: Note note note.

Text Statements. Statements made to identify when a step is to be performed (AT 9:00 A.M. EACH MORNING; UPON RECEIPT OF FORM 1801) or when if–then statements occur (FORM FILLED IN CORRECTLY—Go to Step 6; FORM NOT CORRECT—Go to Step 3) are typed in uppercase beginning at the same tab stop as the step numbers. Leave two blank lines before and after the statement. Note that the instruction part of the if-then statement is typed in upper- and lowercase. This is to distinguish the "then" statement from the "if" statement.

TYPING STANDARDS FOR
THE GRAPHIC LAYOUTS

Any of the graphic layouts (Matrix, Flowchart, Data Flow Diagram, and Illustration) may be used as stand-alone layouts, or in some cases they may be used in conjunction with the written layouts. If a graphic layout is being used as a stand-alone layout, it still requires a Summary, and the typing standards common to all layouts should be followed. If a graphic is being used as an illustration in one of the written layouts, then the standards for that layout are followed. In either case, there are three issues to consider regarding the graphic. These are:

1. Size—How big should the illustration be?
2. Location—Where should it go on the page?
3. Title—What should it be captioned with?

As far as size is concerned, there is a trade-off between readability and un-wieldiness. Basically, the rule is: Make your illustration as large as possible for ease of reading without going beyond the page margins. That means you have 7 ¹⁄₁₀″ in width to work with and about 7½″ in depth. There are two simple rules for placement of illustrations on the page:

1. If the illustration is 4½″ or less in width, align the left-most portion of it with the preprinted Section and Subject fields on the manual page.
2. Conversely, if the illustration is larger than 4½″ wide (to the 7¹⁄₁₀″ maximum), center it on the page between the margins.

Each graphic should be titled by a caption. Try to give them meaningful names, such as "ILLUSTRATION: Loan Criteria" or "ILLUSTRATION: Form 1102," rather than meaningless ones like "Matrix" or "Flowchart."

6.5
ILLUSTRATION PREPARATION
▼

Many of the illustrations in manuals are of forms of the standard 8½″ by 11″ size. Since the space you are working with on the manual page is effectively 7″ x 7½″, some method must be found for reducing these and larger forms to fit on the manual page. The best method is a photocopy machine with a reduction mechanism. If your organization doesn't have one of these machines, reduction can be done commercially for a small fee. Another option is to illustrate only a portion of the form (see Figure 6-7). This method can be especially effective if you are describing how to fill in a section of a form. Forms which are less than 7″ on a side can be illustrated either at full size or reduced. Avoid placing illustrations sideways on the page so that the user doesn't have to turn the manual around to look at them.

An important point to note is that forms should be illustrated as completed by the user, not left blank. If a form is filled in by hand, fill it in by hand for the illustration. If it is typewritten, type it. When your forms are illustrated in this fashion, your readers will be aware of how they themselves should fill in the forms.

All illustrations are bordered. The border serves to delineate the illustration and can be done with black matte tape (1/32″) or drawn in with black felt-tip pens. It is easier and faster to draw a straight line with a pen and ruler than to lay a piece of tape. The rule drawn in pen is finer, but the matte tape gives a sharper, more uniform border. Word processing and text processing software can both produce boxes suitable for framing illustrations as well.

How do you actually get the illustration onto the page? First, fill in the form and make a photocopy, even if it does not need to be reduced. That way, there's no concern about ruining your original and having to fill it in or typeset it again.

Call Placed			
☐ Systems Services	☐ Customer Services		S.N. Keeper
☐ Data Process. Services	☑ Other (specify)	G.J	
☐ Technical Services	Format & Stats Coord.	Supervisor Data Processing	Date
		Joe Carpenter	10/10/--

2 Detailed Problem Description *(print clearly)*

Output program for monthly sales forecast not executing — Error message "Record Size Exceeded".

3 Recovery Action Taken *(print clearly)*

Format & Stats Coordinator called. Application Coordinator was notified of the delay for the Monthly Sales Forecast tape.

4 Problem Resolution *(print clearly)*

Format & Stats Coordinator corrected the output program and tested it. The tape was started again and submitted to the Computer Room — 1½ hrs. off schedule.

5 Problem Closed	Supervisor Data Processing	Date				Format and Stats Coord. or Cust. Eng.	Date			
	Joe Carpenter	Year -|-	Mo. 1|0	Day 1|0		Mary Jared	Year -|-	Mo. 1|0	Day 1|0

FIGURE 6-7   ILLUSTRATING PART OF A FORM

Then, on the photocopy, draw in the borders and trim off the excess paper. An art knife and steel ruler serve better for this purpose than do a pair of scissors since the cut is sharper and straighter. Next, with a blue pencil and ruler draw some guidelines to ensure that placement of the illustration will be straight on the page (don't trust your eyes). Now, apply rubber cement, wax, or glue sparingly but evenly to the back of your photocopy and press it into place on the manual page. Turn the page over and rub gently on the back from the center outwards to ensure that there are no bubbles or wrinkles. Remove any excess adhesive from around the edges.

Some form of *dry-transfer lettering* such as Geotype or Letraset is almost mandatory for illustration preparation. These come in a variety of type styles and sizes and are useful when a typewriter is insufficient and you can't afford expensive typesetting.

The *lettering machine* is an alternative to dry-transfer lettering. This machine makes impressions on a piece of clear tape which is then applied to the page.

The type discs come in a variety of sizes and styles. Generally, this method is faster, tidier, and better looking than the dry-transfer lettering, although considerably more expensive. Compared to typesetting costs, however, it's cheaper.

Try to avoid typesetting whenever possible because of the expense, and because manuals are dynamic, and the time involved in typesetting is simply not justified—unless, of course, you have your own composer.

6.6
PROOFREADING
▼

Proofreading is important to your credibility as a writer and as a professional. Good proofreading often goes unnoticed, whereas the converse is not true. To make sure proofreading is thorough, get someone else to do it for you, preferably from the manuals group or technical writing department in your organization.

Common proofreader's marks are shown in Figure 6-8. Both writers and staff doing the keying should become familiar with them.

Mark	Meaning	Example
⌒	delete	He mowed mowed the lawn.
⌒	close up	He mow ed the lawn.
#	insert space	He mowed the lawn.
¶	begin new paragraph	summer. He mowed the lawn. ¶
⌐	move right	He mowed the lawn. ⌉
⌐	move left	⌈He mowed the lawn.
⌐⌐	center	⌉He mowed the lawn.⌐
⌐⌐	move up	⌐He mowed the lawn.⌐
⌐⌐	move down	He mowed the lawn.
tr	transpose	He mowed lawn the. tr
(sp)	spell out circled words	He mowed the (1st) lawn. sp
stet	let it stand as set	He mowed the lawn. stet
lc	make lowercase	He Mowed the Lawn. lc
caps/≡	capitalize	he mowed the lawn. caps
ital	set in italics	He mowed the lawn. ital
⋏	insert comma	He, Robert mowed the lawn. ⋏
⋎	insert apostrophe or single quote	Its Robert's turn to mow the lawn. ⋎
⋎ ⋎	insert quotes	I mowed the lawn, said Robert. ⋎ ⋎
⊙	insert period	He mowed the lawn ⊙
?/	insert question mark	Who mowed the lawn ?/
⋏	insert semicolon	He mowed that lawn I'll do this one. ⋏
⋏	insert colon	He mowed the following lawns the Roberts', the Williams', and the James'. ⋏

FIGURE 6-8   *PROOFREADER'S MARKS*

6.7
THE CRITIQUE PROCESS
▼

Drafts must be reviewed by the people directly involved in formulating policy, and by management or staff who carry out, or are affected by, the policy or procedure. All too often systems fail because the staff responsible for their success are not kept up-to-date and are not made part of the decision-making process. The same mechanism is at work when line staff are not involved in the development of policies and procedures. This does not mean that clerical staff, for example, should determine policy, but it does mean that for the accompanying procedures to be workable, the staff must be kept informed. Communication is the key. Procedures stand a much better chance of being followed if the staff who must execute them have had a chance to be part of the design team.

However, if your organization is a large one, or if it is very structured, office politics may play a part in draft distribution. Ideally, you would just send the drafts to whomever you wished. But the managers and supervisors of "whomever you wish" may want to decide which of their staff will critique your documents. You should get the go-ahead from these supervisors. Ask the supervisors for help in determining which staff members should be sent the drafts, or if you have a preference, ask for permission to send it to specific staff members. You may have to send it to the supervisor(s) who will then distribute it.

What should the critique committee look for? The critique committee should review the document for

- accuracy
- completeness
- simplicity
- redundancy.

Accuracy, completeness, and simplicity are to be achieved, while redundancy is to be avoided.

There are methods which can be used by the reviewer to simplify the tasks of both the reviewer and the writer/editor and to ensure that all critique notes are noticed. They are:

- Use a colored highlighter pen to mark questionable text.
- Make critique notes in the margins or on the left-hand blank page in red ink.
- Indicate pages on which notes have been made by attaching a paper clip. This is particularly helpful if the draft contains a large number of pages.
- Sign your copy of the draft and return it to the writer/editor. This helps the writer/editor ensure that comments are received from all members of the critique committee.

• Do not communicate comments and corrections by memo, since this practice increases the workload for the writer and critiquer without any offsetting benefits.

Two weeks should be allowed for reviewing first drafts. However, this should by no means be an ironclad rule. More reviewing time should be allotted for drafts of 50 or more pages. For subsequent drafts, less time may be allowed since the reviewer will be more familiar with the material and may only need to check a few key points. Of course, if there are very extensive changes and addition of new material, the normal two-week time frame may be extended.

The complexity of your critique process will depend on your approvals process. If many levels of approval are required to get a document published as policy, then the critique committee and process will be correspondingly large and formal. If, on the other hand, all that is required is one person's approval, then possibly only that person and the one performing the task need review the document.

In a typical situation, the first draft of a document is submitted to the originator, who in turn circulates it among the staff immediately affected by it. The originator, as distinct from the writer/editor, is the primary user or the person who defined the need for the document. When the originator is satisfied with the draft, it is then distributed to the critique group. Psychologically, it is better to define the originator, rather than the writer/editor, as author, since in that case it becomes his or her procedure rather than the writer's.

Additional reviews may be required depending on the manual involved. For example, policy documents submitted for a company's general administration manual need a more extensive review process than those with a very limited readership, such as a computer operations manual. Basically, the rule is that if a person or group is affected by a policy or procedure then that person or group should be a part of the review process. This does not imply that if a procedure affects 80 persons on the clerical staff that they should all review it. Rather a sampling of the clerical staff should review it; perhaps four or five of them.

6.8
APPROVALS
▼

Following the review process, each document is given formal approval indicated by signatures on an *approval form*. There are four reasons for using an approval form rather than signing each page individually. First, if a form is used, there is room for more information than just a signature or two at the bottom of a page. For example, in Figure 6-9, which illustrates an approval form, there is room for the names of the author and the editor and for four approval signatures. If all these names and signatures were required on each manual page there would be much less room for text. Second, an approval form avoids all the signing that would have to be done, and the time it would take, if you were getting approvals for every page of a large portion of a manual. Third, a signature at the bottom of a procedure page introduces a credibility problem when the signator changes positions or leaves the organization. And fourth, inquiries are not directed to the signator. This can be extremely important with government manuals made available to the public.

The *policy/procedure approval form* illustrated in Figure 6-9 contains all pertinent data concerning that document and identifies all staff involved from development to approval. The four signature spaces available on this form meet normal requirements easily. When more than four approval signatures are necessary, further approval slips can be used. Multiple page approvals can be iden-

NADIR Inc.	Policy/Procedure Approval

Document number	Pages	Date
03-03-06	1-4	Jan. 18, 19--

Manual
Personnel

Tab
Hiring

Section
The Selection Process

Subject
Making a Job Offer

Author	Editor
Andres Silva	Chidori Tokuda

Approvals

Signature	date
Donna Davis V.P. Administration	*Jan. 19, 19--*
Andres Silva Manager, Personnel	*Jan. 20, 19--*
Signature	date
Signature	date

FIGURE 6-9   DOCUMENT APPROVAL FORM

tified by a page number in the top right-hand corner, as illustrated in Figure 6-10, and the pages can be stapled together to ensure that they do not get separated.

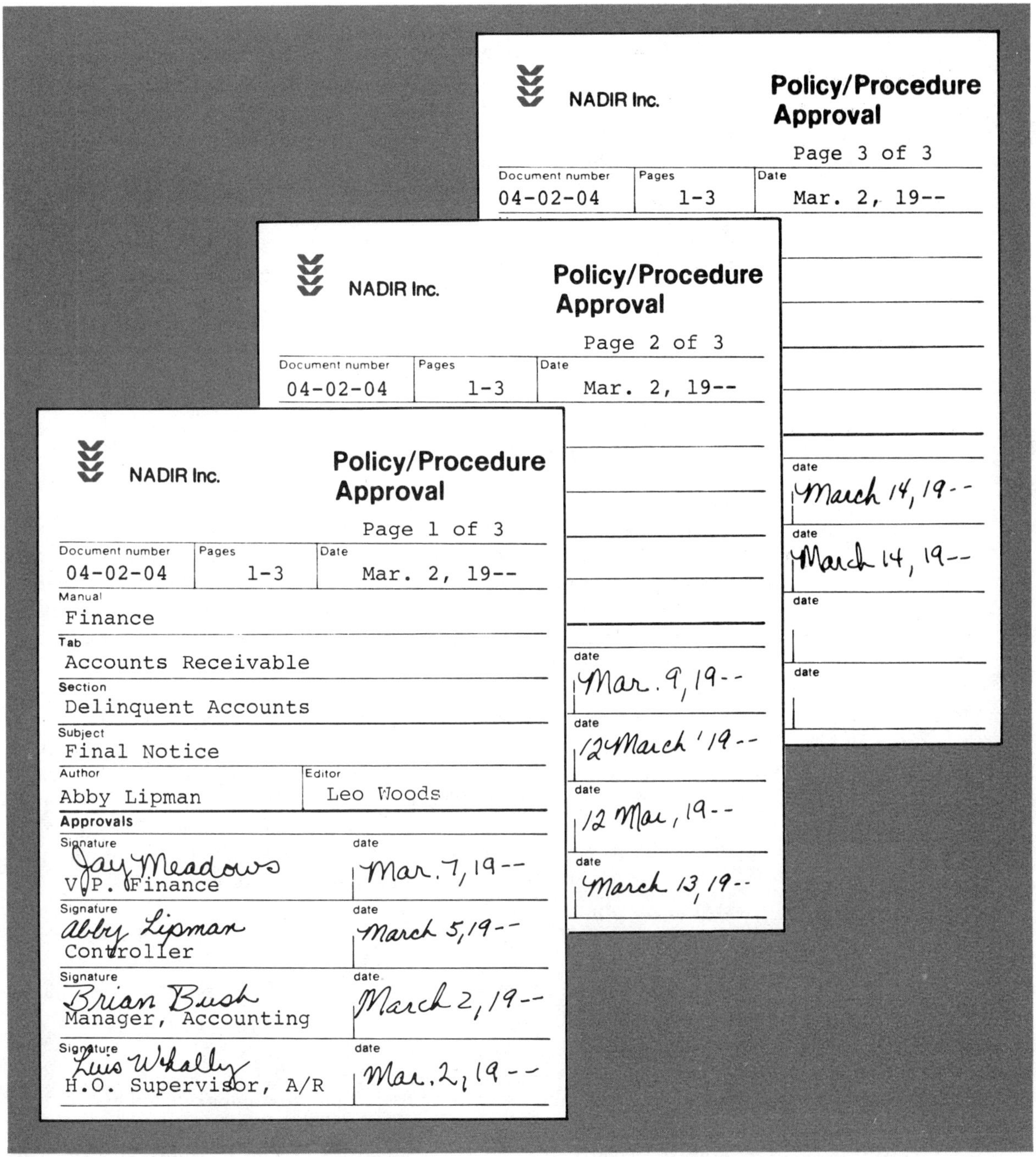

FIGURE 6-10   MULTIPLE PAGE APPROVALS

An alternative for those organizations which average four or more signatures per approval would be to use a larger size, say 8½″ x 5½″, for the approval form. That way, more signatures could easily be accommodated. This larger size is not recommended, however, since an approval process which consistently requires more than four signatures is in danger of becoming unwieldy.

The simplest and best way of determining who should approve a document is to relate the document to the organization chart. Whenever a procedure crosses organizational boundaries, a higher level of approval is required. Even within a specific manual, different levels of approval may be required for separate documents. Each document should be treated individually as regards the need for critique and approval.

The date on the approval form should correspond to the date at the bottom left-hand corner of the document page. The dates opposite the approval signatures are the dates when the signators actually signed the form. Thus, the approval form contains a concise history of the production and approval process.

6.9
PRINTING
▼

Regardless of the manual's size, it is almost always preferable to have it backprinted. Even though very little material may be issued initially, backprinting avoids the problem of re-issuing the material at a later date when the manual becomes full size. The first page of every Subject should be a right-hand page. This practice makes it easy to issue and revise each Subject as a modular unit, something which would otherwise be impossible.

Laser printers can backprint at very high speeds. This equipment usually works on an exception basis, that is, it will backprint everything unless coded not to do so. However, with all other printing and copying methods, you must mark the pages to indicate which are right- and left-hand pages and which pages will or will not be backprinted. This can be done quite simply with a blue pencil, the marks of which will not show up on the printed page. The top right-hand corner of each page is marked lightly with the letter R or L. Right-hand pages (obverse) are always the odd-numbered pages and the left-hand pages (reverse) are the even-numbered pages.

Since each update to a manual is sent to the manual users with a transmittal notice in front, this too should be sent with your documents for printing.

The final version of the documents which goes for printing is called the *printing master*. The printing master, regardless of how it is produced, should be comprised of single sheets and printed one side only to simplify reproduction and to help the printer keep pages in the proper order.

Since your documents will come back from the printer collated according to how they were sent, some care must be exercised in arranging the documents in the order you want them, then correlating this to your transmittal notice. This will usually be in document number sequence to make it easy for the manuals users to update their manuals. However, you may have an eleventh hour addition to the transmittal and not wish to spare the time to retype and proofread the transmittal again, in which case the latecoming document should go in the same order as it appears on the transmittal notice—last. If you are sending documents from two or more different manuals to the print shop, each manual's documents should have their own transmittal.

Producing the printing master may be a very time-consuming matter of typing the material onto the appropriate manual page. If you do not have a word processor or a computer with a quality printer and text processing capability, this will be the only option you have. However, if you use a word processor, an automatic sheet feeder to feed your pre-cut manual pages will ensure accurate and consistent placement of the text on the page, and will also increase throughput speed. An alternative with automated systems, used if the printer cannot feed single sheets, is to print the text onto continuous paper, burst it into single sheets, and then overprint the text onto the manual page using a photocopy machine. But this is not a recommended method, since it is more cumbersome and time-consuming.

PRINTING METHODS

If you want to produce hard copies of your manuals, decisions need to be made about where the printing should be done (in-house or contracted out), and what quality is needed.

Dispense with the notion of typesetting your manuals because of the expense and time involved. Unless you have your own phototypesetting machine (preferably hooked up to your computer or word processor), typesetting manuals will create more problems than it's worth. Small volume printing (30 copies or fewer) of a manual can be achieved with a photocopy machine which has a collator. However, if your photocopier is not equipped with a collator, or if it does not feature two-sided copying, it may be worth your while to get some quotes on printing from print shops. The convenience of having it done close at hand (in-house) and the expense and the time it takes to have it done elsewhere must be considered.

Whether your manuals are printed in-house or at a commercial printer, the printer will need to know what type of paper to use, the number of left- and right-hand pages, collating instructions, hole-punching instructions, the number of copies, etc. All this information is illustrated on the "Innovations Ltd. Requisition for Printing and Mailing," Figure 6-11.

TYPES OF
PAPER TO USE

Since your manuals will be printed on both sides, a paper which is opaque enough not to hinder the reading of text on either side must be chosen. The

Innovations Ltd.

Requisition for Printing and Mailing

Note: Please press hard, you are making 5 copies.

Division	Date ordered	Job title	Form I.D.
Marketing	April 17, 19—	Marketing Manual	0682

Acct code 8310

Printing Service

Printing Service	Quantity	Cost ($)	Charge
Masters	175	.25 each	
Copies per original 105 ×	100	16.50 per M.	
[X] Collate		4.00 per M.	
[ ] Staple		3.00 per M.	
[X] Punch		1.00 per M.	
[ ] Machine fold		2.50 per M.	
[ ] Hand fold		13.00 per hr.	
[ ] Pad		2.00 per M.	
[ ] Trim		1.00 per M.	
[X] Overprint 70 ×	100	11.00 per M.	
Other Costs			

Note: Minimum printing charge $5.00.

Total printing costs

Type of stock	Paper size	Color
Bond	11 × 8½	White

Special instructions

Mailing Service

Mailing Service	Quantity	Cost ($)	Charge
Stencils/Typing		.35 each	
Addressing		13.25 per M.	
Envelope [ ] First Class [ ] Printed Matter Size			
Label — Machine		11.00 per M.	
— Hand		13.00 per hr.	
Fold — Machine		2.50 per M.	
— Hand		13.00 per hr.	
Insert — One		6.75 per M.	
— Two		7.00 per M.	
— Three		7.50 per M.	
— Four or more		7.75 per M.	
Hand Insert Number of inserts		13.00 per hr.	
Metering hand insert mail		13.00 per hr.	
Other costs			

Note: Minimum mailing service charge $15.00.

Total mailing charges

Postage

Total

Special instructions

Deliver to: N. B. Moncton
Manuals Coordinator

Originator (Please print)	Phone number	Date required (Do not use A.S.A.P.)	Authorized signature
N.B. Moncton	2118	April 24, 19—	Ned Moncton

ACCOUNTING

FIGURE 6-11   REQUISITION FOR PRINTING AND MAILING

major factor in determining opacity is weight. Paper type and grade are others.

Printers refer to paper weights in two ways—M and lb. (or #). The letter "M" represents the weight of 1,000 sheets measuring 17″ x 22″. Paper of equal quality and size, but purchased in reams (a ream equals 500 sheets) is designated by "lb" or "#" following the weight. Thus 32M is the same as 16#. Paper of 40M (20lb.) is the minimum weight suitable for printing both sides of the page. It is possible to use a heavier paper than 40M for the manual page, but keep in mind that it will be more expensive and take up more space in the binder. For the title page/amendment record, card stock of 220M is recommended. Refer to Table 7-2 in Chapter 7 for binder capacity of various weights of paper.

There is considerable variance in paper quality from region to region, and even among paper manufacturers. The best way to determine which paper to use is to have a number of suppliers give you some samples of, say, two different grades and three different weights and test these with the actual printing method you'll be using. The visibility of print through a page also depends on such variables as the individual printing press or photocopier and the ink or toner.

Standard paper color is white, and most applications call for black ink. Economy is the main reason for printing black on white but this combination does not always produce the most satisfactory results in terms of legibility. Legibility tests have established the color combinations that work best. In these tests, six colors of ink and paper (black, white, green, blue, red, and yellow) were tested in combination. The test results are shown in Table 6-3.

Order of Legibility	Ink Color	Paper Color
1	Black	Yellow
2	Green	White
3	Red	White
4	Blue	White
5	White	Blue
6	Black	White
7	Yellow	Black
8	White	Red
9	White	Green
10	White	Black
11	Red	Yellow
12	Green	Red

TABLE 6-3   LEGIBILITY OF INK AND PAPER COLOR

As you can see, black ink on yellow paper proved to be the most legible combination, while the traditional black on white was only sixth in order.

PRINTING ILLUSTRATIONS

While it does not generally pay to have text typeset, sometimes it is easier to have a *photo-mechanical transfer* (PMT) made of your illustrations, especially when the illustration is too detailed or the print too small for effective reproduction with a typewriter and a photocopier. The artwork should then be kept separately from the printing masters. Do not use the artwork to paste on the printing master, since future changes of text could necessitate a new PMT where none would otherwise be necessary. A photocopy of the PMT will suffice for creating the printing master.

HOUSING

7.1
BINDERS

▼

Vinyl binders are the most convenient method of binding loose pages and storing them on a shelf. Good binders have the following characteristics:

- they are rigid so that they stand up well on a shelf
- they display good spine visibility while on a shelf
- they protect their paper contents so the paper wears well
- they are durable.

There are many second-rate products on the market which, unfortunately, do not possess any of these characteristics. Chief among these culprits is the so-called school binder, millions of which are sold in stationery and department stores each year. This type of binder is simply not good enough for a manual, since it seldom lasts longer than a year before the cover rips or the ring fitting breaks. A little extra money invested in custom-made, high quality binders will pay off in the long run; although they may cost 50 to 75 percent more than the mass-produced ones, they will last 10 to 15 years longer.

A binder consists of a vinyl cover, a board (for rigidity), a ring fitting, tab dividers, and page lifters. Each of these features will be discussed in detail.

VINEL COVERS

◆

High quality virgin vinyl should be used for binders because it is more durable than reprocessed vinyl. Specify at least 14-gauge, meaning 14 thousandths of an inch in thickness, to achieve the proper qualities of strength and durability. In cold climates, the vinyl must be able to withstand temperature extremes. A *coldcrack* (the terminology to express temperature specifications) of −20° Fahrenheit protects against, for example, leaving the binder in the car overnight, or shipping it to another city where it might be left on an unheated loading dock or truck.

While the vinyl is the most important factor in determining binder strength and durability, the manner in which the vinyl is bonded at the edges of the binder is also of prime importance. The blind-edge weld is far superior to any other process of bonding, and will prolong the binder's life. Figure 7–1 illustrates

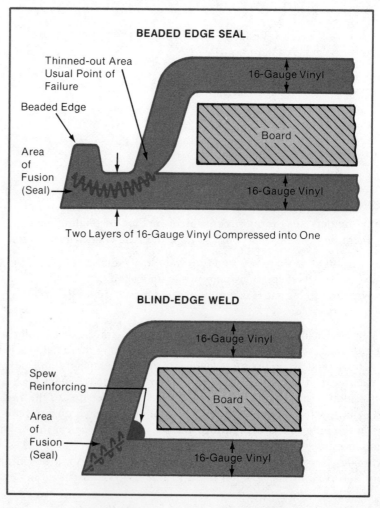

FIGURE 7-1   THE BEADED EDGE SEAL COMPARED TO THE BLIND-EDGE WELD

both (A) the traditional *beaded edge seal* and (B) the latest development, the superior *blind-edge weld*.

The fault of the standard beaded edge seal is that the protruding lip or bead tends to wear, get caught on things, and eventually cracks. Even standing still on a shelf, downward pressure is exerted on the seal, causing wear. No such wear occurs when the electrostatic sealing causes the vinyl to bead on the interior of the weld; then there is no edge to catch or bend.

Another recent advance in binder vinyl technology is in the hinge design. The standard hinge is a *plain bar weld*, as illustrated in Figure 7–2. This is the same sort of weld as in the standard beaded edge seal, and suffers from the same weaknesses. That is, it is very fragile and tears easily. On the other hand, the new *island spine* provides many times the strength of the old spine. This is illus-

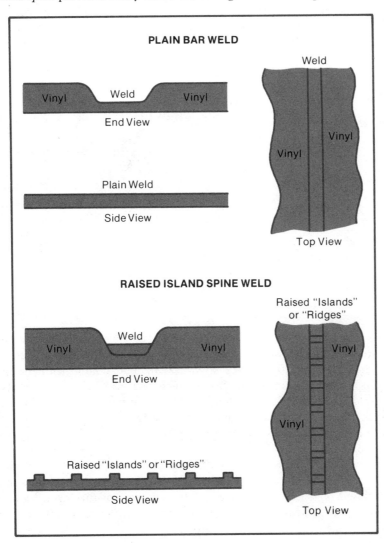

FIGURE 7-2   THE PLAIN BAR WELD COMPARED TO THE RAISED-ISLAND SPINE WELD

trated in Figure 7–2 as well. The extra vinyl in the spine, and especially the ribbed construction, provides the increased strength and durability. The bar weld spine is easily ripped, but the island spine is extremely difficult to tear. One manufacturer of these binders built a machine to test the durability of the new island spine compared to the old spine. The old spine broke after a few thousand openings and closings of a binder, but the binder with the island spine eventually outlasted and broke the testing machine!

BOARD INSERTS

♦

Pasted chipboard is sandwiched between the vinyl to maintain rigidity. Avoid flexible binders since they do not stand up well in bookshelves and the rings can press through the cover and damage it. Table 7–1 shows the recommended thickness of board for various binder sizes.

TABLE 7-1
RECOMMENDED
THICKNESS OF BOARD
INSERTS

Binder Size	Board Thickness
Up to 1″	.080″
1¼ to 1¾″	.100″
2″ and larger	.120″

Although the table indicates binder sizes of 2″ and larger, a binder larger than 2″ can be heavy and unwieldy, especially when filled to capacity.

RING FITTINGS

♦

Not long ago, all ring fittings were round, in imitation of book bindings. Then came a big improvement, the *D ring,* and finally the current state of the art, which is the *slant D ring* (see Figure 7–3). The trouble with the original round ring is that the actual capacity is much less than the ring diameter, and the shape of the ring causes the binder contents to hide the tab dividers at the back of the binder. The latest slant D ring, on the other hand, offers up to 30 percent more capacity than the same size of round ring, and all tab dividers are clearly visible.

A serious problem with the old-fashioned school binders is that the ring fitting is attached to the spine. This means that if you lay one of these binders flat but closed on a desk, then open it, the contents of the manual are pulled along with the ring fitting as it changes positions from the vertical to the horizontal. With the slant D ring, the ring fitting is rivetted to the back cover of the

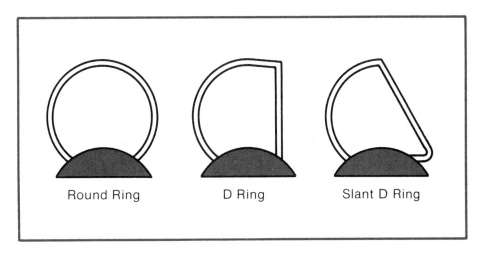

Round Ring   D Ring   Slant D Ring

FIGURE 7-3   RING FITTINGS

manual instead of the spine, thus keeping the binder contents stationary during opening and closing, producing much less wear on the paper. In addition, mounting the ring fitting on the back cover of the binder does not mar the appearance of the spine. With the slant D ring, you avoid having to reinforce the front pages to protect them. Round and slant D ring fittings in the open and closed positions are shown in Figure 7–4.

Another problem with the round ring is that the paper catches in the joint of the ring itself. A look at Figure 7–5, which shows an enlargement of the round and slant D rings, shows that the paper in a slant D ring binder never actually comes into contact with the joint, whereas in the round ring binder, the paper contents are always in contact with the joint when the binder is closed. Also, the crown on the highest portion of the slant D ring is actually higher than the joint, so that the vinyl of the binder cover does not come into contact with the joint either.

Some ring fittings have *boosters*—triggers for opening and closing the rings— but it is recommended that you not order ring fittings with boosters for several reasons:

- Most people open the ring by grasping it in the middle and pulling it apart instead of using boosters.
- The triggers represent a weak point in the construction of the ring fitting and are almost guaranteed to fail even after light usage. Eliminating them allows the whole fitting to be strengthened.
- After some use, when they become distorted, the boosters scratch the surface of whatever they're stored on.
- Thumbnails can be damaged by pressing the triggers.
- Boosters can interfere with the motion of the pages as they are turned.
- The boosters can add up to 20 cents to the cost of each binder.
- Finally, it's just as easy to open the ring without the boosters.

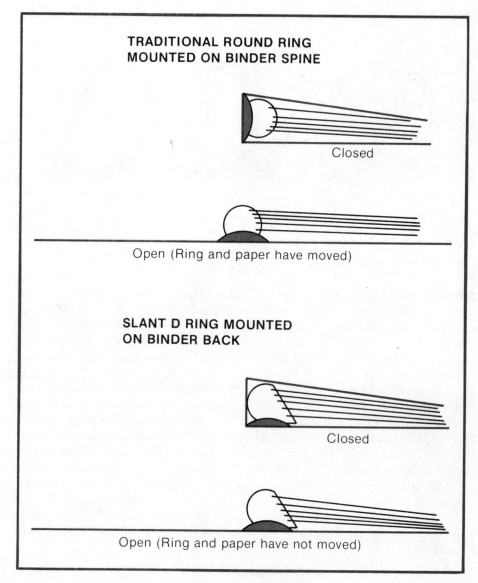

**TRADITIONAL ROUND RING
MOUNTED ON BINDER SPINE**

Closed

Open (Ring and paper have moved)

**SLANT D RING MOUNTED
ON BINDER BACK**

Closed

Open (Ring and paper have not moved)

FIGURE 7-4   RINGS IN OPEN AND CLOSED BINDERS

The number of rings you need on the ring fittings should be considered. Three is the standard number for 11″ × 8½″ paper, but four rings are used for metric binders, which are 11¾″ × 8¼″. You could go to a custom ring fitting of five or more rings if it is important that only material designed for the binder goes into it. However, each additional ring will add to the cost of the binder.

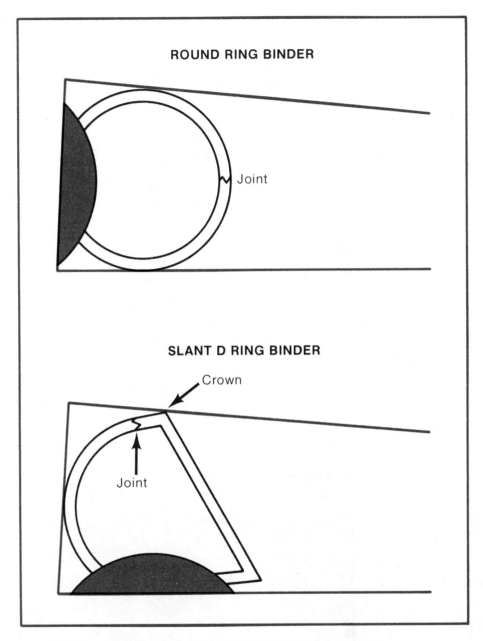

ROUND RING BINDER

Joint

SLANT D RING BINDER

Crown

Joint

FIGURE 7-5   BINDER RINGS AND THE POSITION OF THEIR JOINTS

When you are discussing binder size with a vendor, always quote the binding edge first. Thus 11″ × 8½″ means the 11″ side is the binding edge. Do not make the mistake of asking for 8½″ × 11″ and being disappointed when your binders arrive and the binding edge is only 8½″, as in Figure 7–6.

214
CHAPTER 7

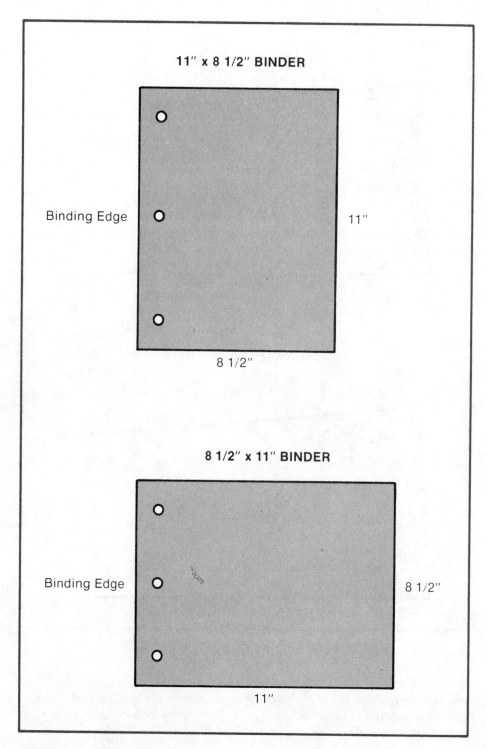

11" x 8 1/2" BINDER

Binding Edge

11"

8 1/2"

8 1/2" x 11" BINDER

Binding Edge

8 1/2"

11"

FIGURE 7-6   BINDING EDGES

Table 7–2 compares the capacity (expressed in numbers of sheets of paper) of round ring binders to the same size binder with a slant D ring fitting. The capacity of a 2½" round ring binder is shown to illustrate that its capacity is even less than that of a 2" slant D ring binder. This capacity chart makes the superiority of the slant D ring evident.

Ring		Inches	Effective Capacity								
			Sheets of Bond			Sheets of Uncoated Book Stock			Sheets of Coated Book Stock		
Type	Size		16 lb 32 M	20 lb 40 M	24 lb 48 M	60 lb 120 M	70 lb 140 M	80 lb 160 M	60 lb 120 M	70 lb 140 M	80 lb 160 M
Round	1"	.720"	202	166	140	164	148	121	240	200	175
Slant D	1"	1.000"	270	220	190	220	200	160	320	270	235
Round	1¼"	.960"	269	221	187	218	197	161	320	266	234
Slant D	1¼"	1.156"	320	260	220	260	230	190	380	315	280
Round	1½"	1.040"	292	240	202	289	213	175	346	289	254
Slant D	1½"	1.500"	410	337	285	335	300	245	485	405	355
Round	2"	1.584"	445	366	309	440	325	266	527	440	386
Slant D	1¾"	1.719"	475	390	330	385	345	285	565	470	415
Round	2½"	1.952"	548	451	380	445	400	328	650	542	476
Slant D	2"	2.100"	580	480	400	470	420	350	690	575	505

TABLE 7-2   BINDER CAPACITIES OF ROUND AND SLANT D RING FITTINGS

This capacity table can be used to determine the size of binders you need. To estimate the number of pages in your manual, use an average of three pages per Subject, then add 15 percent for the Controls. Take into account the title page and your tab dividers, each of which, depending on its weight, is equivalent to three to five sheets of 20 lb. paper.

HOLE PUNCHING

Since ring thickness increases with binder size, the size of hole that you punch (or drill) in the paper must also vary to accommodate the ring and prevent tearing of the paper. For binders less than ¾" in capacity, a ³⁄₁₆" hole is recommended; for ¾" or 1" binders, use a ¼" hole; and for any binder larger than 1" (the most frequent situation in business applications), drill a ⁵⁄₁₆" hole. These hole sizes ensure that the holes are large enough to fit over the rings comfortably, and that they allow freedom of motion in flipping pages. There should also be a margin (or throat) between the edge of the paper and the leftmost edge of the hole. This throat should be ¼″ wide for all paper with ¼″ or ⁵⁄₁₆″ holes, but a ³⁄₁₆″ throat is best for paper with only a ³⁄₁₆″ diameter hole. Figures 7–7 and 7–8 illustrate the recommended sizes and positions of holes for 11″ × 8½″ and 8½″ × 5½″ paper respectively. It is assumed that the paper will go into binders with

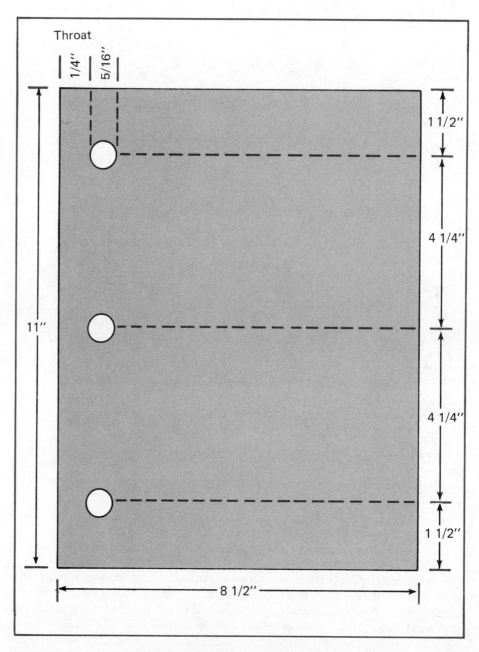

FIGURE 7-7   RECOMMENDED HOLE PUNCHING FOR 11″ × 8½″ PAPER

a capacity greater than 1″. For smaller capacity binders the hole diameter and throat width would be scaled down accordingly. For metric sizes and nonstandard numbers of rings, a manufacturer will be able to make appropriate recommendations.

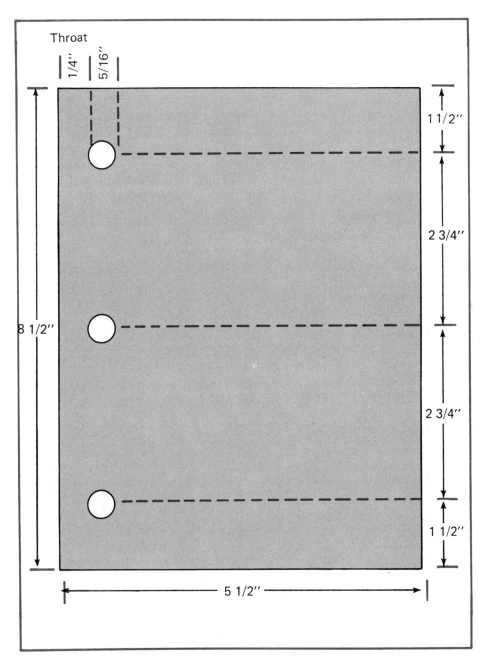

FIGURE 7-8   RECOMMENDED HOLE PUNCHING FOR 8½″ × 5½″ PAPER

Note that the dimensions from the top, bottom, and left edge are the same regardless of the page size. Also, the reason for earlier choosing ⁷⁄₁₀″ (7 character spaces) for the margin size is now readily apparent (see Page Design and Format in Chapter 2). Even allowing for a little inexactitude in punching and aligning, there is no danger that any information on the manual page is going to be obliterated by the holes.

EASEL BINDERS AND FLIPCHART BINDERS

Easel binders, which have a bend in the middle enabling them to be propped up, are a convenient way to house manuals for employees who must carry out hand-eye coordinated tasks while referencing the manual. Examples of these employees are data entry operators, typists, cooks, and equipment operators. Without the convenience of an easel binder they would either have to change their sightline drastically or prop the binder up with a device of some sort. Figure 7–9 illustrates a schematic easel binder viewed from the side.

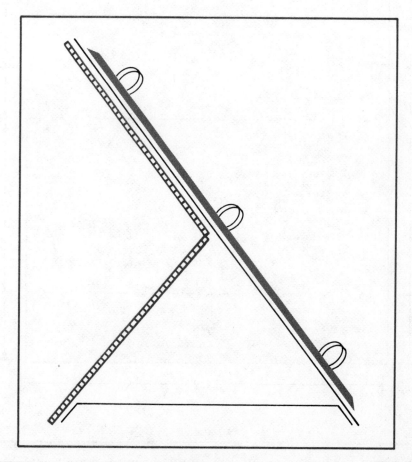

FIGURE 7-9   EASEL BINDER—SIDE VIEW

Flipchart binders are a fairly recent development in binder technology. Flipchart binders can be used for sales or promotional manuals and for presentations. One type has an extra cover welded on to provide a kind of three-legged stool effect, allowing the binder to stand upright on its own so that the pages can remain vertical. Another type of flipchart binder looks like a capital A when it is in use, with a brace supporting the two covers, and the ring fitting at the apex of the A. Figure 7–10 shows schematic drawings of both types.

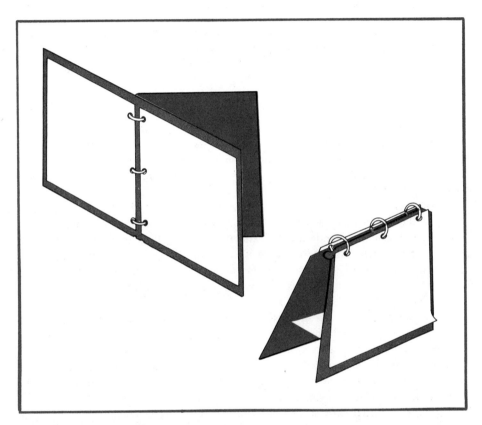

FIGURE 7-10   TWO TYPES OF FLIPCHART BINDERS

7.2
VISUAL IDENTITY
▼

Manuals must be attractively packaged to achieve the optimum impact. Compared to the cost of writing a manual, the cost of housing it is very small, sometimes as little as 1 percent of the writing cost. There are ways you can save money on housing, and these will be discussed in some detail, but scrimping on looks and quality should not be one of them.

There should be one person to control and coordinate the binder effort so that consistency of design and quality can be maintained and the best prices obtained. This person would ensure that

- duplicate colors are not issued to different departments if each is allowed its own
- the graphic signature (company logo plus company name) is a consistent size, type style, and weight of type, and is positioned similarly on all of the organization's binders
- standards for print style in the manual name are consistent
- proper binder sizes and capacities are ordered
- the type of information on all company binders is similar.

There are three aspects of cover design to consider in choosing a binder for your manuals—color, information, and decoration.

COLOR

Binder manufacturers offer a wide variety of standard colors besides the old stand-by, black. These include blues, reds, greens, yellows, oranges, browns, and many others. Although the trend in the past has been toward somber tones such as navy blue, dark brown, and wine red, in recent years the colors have become livelier, with brilliant reds, yellows, and greens gaining ascendancy along with pastel shades.

Another option open to you is a special or nonstandard color, and manufacturers will custom-match any color that you desire. Naturally, this is more expensive than choosing a standard color, and there is usually a minimum amount of vinyl that they will produce to make it economically feasible, equivalent to say 5,000 or more binders. Unless you have a very large organization which has an unusual characteristic color, this will probably not be worthwhile.

Choosing a color for your binders is no trivial matter, especially if your manuals are going to be read outside the organization. Binder color conveys an image, and some thought must be given to the type of image you wish to present to the public. For instance, a solid, conservative image can be transmitted through a dark blue or dark brown binder while an upbeat, contemporary image will be conveyed if you choose orange or fuchsia binders. Light grey or mushroom transmit a quiet elegance.

If your manuals are strictly internal affairs, it is usually best to use one standard color for all manuals instead of different colors for each division. This allows you to order binders and spine inserts in large quantities, producing savings in cost and administration, and eliminating long lead times since binders can be stocked conveniently. Individual users or departments can then get smaller numbers of binders at lower prices than if each order has to be placed separately. Also, there is no danger of running out of suitable colors if all manuals are the same color.

INFORMATION

The second element to be considered in binder design is the information you wish to have on the binder cover and spine. This information will consist of things such as company logo, company name, division or department name, and manual title. It should not include items such as names, addresses, and telephone numbers, since these can change frequently and outdate the binders.

The normal practice with regard to the information placed on the binder is to put the same data on the front cover and on the spine, but this is not absolutely necessary. It is necessary, however, to place sufficient information on the spine to identify the manual to a potential user when the binder is standing upright on a shelf. A few tips are in order here.

- The spine only needs to be read from a distance of 6 to 12 feet, so the lettering does not have to be huge.
- The lettering should be in a simple, clean type style for readability—Helvetica or Univers (sans serif) is fine. Under no circumstances should you use a decorative typeface for the manual title because these are hard to read. See Figures 7–11 and 7–12 on pages 222 and 223 for a few samples of what to use and what not to use.
- Use upper- and lowercase letters where possible for the manual title to aid readability. However, your company name can be in uppercase if that's the way it is ordinarily depicted.
- Avoid the use of Chinese-style lettering on the spine, that is, aligning the letters vertically one above the other. Figures 7–13 and 7–14 on page 224 illustrate the right and wrong ways to arrange the lettering.

There are very good reasons for not designing a binder spine with vertical lettering:

- Our alphabet (the Roman alphabet), unlike Chinese ideograms, was designed to be printed horizontally, left to right. Roman letters are not all of equal width, so when printed vertically they appear unbalanced. "I," for instance, is not as wide as "H" or "M." If you were to look at the whole alphabet printed vertically it would not appear to be at all consistent.
- Reading tests have shown that it takes much longer to read and comprehend vertical writing than it does to read horizontal writing. This is because our brains have learned to recognize words and groups of words as complete images and not as collections of individual letters.
- Hand in hand with the previous two reasons goes the fact that the optical centerline of some letters is different. The optical centerline of the symmetrical letters such as "A," "H," and "O" is dead center. In asymmetrical letters such as "E" and "K," it is more to the left; in "J" and sometimes "Y" (depending on the typeface), it is to the right. This forces a choice between lining up the letters optically, so the eye can move in a straight line vertically down the spine, but leaving the margins unequal, or geometrically, in which the margins are equal, but the eye must move from left to right as well as vertically. Neither choice is satisfactory.
- As difficult to read as vertical printing is on the shelf, it is almost impossible to read if the binder is lying flat on a desk, at least without craning your neck. Such is not the case with normal printing, however.

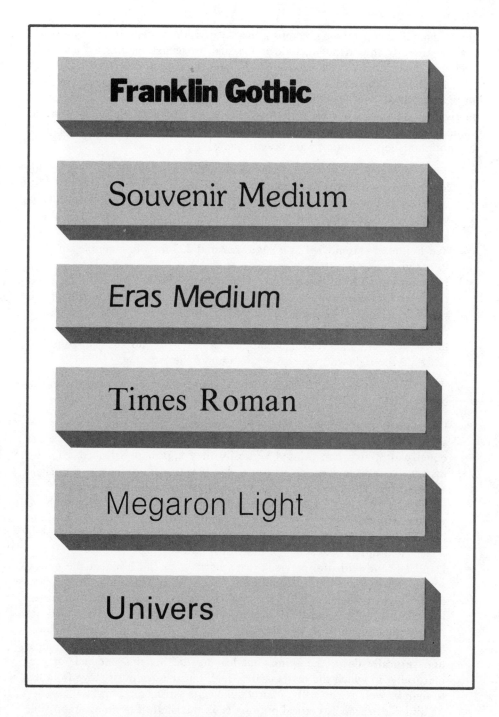

FIGURE 7-11   APPROPRIATE TYPE STYLES FOR BINDER SPINES

FIGURE 7-12   INAPPROPRIATE TYPE STYLES FOR BINDER SPINES

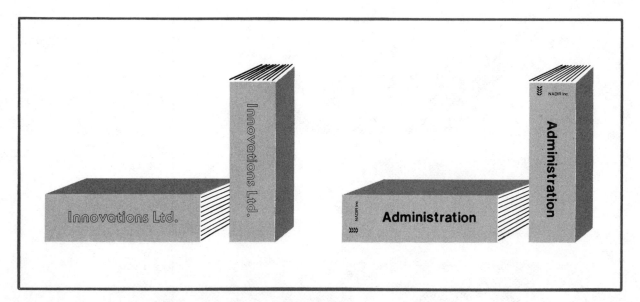

FIGURE 7-13   PROPER ARRANGEMENT OF SPINE LETTERING

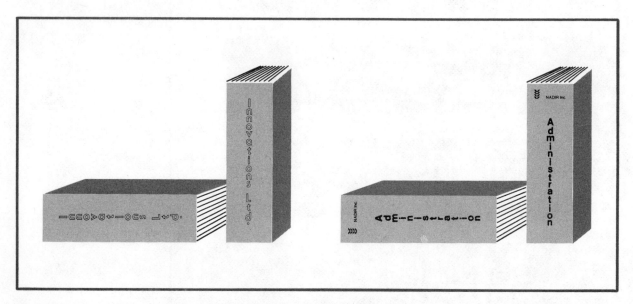

FIGURE 7-14   IMPROPER ARRANGEMENT OF SPINE LETTERING

- Since letters are taller than they are wide, all titles will take up more space if printed vertically than if they are printed horizontally. Thus, for longer titles, the size of the letters has to be reduced.

Note also in Figure 7–13 that the titles "Innovations Ltd." and "Administration" are set from top to bottom, so that they can be read easily when the binder is flat on its back on a desk. Setting the title to be read from the bottom up is much more awkward.

DECORATION

The third element of binder design is the decoration of covers. Full rein can be given to one's creativity in designing these binder covers. Most covers are decorated only on the front, but some remarkably good effects can be created by extending the design around the spine to the back cover as well. Most commercial firms want a design with a combination of name, logo, message, and decorativeness. This combination of factors can be very powerful in conveying the appropriate corporate image.

Try to keep the design simple and straightforward. The Scotchkote Protective Coatings binder of 3M Company is a prime example of visually portraying a message about manual content with a very simple design. This binder depicts a solid surface with four or five stylized arrows bouncing off it—effectively stating that whatever is represented by the arrows cannot penetrate material coated with Scotchkote. Another good example, but one which is a little more subtle, is the Toro Marketing Guide for Snow and Debris Equipment. It depicts a symbol consisting of half a snowflake and half a maple leaf.

Silk screening is one of the many techniques which can be used to make binder covers more attractive and more effective. Binders are silk screened much as prints are silk screened by artists. Silk screening is attractive and effective, and it is the most common technique, combining reasonable cost with aesthetic looks. If silk screening is used, wider letter spacing than normal is required since there is a tendency for the ink to bleed slightly on the vinyl. Also, silk screening a very large area should be avoided since the usually lighter colors of the screen scuff very easily, and soon the binder begins to look messy.

A cheaper alternative to silk screening is *hot foil stamping*, which can be used for small prints, but is less permanent. The foil (usually gold or silver in color) is heat sealed onto the vinyl, but eventually it oxidizes, since it's not real gold or silver, and then chips off easily.

Appliqué (vinyl welded on vinyl) produces a raised print. This method costs a little more and is limited to small areas, but adds prestige and color to a binder. Additionally, it is the most permanent method of printing on vinyl. Appliqué is used mainly for highlighting a logo or a name, and is very attractive in combination with silk screening.

Embossing is another common technique whereby a logo or other design is raised, simply by lowering the surrounding area. The logo is thus at the same level as the major portion of the vinyl cover—but is enclosed by a depressed portion to make it stand out. This is done by pressing a die into the vinyl.

Debossing is the opposite of embossing. A debossed binder cover has the design depressed into the vinyl with a die. Both embossing and debossing can be used to good advantage in conjunction with a technique such as silk screening or hot foil stamping. And either can be used in combination with appliqué. For example, you could emboss your logo on a piece of blue vinyl, then apply the embossed logo (appliqué) to a white vinyl cover.

The latest binder decoration technique, still in the developmental stage, is called *flow molding*. Flow molding produces the same effect as appliqué, but promises to be cheaper, since only one piece of vinyl is used, whereas two pieces are needed for appliqué. Basically, in this technique, a mold is made of the desired design, and the vinyl is pressed against it. Flow molding requires thicker vinyl than other techniques, usually 18-gauge, which will increase the cost slightly.

In summary, there are two techniques to apply color to the vinyl—silk screening and hot foil stamping. Additionally, there are four techniques to shape the vinyl into a design. These are appliqué, embossing, debossing, and flow molding.

PADDING

Padding consists of gluing a ⅛″ or ¼″ sheet of foam (such as polyurethane) to the chipboard, before it is placed between the vinyl sheets, which gives the cover a "cushion" effect. The most common applications for padding are binders for presentations, photographs (for weddings and the like), stamps, scrapbooks, and other items where thickness is associated with quality. For most commercial applications, forget it, unless you're giving away your binders with something like sales or marketing material inside, and wish to create the image of substantiality.

TEXTURED VINYL

These days, vinyl can be made to feel like just about anything. The most common nonvinyl textures are suede and leather. These specialty textures are also used mainly to create a quality image for promotional material or the like. Naturally, this is a little more expensive than ordinary vinyl.

7.3
TAB DIVIDERS

Tab dividers are an important part of your binders. They carry the same number as the Tab, representing the first two digits of the document number. There are two exceptions to numbered tab dividers, the "Indices" and "Appendices." As for the others, they are numbered consecutively from 01 to however many Tabs there are in the manual.

This method of numbering tab dividers provides an easy reference and aids retrievability. Note that you should not have the Tab names printed on the tab dividers, since you won't be able to use them again if you change the name of a Tab (for instance, if a large Tab is split into two smaller ones).

The paper used for tab dividers should not be too heavy—a good tab stock of 80 to 100 lb. is quite sufficient. The tabs and holes should be reinforced with mylar, which is more durable than acetate reinforcements.

Tab dividers can be made in any number per row or bank, but they should not be too small to provide a good grip for thumb and forefinger. A single bank and a double bank of dividers is illustrated in Figure 7–15. Coordinate the colors of the tab dividers to match your binder color.

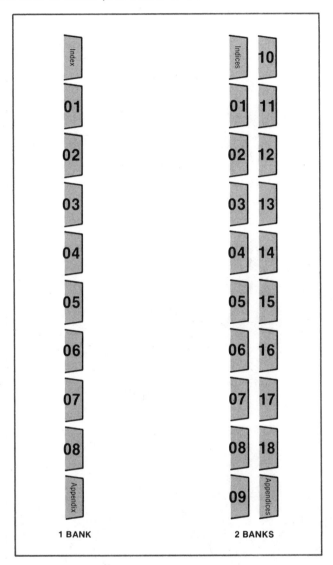

FIGURE 7-15   TAB DIVIDERS

7.4
PAGE LIFTERS
▼

Page lifters (sometimes referred to as sheet lifters) are used to assist in returning the binder contents to the closed position. The use of a page lifter allows you to close the binder by lifting the front cover and returning it to the closed position without actually forcing the pages with your hands. The page lifter should be made of heavy-duty polyethylene and placed *on top of the binder contents*. The polyethylene should be transparent enough so that the information on the title page is visible through it. For binder capacities up to 1″, a 3″ page lifter is sufficient, but for binder capacities greater than 1″, use a 5″ page lifter. Figure 7–16 shows how the page lifter works.

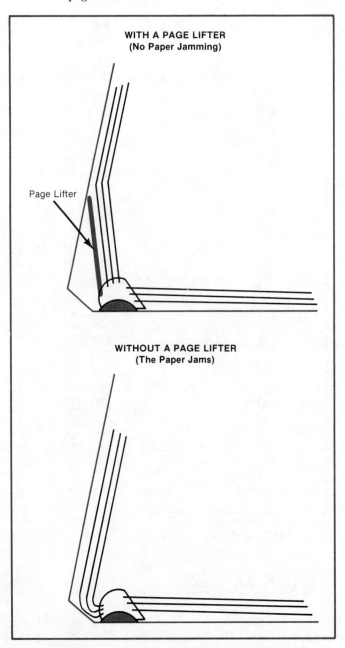

WITH A PAGE LIFTER
(No Paper Jamming)

Page Lifter

WITHOUT A PAGE LIFTER
(The Paper Jams)

FIGURE 7-16   BINDER WITH AND WITHOUT PAGE LIFTER

It is useful to place a blank page or sheet of card stock at the back of the manual to prevent the last page from sticking to the vinyl. When the reverse of the last page has printing on it, the print is sometimes transferred to the vinyl, detracting from the appearance of the inside back cover. The extra sheet, particularly if it's card stock, prevents both the page from sticking to the cover and the transfer of print.

7.5

POCKETS
▼

Plastic *spine pockets* are used to hold a card containing the manual name. The size and location of the pocket should be standardized for all manuals regardless of size. This

- maintains a consistent appearance
- simplifies artwork preparation
- enables grouping of orders for printing
- creates flexibility.

The standard pocket should be no wider than the smallest binder likely to be used. If, for example, a 1″ binder will be the smallest size, then the pocket can be welded to the hinge. On larger binders the pocket will be centered on the spine. Then all spine inserts can be 1″ wide by whatever length desired.

Flexibility is the most important reason from the user's point of view for using spine pockets with cards. When the contents grow, simply transfer the contents and the title card to a new binder. Thus, when a large manual is split into separate manuals, it is only necessary to buy the new inserts (provided you maintain a stock of binders); so money is saved. The size and arrangement of type on the spine insert should be common to all manuals, regardless of binder size.

When using spine pockets, the front of the binder should not have the manual name on it. The upper portion of the spine can accommodate the organization name and logo, and the lower portion, the manual name. Don't use a plastic pocket on the front binder cover because it detracts from the appearance of the binder, and the motion of removing and replacing the binder on the shelf can tear the plastic.

Another application for plastic pockets is to put one on the *inside* front cover to contain a business card. If you do this, make sure that the opening and closing motion of the binder does not cause the page lifter to rub against the business card pocket, as this will eventually tear it.

Figure 7–17 shows some Nadir, Inc., binders of different sizes. Note the consistent appearance of the spine pockets and the title cards. Also note that the size and position of the company name and logo is the same for all binders regardless of capacity.

A variation on this theme is, instead of using card inserts, to use clear vinyl inserts with the manual title silk screened onto the clear vinyl. This method has the advantage of obviating the problem of color matching the card inserts with your vinyl binder cover. On the other hand, the vinyl inserts are more expensive and are very flexible, making the insertion more difficult than it is with the firm card inserts. There is also a danger of type transfer from the vinyl insert to the spine pocket, which may prevent reuse of the binder for another manual.

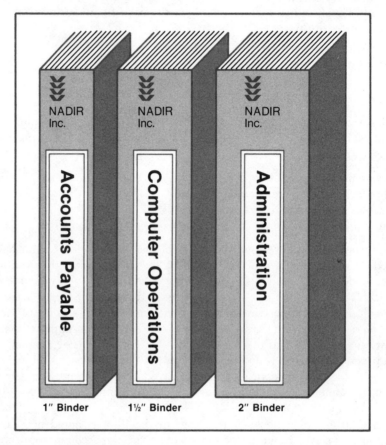

FIGURE 7-17   SPINE POCKETS

7.6

BINDER SPECIFICATIONS
▼

By this time you've made all the necessary decisions about what your binders are going to look like: how big they will be; how many you're going to order; how many tab dividers you'll need; and so on. To put all this information together in a format that can be useful both to you and to your binder supplier, a form such as WMC's Specifications for Binders and Tab Dividers, illustrated in Figure 7–18, is very useful. This form tells the supplier exactly what you want, allowing no margin for error. Note that much of the information is preprinted on the form: for instance, the specifications for vinyl, board, ring fitting, and page lifter. Since these are constant for all of Widget Manufacturing Company's manuals, this saves typing the information each time.

Widget Manufacturing Company	11070 Tuscaloosa Street Chicago, Illinois 60609-1256	**Specifications for Binders and Tab Dividers**

Job name	Contact	Telephone number
Sales Administration	Byron Lang	(312) 789-4022

Binder Specifications

Quantity	Page size	Capacity	Color outside	Liner
200	11" x 8½" plus ½" tab extension	1¼"	#102 Red	#102 Red

Vinyl

16 gauge (.016) thick, Virgin vinyl, grade D, class 120, cold crack -20°F, Microfine surface

Board	Ring fitting
Pasted Chipboard	Slant D ' ring fitting without triggers, mounted on back cover with exposed rivets

Page lifter	Construction
Standard Polyvinyl	Blind edge weld, with ridge reinforced island hinge

Printing instructions

Silk screen on cover and spine, in white

Pockets

Spine pocket to fit insert 1" x 7½" pocket centered on spine and positioned ¼" from bottom

Other instructions

None

Artwork

[X] To be supplied by WMC   [ ] To be supplied by vendor   [ ] Other

Tab Divider Specifications

Sets (quantity)	Tabs per set	Tabs per bank
200	10	10: Index, 01-08, Appendix

Printed	Tabs mylar reinforced in:	Sheet size
[X] One side [ ] Two sides	01-08 in white, Index and Appendix in red	11" x 8½" plus ½" tab extension

Stock	Punching	Collated
100 lbs. — White	3 hole punched, 4¼ c. to c. ¼" diameter, holes mylar reinforced in clear	by supplier

Artwork	Specifications authorized	Date
When supplied by WMC is to be returned to WMC	*Byron Lang*	*Sept. 27, 19--*

FIGURE 7-18   SPECIFICATIONS FOR BINDERS AND TAB DIVIDERS

DISTRIBUTION

8.1   Analysis of Requirements
8.2   Security
8.3   Assembly and Numbering
8.4   Issuing and Controlling the Manual

8.1
ANALYSIS OF REQUIREMENTS

▼

The first step in determining manuals distribution is to establish who should receive copies and why they should receive them. Manuals are issued on a need-to-know basis, which means that if a person needs a manual to perform his or her job, then that person should be issued one. It does not necessarily mean that each of these persons needs a personal copy, just access to one. A group of two to six people can share a manual when it is not needed constantly. However, this is not to imply that a manual should be kept in a supervisor's or manager's office, as experience shows that staff will be reluctant to take the manual out of the supervisor's office. Better that the supervisor or manager should have to come out of his or her office to have access to the manual. Some organizations adopt the policy that the first line of supervision over those that need the manual is entitled to a manual as well. This is also a reasonable method of determining distribution requirements. The thing to avoid at all costs, however, is the situation where only management personnel have manuals. In this milieu it becomes a status symbol to have many manuals on your credenza, and if that's the situation, your organization may as well not have manuals at all.

If manuals are not issued to staff who need them to do their jobs, staff members may acquire unauthorized copies of the manuals, usually by photocopying someone else's manual. These unauthorized copies, however, never get updated and can lead to costly errors.

One effective method of categorization for manuals distribution is the following:

- automatic
- on request
- restricted.

Using this method, designated staff are automatically entitled to certain manuals. Staff not automatically entitled to a manual may be issued one upon the request of their supervisor or manager. Manuals designated as restricted are issued only to authorized staff—there should be a list of such staff available to the distribution controller.

One way of representing this method of distribution is by a matrix: a list of job titles on the vertical axis, manual names on the horizontal axis, and codes to represent the distribution categories in the body of the matrix. That way, the distribution controller can tell at a glance whether or not to issue a manual to a particular individual.

It is imperative that the person controlling distribution be made aware of staff commencement, changes, and terminations, so that the appropriate manuals may be issued and retrieved.

The method described here is a fairly rigid, formal distribution scheme. Yours need not be so complicated. It may be as informal as a single person more or less arbitrarily deciding, upon consultation, whether a manual should be issued. It should not, however, be so informal that anyone can decide to obtain any manual, for then problems of unnecessary proliferation or a lack of manuals where they are most needed can occur.

The principle of issuing manuals on a need-to-know basis has been taken to an extreme in some organizations. A method called Tab distribution is used, in which a person who would reference only a portion of a manual is issued only that portion. Superficially, this may seem reasonable. However, in practice, it does not work, and it is strongly recommended that this method *not* be used for a number of very good reasons.

- Managing a Tab distribution system is very difficult, requiring that each Tab so distributed be put on the distribution list and the distribution matrix.
- Separate alphabetic indices must be maintained for each Tab, as well as for the complete manual.
- The numbering system no longer applies; i.e., the first two digits are meaningless.
- Distribution of Tabs results in a waste of oversized binders, ordering binders of different sizes, or the use of nonstandard binder covers, all of which defeat the purposes for setting organization standards.
- Large Tabs, say 100 pages or more, are entering the size range where they perhaps should be considered as unique manuals anyway.

The use of Tab distribution is another example of how interlocking standards are eroded when one standard is violated (the use of Narrative and Headline layouts, mentioned previously, was another).

8.2

SECURITY
▼

Every day our society becomes more security conscious. Security is of the utmost importance with computer systems, but it can apply equally well to other functions. When analyzing distribution requirements for a manual, security must also be taken into account. Maintaining proper security is a difficult task, and it becomes more complex the more that is documented. Security requirements must be considered for

- issuing manuals (Is there a need to classify the manual as restricted?)
- retrieving manuals from terminated or relocated staff (Some organizations withhold the final paycheck until all manuals and other company property are returned.)
- disposing of obsolete copies.

Disposal can be a particularly thorny problem if it is not addressed properly. Manuals which contain confidential or potentially dangerous information should be shredded before being thrown out. These days, it is not good enough to throw things out in the garbage. News reporters have been known to sift through the garbage of government agencies or large corporations hoping for a scoop of some kind. Furthermore, there is always the danger of malicious pranks by juvenile and not-so-juvenile delinquents. The telephone system of a major American city, for example, was nearly brought down by kids who found a manual with computer access codes in a waste bin behind the telephone company. Almost daily we hear about someone illegally accessing supposedly top secret computer systems and wreaking havoc. Don't let something similar happen to you. All it takes is a few simple precautionary measures, such as physically retrieving restricted copies of manuals and disposing of obsolete documents by shredding or incineration.

8.3

ASSEMBLY AND
NUMBERING
▼

All the components of the manual should be assembled by the person responsible for distribution. These components are:

- binder
- spine insert (optional)
- page lifter
- Title Page/Amendment Record
- tab dividers
- documents.

Once you know how many copies of the manual are required, it is advisable to keep a small surplus stock to fill additional needs due to hiring and promotions. It is important not to overdo this, however, since these spares must be updated by the person responsible for manuals distribution. And updating a shelf-full of manuals which are never used can be an extremely demotivating task.

Do not issue a manual which is not up-to-date, since this can create frustration and a negative impression on the part of a new manual holder. No one wants to be handed a manual with a few updates to make before it is operable. Further, when you receive a manual from someone who has either left the company or no longer needs it, you should not re-issue it until the contents have been carefully checked. A simpler and less time-consuming method, if you have a volatile distribution system, is to throw out the contents of any manuals returned and simply replace them with the latest version.

In order to maintain proper control, each manual must be numbered. An adhesive label or felt marker is sufficient for this purpose, and the Title Page, or if you prefer, the Amendment Record, is a good place to put this number. The number should not be put on the binder itself since glue will not adhere to vinyl for long and ink is unsightly. There is no real reason that this distribution number needs to be visible when the binder is on the shelf, so it should not be located on the spine pocket if you have one. That would detract from the binder appearance. One solution is to print a box entitled "Manual Number" in the lower portion of the Title Page and just write in the number as you assemble the manual.

8.4
ISSUING AND CONTROLLING THE MANUAL
▼

The distribution system consists of the following:

* a distribution list
* a printing and distribution log
* a mailing list.

Each of these items can be kept manually; that is, they may be paper logs and lists updated by hand; or the logs and lists can be keyed in at a terminal, stored and updated, and then printed when required. Manuals management is much easier if it is automated wherever possible.

THE DISTRIBUTION LIST
◆

The distribution list is a simple columnar page used for entering the title and/or name of the manual holder against the appropriate manual number. Manuals should be *assigned to positions,* not to individuals, since it is the position which creates the need; however, they should be *issued to individuals.* To understand this distinction study this example: The product managers may be entitled to the company Sales manuals and Marketing manuals by virtue of their position; however, the manuals are issued to the individual product managers in order to control the manuals and to create responsibility for them. Issuing a manual to an individual rather than to an area or a department means that the individual is responsible for its welfare and upkeep. No such responsibility can be assigned to a department, at least in practice. Figure 8–1 illustrates a sample distribution list. Manual No. 1 should be retained as the master manual by the area responsible for distribution. One copy of each manual should be issued to the internal auditors, and one copy must, of course, be issued to each writer who is working on the manual. The date of issue and the signature of the recipient are optional, depending on how your own organization views their importance.

THE PRINTING AND
DISTRIBUTION LOG

This log, illustrated in Figure 8–2, keeps track of manuals and amendments through the various production stages. If you have a number of manuals being controlled by one individual or area, a printing and distribution log is essential. The printing and distribution log comes into play when the amendment package (although it could also be a new manual or a portion of a new manual) is submitted to the distribution controller. The controller logs in the transmittal number and date, then prepares the amendment to send it for printing. Using this method, the distribution controller does not have to depend on memory to determine when a document was submitted to the printer or when it was distributed, etc. It's all there in black and white.

Thus, the printing and distribution log serves a dual purpose:

1. It allows the individuals who are controlling manuals distribution to track each manual and amendment through the production process.
2. It provides a ready source of information for any inquiries which may arise, especially from the writer/editors (Where is my amendment?, etc.).

The amendment, itself, plus a transmittal notice (which is simply a standard, stylized memo and is described in Chapter 9) make up what is referred to as a *transmittal*. Each transmittal (for each manual) is assigned a unique, sequential transmittal number, in order to control it.

THE MAILING LIST

The mailing list consists of the addresses of the manual holders. It is used to route amendments to them. Labels, which can be used with any plain bond copier, are a very good method for preparing mailing lists. The list is typed once and then photocopied onto the labels as required. Or, the list can be typed and updated on a terminal and printed onto continuous labels. The very first label should contain the name and address of the issuer—so that it can be placed on the transmittal notice (in the "From" field) before being sent for printing. However, if all of your transmittal notices are issued from the same location, this

 NADIR Inc.

Manuals Distribution List

Manual Name: *Administration*

No.	Assigned to: Position	Issued to: Name	Signature	Date
1	Manuals Controller	Linda Sand	*Linda Sand*	Mar.1,19--
2	Internal Auditor	Elizabeth Lee	*Elizabeth Lee*	Mar.1,19--
3	Director, Systems	Charles Katon	*Charles Katon*	Mar.1,19--
4	V.P. Administration	George Fair	*George Fair*	Mar.4,19--
5	Office Manager	Karen Sellens	*Karen Sellens*	Mar.1,19--
6	Technical Writer	Emily Gordon	*Emily Gordon*	Mar.6,19--

FIGURE 8-1   SAMPLE DISTRIBUTION LIST

Widget Manufacturing Company

Printing and Distribution Log

Date Documents Received from Writer	Manual Name	Trans. No.	Transmittal Date	Date Sent for Printing	Where Sent	No. of Pages	No. of Copies Req'd	Date Copies Received from Printing	Date Copies Distributed
Sept.8,--	ADMIN	27	Sept.8,--	Sept.9,--	RAPID PRINT	48	110	Sept.12,--	Sept.13,--
Sept.9,--	FINANCE	6	Sept.6,--	Sept.9,--	PRINT SHOP	16	22	Sept.16,--	Sept.19,--
Sept.14,--	DATA ENTRY	11	Sept.13,--	Sept.14,--	''	21	40	Sept.20,--	Sept.21,--
Sept.30,--	ADMIN	28	Sept.29,--	Sept.30,--	RAPID PRINT	33	110	Oct.4,--	Oct.5,--
Oct.8,--	PERSONNEL	15	Oct.7,--	Oct.8,--	PRINT SHOP	26	29		

FIGURE 8-2   PRINTING AND DISTRIBUTION LOG

name and address could be preprinted on the form itself. A typical Transmittal Notice is illustrated in Figure 9–1, page 244.

If you actually have to mail your manuals (to customers or to branch offices, for instance), a binder manufacturer will be able to supply you with a good strong box capable of withstanding all but deliberate, determined abuse. These mailing cartons resemble pizza boxes in construction.

MAINTENANCE

9.1
RESPONSIBILITIES
▼

Maintenance of anything, whether it be a computer system, an automobile, or a manual, is often viewed as a necessary evil or an unpleasant chore. This need not be the case with manuals, however, if maintenance is handled correctly. Just as it is cheaper and less time-consuming in the long run to maintain a car properly, so it is with a manual.

Over the years, some pretty amazing maintenance methods have come to light, as illustrated in the following examples:

One manager simply filed all the updates to his manuals in his bottom drawer.

Another decided that rather than having many manuals, it would be better if she had just one. So she bought herself the largest binder she could find and put the contents of her three manuals into it—in numerical order. All the 01-01-01's were together, then all the 01-01-02's, etc.

Another supervisor returned all his manuals and those of his staff to the department controlling updates and distribution, asking that the manuals be audited to see if they were up-to-date. Of course, they weren't, and he knew it. None had been updated for two years! Rather than update them, the contents were thrown out and this supervisor and his staff were issued completely new copies, along with a stern reprimand.

In the organizations which fostered such actions, the user's responsibility for maintaining the integrity of the manuals and ensuring that they were up-to-date was not made clear. Defining these responsibilities should be of prime importance. Although the responsibilities of persons involved in the manuals program have been defined throughout this book, these responsibilities are brought together here for review.

COORDINATION

A specific group or person in the organization should be responsible for coordinating the development, production, and distribution of the organization's manuals. Governments and very large corporations may wish to divide these responsibilities among their separate divisions, departments, agencies, or regions.

DISTRIBUTION AND CONTROL

One person or group, if possible, should be responsible for the physical distribution and control of the organization's manuals.

STAFF CHANGES

Supervisory staff are responsible for informing the person in charge of the distribution system of employee commencements, transfers, and terminations. This allows proper control over issuing and retrieving manuals.

AUTHORING PROCEDURES

It is usually the responsibility of the sponsoring area to initiate and author its own procedures, or at least to provide the writing staff with a rough draft or the raw material necessary to construct the documents from scratch. Whichever method is used (and it will vary from organization to organization, from manual to manual within the same organization, or even within the same manual), someone in this sponsoring area, not the writer/editor, should be designated as the document's author. This conveys ownership to the sponsoring area, where it belongs, rather than to the writing area, where it does not belong.

EDITING

The manuals development area is responsible for editing the author's draft documents to the proper standards. Depending on how good the submitted raw material is, editing may involve a simple rewrite to standards, a complete rewrite, or an analysis and rewrite.

AMENDMENTS

Each manual holder is responsible for

- reading all amendments when received
- logging the receipt of updates on the Amendment Record
- updating the manual.

MAINTAINING INTEGRITY

Manuals must be maintained as issued. Staff should be prohibited from altering either the binder or its contents and from changing the location of documents within the binder, unless instructed to do so by means of a transmittal notice. This keeps the manuals as accurate as possible. Most of these responsibilities can be conveyed to the manual holders by way of the Management Endorsement (see Chapter 3).

9.2
REVISIONS

Errors and other requests for revision should be brought to the attention of the person or group responsible for coordination of the manuals program. Depending upon how formal your organization wishes to make this process, these requests for revision can range from a simple telephone call or other verbal request to a formal written request on a form or memorandum. Both methods, verbal and written, have advantages and disadvantages. The verbal request is easier for the manual user, since it takes up less of his or her time than the written request. If the manual user has to put it in writing, it may not be worth the bother. On the other hand, a formal written request is less likely to be lost in the shuffle or forgotten than is a verbal request. Whichever method you choose, it should be explained in the Management Endorsement.

If the revision amounts to no more than a simple error correction, then the document can be reissued without further approval. If the change requested is a change in policy or a serious change in procedure or standards, then the revised document should proceed through the normal critique and approval process (see Chapter 6).

When documents are revised and reissued, they must reflect the current date in the lower left-hand corner of the page. For a minor correction, with no further approval, it may be wise to make a note on the approval form to the effect that a correction has been issued on such-and-such a date. For example, the initial date on the approval form could be stroked out and the revision date entered by hand with a brief explanation. This simplifies the task of correcting errors and maintains an audit trail.

A frequent complaint about procedures is that people are too busy to read everything that crosses their desks. One way of reducing the amount of reading is to mark any corrections or revisions in the margins of the revised documents. For example, a one-line revision or error correction can be noted by an arrow (→) or an arrowhead (▶). Revisions which cover a few lines of text can be indicated by a single line or by double vertical lines or bars in the margin. This method provides the reader with an immediate identifier and serves as a beacon to all changes. Naturally, if major changes are made, no such identifier would be present and the manual holder would be expected to read the entire document.

TRANSMITTAL NOTICE

The *transmittal notice* is the principal means of communicating revisions (amendments) to manual holders. Figure 9–1 shows a typical transmittal notice. Note the use of labels for identifying "To" and "From." The transmittal notice also contains simple instructions for use. The illustration shows the Add, Delete, and Comments columns in that order. But, if you prefer, you could reverse Add and Delete. It depends on which you think is more important. Sometimes, you'll only have Add instructions; an argument for having Add first. However, it could be argued that the sequence of events should be: (1) delete old document; (2) read new document; (3) add new document; in which case, the Delete column should be leftmost on the form. Which column you use first is not all that important, so long as you realize that instructions for updating the manual should be printed on the transmittal notice.

The Comments column on the transmittal notice is the means for advising users exactly why a document is being added or deleted. Comments such as "New," "Revised," "Obsolete," or "Typo Correction" are simple and self-explanatory. These comments also help to inform the user how much of the document needs to be read: for example, all of a "New" document, but only the indicated portion of a "Revised" document.

AMENDMENT RECORD

The Amendment Record (see Figure 3–2) is essential for proper maintenance of a manual. On it, the manual holder records the date on which the latest transmittal is received against the transmittal number corresponding to the preprinted number on the Amendment Record. The Amendment Record, which is common to all manuals, is printed on the reverse side of the Title Page. To save money on printing, have the Amendment Record for all manuals printed in bulk, then have the individual Title Page for each manual printed on the blank side as required.

244

Widget
Manufacturing
Company

Policy and Procedure Transmittal

Transmittal Number
26

Date
Aug.6, 19--

Manual name: Corporate Finance

To:	From:
Mr. Dan Alighieri, Controller WMC Branch Office 980 Birmingham Avenue Cincinnati, Ohio 45111	Manuals Coordinator WMC Head Office 11070 Tuscaloosa Street Chicago, Illinois 60609

Instructions:

1. Check the list of pages in the Add column with the contents of this package. If any pages are missing, contact the sender immediately.
2. Read the attached pages and insert them in the manual.
3. Remove and destroy all obsolete pages.
4. Update the Amendment Record.

Add		Delete		
Document No. / Page No.	Date	Document No. / Page No.	Date	Comments
02-02-01 / 1	Aug.2,'--	02-02-01 / 1	Mar.26,'--	Revised
		02-02-09 / 1-5	Mar.26,'--	Obsolete
04-03-01 / 1	Jul.31,'--			New
04-03-02 / 1-4	Jul.31,'--			New
04-03-03 / 1-2	Jul.31,'--			New
04-03-04 / 1-2	Jul.31,'--			New
04-03-05 / 1-4	Jul.31,'--			New
05-02-04 / 1-3	Aug.1,'--	05-02-04 / 1-4	Jan.17,'--	Revised
05-02-06 / 1-4	Aug.1,'--	05-02-06 / 1-4	Jan.17,'--	Revised

FIGURE 9-1   TRANSMITTAL NOTICE

An Amendment Record serves two important purposes:

1. The manual holder knows when a transmittal has been missed.
2. The department or person responsible for manuals coordination can tell at a glance how up-to-date a manual is when conducting an audit or before reissuing a manual.

PROCESSING AMENDMENTS

All amendments must be handled and coordinated by one area (ideally by one person) or department to ensure proper administration of the system. The specific areas of concern are:

- *Assigning transmittal numbers.* The more people you have working on one manual and the more manuals you have, the more complex this task becomes. A simple transmittal log, such as the one illustrated in Figure 9–2, may be necessary to control this effort and to prevent the embarrassing situation in which two writer/editors issue an update to the same manual, both with the same transmittal number.
- *Grouping amendments.* This reduces the number of transmittals and makes everyone's job easier. It may mean retaining an amendment until there is a convenient-sized transmittal. Obviously, though, if something is urgent, it would not be held up for convenience's sake.
- *Revising the table of contents and indices.* Updating these documents every time you issue an amendment usually involves considerable extra work. A little common sense must be employed in updating indices. Again, urgency must be weighed against convenience before making your decision. If documents are being issued for a manual once a week, for example, revised indices could be issued, say, every month. On the other hand, if an amendment is issued every few months, the indices could be updated each time. And, if your table of contents refers to the section levels only (remember the alpha subject index is for retrieval), it will seldom need to be revised.
- *Obtaining sufficient copies of amendments from the printer.* This involves liaison with the printer and must take into account how many manual holders there are and what, if any, spare copies are on hand. They, too, must be updated. Refer to Figure 6–11, Requisition for Printing and Mailing.
- *Distributing transmittals and updating spare copies.* This could be as simple as walking around the office and giving each manual holder an update; or, it could be more complicated, involving internal mail delivery service, courier service, postal service, or electronic transmission. Updating spare copies may mean updating document files rather than manuals, if that is your choice. Some organizations prefer a method of storing spare copies of manuals by keeping a file folder for each document, and putting however many copies of each document are needed in the appropriate file folder. Then, when the time comes to issue a spare manual, it is simply assembled from the document files, put into a binder, and issued. This involves a little less work during maintenance, but a little more work during distribution.

 NADIR Inc.

Transmittal Log

Manual Name: *Administration*

Transmittal No.	Issued by	Date
1	Alice Klempe	Jan. 18, --
2	Simon Redeker	Mar. 2, --
3	Alice Klempe	Mar. 17, --
4	Teresa Robbins	Apr. 29, --
5	Teresa Robbins	June 26, --
6	Alice Klempe	Sept. 15, --
7	Simon Redeker	Sept. 30, --
8	Jack Killinger	Nov. 8, --
9	Simon Redeker	Dec. 11, --

FIGURE 9-2   TRANSMITTAL LOG

- *Handling inquiries from manual holders.* No system of distribution and maintenance can be perfect; somewhere along the line a user will not get an amendment, or will forget to update a manual. Then, you're going to need someone to handle the ensuing phone call from the user who will explain the situation and then proclaim his or her innocence from fault! Is that cynical? You bet!
- *Mailing label preparation.* This has been described in detail in the Distribution chapter.

All these activities are of a strictly clerical nature and are best handled by support staff rather than procedure analysts or writer/editors.

SCHEDULED REVISIONS

Periodic scheduled revisions should be a part of every maintenance program to ensure that the documents in your manuals are not visibly outdated. Part of the editor's time should be set aside for this review. All that's needed to avoid an outdated appearance is an informal review of the manual's contents once every year or two. If there are a number of manuals, you may choose to schedule your reviews so that they don't all come at once, spacing them out over the year.

To conduct a review, simply ask the person(s) who approved the documents in question whether they are still valid and up-to-date. If they are, reissue them with the current date; if they are not, the review has served its purpose.

9.3
MASTER AND CONTROL MANUALS

One Master Manual and one Control Manual are kept for every manual that is written or revised in the manuals program. It is imperative that these manuals be kept completely up-to-date; that is, updates must be recorded faithfully on the Amendment Record and additions and/or deletions must be made accordingly.

The *Master Manual* is the official copy of the manual. It is kept in the area responsible for manuals coordination and is not loaned out to anyone. It is, however, used for reference purposes, to answer inquiries from users and other interested parties, and as a kind of bellwether against which user manuals are audited. Pages must not be removed except under authorization of a transmittal notice.

The *Control Manual* is the writer's own copy of the manual. If more than one writer is working on any given manual, designate one person as custodian of the Control Manual. These control manuals are used as working drafts by the writers for editing and planning purposes. Pending revisions may be made directly onto the pages of these manuals. For instance, telephoned or written requests for revision can be put in a Control Manual until such time as the revised document is ready to be issued. Unlike the Master Manual, which is necessary as an audit check and to answer queries, control manuals are not an absolute necessity and many writers get along quite well without them.

BACKUP

Just as it is important for data on computer systems to be backed up for safety, so it is with manuals. The master and control manuals which provide some backup have already been discussed, but more backup than that is necessary. At least one of the two following methods should be considered—off-site storage or vault storage. Either method provides fairly inexpensive insurance against extreme disaster such as fire or flood. If your manuals are stored on a computer or a word processor, you should consider off-site tape or disk storage of all your current manuals documentation. Because electronic media for the storage of data are very fragile, you should always have more than one copy securely stored and it must be updated every time an amendment is issued in order to be current. Therefore, you should set up a backup program similar to those run by EDP departments. The frequency of backup could be weekly or monthly, depending on the volatility of your manuals. If, on the other hand, your manuals are all hard copy, then store a copy of each in a vault or off-site. One designated person—the manuals coordinator or a clerk—would then be required to update these manuals occasionally—say, once a month.

For convenience's sake, some organizations send their updates off-site and don't actually update the manuals, thereby saving themselves that labor. Updating the backup manuals is then only necessary in case of disaster.

9.4
WRITER/EDITOR'S FILES
▼

Five files are maintained for each manual, either by the writer responsible for the manual or, if more than one writer, by the person or department designated as responsible for manuals coordination. These are:

- printing master file
- approvals file
- transmittal file
- archives file
- artwork file.

In addition, each writer should keep a personal file of working papers.

PRINTING MASTER FILE

The *printing master file* contains the original documents used for reproducing the manual. It is important that the whole manual be kept together, in document number order, to simplify the task of printing additional copies when this becomes necessary, or for retrieval when one or more documents or pages needs to be found. To avoid damage to the originals, do not clip or staple them, and do not punch holes in them. Originals should never leave the file except for printing; they should not even be sent out with the approvals form when you are obtaining sign-offs. Send a photocopy instead. This will save any unnecessary handling and will prevent the possibility of damage. It will also avoid the possibility of someone making last minute corrections on your printing master.

APPROVALS FILE

The *approvals file* contains the approval forms for the documents currently in the manual. For each document in the printing master file, there should be a corresponding form in the approvals file, except, of course, for the table of contents, indices, etc. These approvals are also filed in document number sequence. The purpose of storing the approvals separately from the originals is twofold:

1. It prevents the damage mentioned previously.
2. It avoids time wasted in unclipping and reclipping when documents need to be copied or printed.

TRANSMITTAL FILE

The *transmittal file* (or update file) contains, in chronological order, all transmittals distributed for the manual. Each transmittal consists of the transmittal notice and all documents sent out with it. The purpose of the transmittal file is to provide easy access to the content of each transmittal, to answer inquiries regarding missing transmittals, and to make replacement copies without having to assemble documents from the printing master. It should not often happen that someone misplaces or does not receive a transmittal, but when it does occur, it's a lot easier for the manuals coordinator to simply photocopy the transmittal rather than pick out each document or page from the printing master file.

When the manual is first issued, the initial documents are distributed in the binder. Thus, Transmittal No. 1 consists of the initial content of the manual.

ARCHIVES FILE

When a document is obsolete (either revised or reworked), the document and its approval form are removed from their respective files, stapled together, and filed in document number sequence in the *archives file*. This maintains a record of all previous versions of each document in order to answer inquiries, or, if necessary, even to reissue a former document. Reissuing a former document happens so seldom in most organizations though, that it's not worth the trouble to keep separate archives files for approvals and printing masters. The flow of documents through these files, their contents, and their filing methods are illustrated graphically in Figure 9–3.

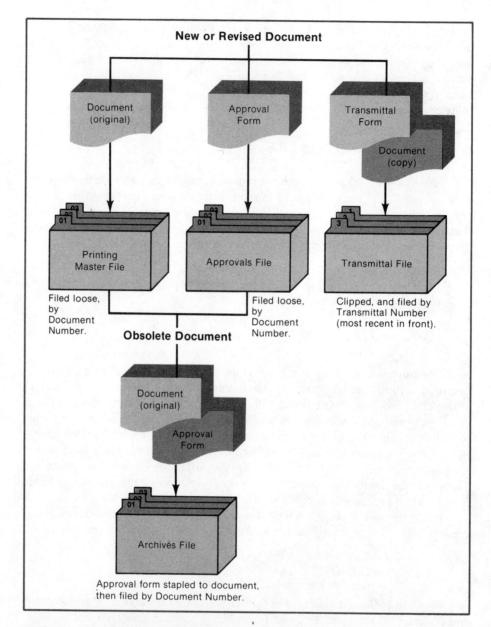

FIGURE 9-3   FLOW OF DOCUMENTS THROUGH FILES

ARTWORK FILE

Each manual should have its own file for artwork. Copies of illustrations should be made and used for the printing master, thereby leaving the original intact for reuse at a later date. These originals and PMT's of forms, matrices, charts, flowcharts, and data flow diagrams should be stored in the artwork file for safekeeping. The reasons for this are clear: Although the text of a document might change, the illustrations may not. Thus, you may be able to save considerable time just by photocopying the original illustration and gluing it to your revised document. A large envelope is better for this purpose than a file folder since much of the artwork will be larger than it is on the manual page. Also, small pieces of artwork are not as likely to slip out of an envelope.

WORKING PAPER FILE

Each writer/editor should keep his or her own file of working papers, probably one Subject to a folder. Each folder will contain any initial material and drafts of the Subject. How long you keep your working files is entirely up to you or your organization. Some writers throw out all working papers as soon as a document is published and some keep them almost forever. It's largely a matter of personality, preference, and space.

9.5
DIRECTIVES AND INTERIM PROCEDURES
▼

Standards must be set for publishing documents which are out of the ordinary or which cover unusual circumstances. Such documents can all be classified under the category *interim procedures*. How do these interim procedures differ from the normal policy and procedure documents? Well, they could be special bulletins or updates which occur as a result of sudden policy or procedure changes made by management. In the manuals field, these are called *directives*, and they may have a significant effect on day-to-day operations. Therefore, they must be distributed to staff who "need to know" immediately. The difference between a directive and a normal Subject published in manuals is basically the time frame needed to get the information published and in the hands of the manual's audience.

In addition to directives, you may have documents describing activities which will only be in effect for a specified, usually short, period of time. An example might be a surcharge which must be added to the cost of an item for one month only, or your head office might announce that they are going to give a summer discount to certain customers. In these instances you would publish the document knowing full well that it must be deleted as soon as the specified time is up. These are true interim procedures, and again, the only difference between these documents and normal Subjects may be the time frames; that is, the time available to prepare the document and the time during which the document will be in effect.

Other types of interim documents might be emergency or contingency documents which must be published and followed during an emergency only. Again, time is a major factor. However, careful consideration should be given to these documents, for you may find that you need to set aside a part of a manual just for them. For example, suppose you have certain procedures that must be followed if there is a mail or a trucking strike. Such procedures may be completely different than those normally followed. Thus, they must be published as well as the normal procedures. But if mail or trucking strikes are common occurrences, why publish and then delete? You might just as well house the emergency procedures permanently, but separately, within their respective manuals. Having such interim documents immediately available may very well save hours of "crisis management."

To summarize then, interim procedures consist of subject matter which (1) must be published in a hurry and/or (2) will only be in effect for a short period of time. In either case, these interim procedures can be handled in a similar manner. The distinction between the two (i.e., a directive and an interim procedure) is really moot.

LAYOUTS

Under normal circumstances, the most appropriate layout is used to ensure that the Subject is always presented to the audience in the simplest and most effective manner possible. However, it has been found that in the case of directives and interim procedures, there sometimes is not enough time for the writer to produce to the high standards set for the program. In other words, there may not be time to analyze and come up with a good Matrix or Playscript in, say, a couple of hours or a day. Because time is of the essence, it is recommended that you write these documents as quickly as possible, using whichever layout you are most comfortable with. Usually Caption layout will suffice.

Once the document has been issued, it is the writer's responsibility to immediately begin to investigate:

- All the ramifications of the document. Does it affect other material already published? Will that material need to be revised? Will the document be used again after the initial period of time is up? Do you need a Tab in your manual for contingency procedures? Are there more documents that should be written?
- Whether all the policy and procedure facts have been presented in the interim document.
- Which layout should be used when the document is issued in final form.

NUMBERING

If the interim procedure replaces an existing Subject in the manual, then the same document number currently used should be used again. However, if the subject matter is new, the interim procedure should be assigned a new document number in the appropriate Tab and Section of the manual. This is assuming that the interim procedures are not emergency procedures, which you may wish to house permanently in a Section or Tab of their own (as mentioned previously).

Interim procedures and directives should be printed on the standard manual page you always use. However, it is recommended that they be printed on colored paper to distinguish between these unique documents and others in the manual. For instance, an interim procedure could be printed on blue or yellow paper—something that stands out. This aids in identification and retrievability for the manual user simply because the color is different from the norm.

If a print shop is used for producing your pages, specify the color of paper required. If the originals are photocopied, load the appropriate colored paper into the photocopy machine.

APPROVALS

Since most interim documents must be published in a hurry, it may be necessary to bypass the normal approval "sign-off" process. It may simply be impossible to get all the signatures required in the time available. For this reason, get one signature only—that of the person at the top. This signature should be obtained on your standard approval form.

When the document has been rewritten to standards, the normal approval procedure for obtaining sign-offs can then be followed (see Section 6.8). Don't let the fact that you only need approval at the top for interim documents convince you that this is so for *all* documents. It's true that the support of upper management is required for good documentation, but the support and cooperation of line staff and middle and first-line management is needed as well. They too must support your documentation.

DISTRIBUTION

Interim procedures should be distributed immediately under cover of a standard transmittal notice.

DELETIONS

An interim procedure is removed from the manual when it becomes obsolete, or when the final document has been written to standards and approved. In either case, the transmittal notice should be used for this purpose.

9.6
OTHER CONSIDERATIONS

The topics discussed so far in this chapter are crucial to a well-run maintenance program. There are, however, other miscellaneous items which don't conveniently fit into a category such as Production or Maintenance, but which will nevertheless be grouped here. These are things such as user education, cross-referencing, working relationships, auditing, and supplies maintenance. Proper attention to these items can help make your program more effective.

USER EDUCATION

User education should begin at the outset of the manuals program and should continue throughout the program. Initially, all personnel should be advised as to how the program will be run, what standards will be in force, and how the manuals are structured. Then, when the program is under way, specific situations can be dealt with as they occur. For example, it is very useful to conduct user walkthroughs with particularly complex, or contentious, new procedures, standards, or policies, just as it is in systems development. The personal touch goes a long way toward achieving acceptance of new material.

The *walkthrough* is just what it says—the leader holds the user's hand, figuratively of course, and walks the user through the procedure step-by-step. Walkthroughs can be simple or structured, ranging from a one-to-one demonstration at the user's workplace to a presentation in front of a dozen or more people. Regardless of how large or formal the walkthrough is, questions must be encouraged. If the group feels constrained to keep silent, then the walkthrough won't accomplish anything. To encourage participation, ask frequently if there are any questions. And stop to give people a moment to think about questions—don't carry on immediately, since this will discourage these queries. Ask a specific person if he or she has any problems or doubts. Or ask someone to clarify a point—perhaps a technical issue or a policy decision. You can even stage-manage little dialogues by setting them up in advance. To do this, arrange it with a colleague beforehand, or pick someone out ahead of time to ask you a prepared question. That can get the ball rolling very well, and the prepared question can lead to further questions and discussion by others.

All this sounds a bit Machiavellian, but it's really not. All you are trying to do is to provide an open atmosphere in which no one will feel hesitant about speaking up. You are trying to ensure that once the procedure (policy, standard) is published, it will be correct, understood, and readily accepted.

To borrow another phrase from systems development, procedures can also be user tested. The *user test* is quite simple. You give the user a copy of the procedure, and ask the user to follow it step-by-step to see if it works. You'll be surprised at how many times a form disappearing into thin air or a vital missing step is found due to user testing. Of course, you should check the procedures before the user does to keep these errors to a minimum.

User education really begins with the review process. Often, especially with procedure documentation, the writer/editor is documenting what is already taking place, and as far as the user is concerned, this documentation may do no more than put procedures that the user is already following into black and white. In that case, the review process may induce the user to think of better ways to get the job done, or to eliminate costly or wasteful steps.

In most cases, policies and procedures will be self-explanatory, and the transmittal notice and the document itself will be sufficient for the manual users to orient themselves toward the new way of doing things. Only in exceptional cases would a walkthrough or a formal user test be required. However, this does not mean that the appearance of a transmittal notice should be the first time a user hears of a new procedure. By all means, keep the users informed of what you are doing so that they have as few unpleasant surprises as possible.

CROSS-REFERENCING

Although this topic has been mentioned before, it is a good place to reiterate that cross-referencing in manuals should be kept to a minimum, due to the difficulty in keeping it up-to-date. Few things are more annoying and wasteful than attempting to change references to other documents and manuals when a Subject is under revision. If it is absolutely necessary to refer to another Subject in a document, refer to it by Subject or Section name rather than by document number, since Subject and Section names are less likely to change. Actually, you'll do better in the long run to avoid cross-referencing altogether.

WORKING RELATIONSHIPS

Manuals writers must have close working relationships with users, but there are other areas of the organization which must concern the writers as well. The two most prominent among these are systems and forms. Historically, systems departments developed out of methods and procedures. Today, manuals writers are often found in systems departments, and in some cases, manuals people, forms people, and systems people are all found in the same department.

After the writer-user relationship, the second most important working relationship of manuals developers may be with the forms designers. Since a good portion of most manuals is forms, it is easy to see why. The most important aspect of this relationship is communication—the manuals writers must keep the forms people informed so that they can function properly and in a timely manner. Forms people need to assign form numbers, order PMT's, design the forms, etc. In fact, it can be argued with good reason that the manuals writer and the forms designer are a team—every form exists because of a procedure (written or not). Therefore, any change to a form can have an impact on the procedure, and changing the procedure can reduce or enhance the effectiveness of the form.

AUDITING

It's very simple to conduct an audit of a manual; much easier than most other audits. The manuals audit is designed to reveal exactly one thing: Is this manual complete and up-to-date? The staff who conduct the audits will usually, but not necessarily, be from the same area or department which coordinates distribution and maintenance. To perform the audit the staff need the Master Manual and the user's manual which is going to be audited. There are three steps to auditing a manual. They are:

1. Check that the manual is still in the possession of the person to whom it was issued.
2. Check that the Amendment Record is complete and up-to-date.
3. Spot check a number of documents in the manual, looking particularly at document numbers and dates.

The depth of the audit you conduct and the frequency of the audits will depend on:

- the number of manuals in the organization
- how many copies of each are in circulation
- how bad or good the current audit reveals the manuals to be
- what previous audits have shown
- the availability of staff to conduct the audit.

Generally speaking, an audit should be performed on a manual once every year or two. But if you discover a lot of incomplete and/or out-of-date manuals in your organization, conduct audits more frequently until the situation improves.

How many of the extant copies of a particular manual you audit depends upon the factors mentioned previously. If, for example, there are only half a dozen copies, each in a different department, then you would probably wish to audit all of them. If, on the other hand, there are a hundred or more copies, you may wish to spot check them only. A middle course, which is often satisfactory, is to spot check only those manuals with accurate Amendment Records, but to delve a little more deeply into those with inaccurate Amendment Records.

Two more points regarding audits: (1) they should be planned and scheduled, and (2) records must be kept. Regarding planning and scheduling, most organizations find it preferable to spread out their audits over the calendar year rather than to perform a blitz audit over a period of days or weeks. That way, the audit does not interfere with the routine day-to-day operation of business. Keeping records helps you to realize what the tendencies of individuals and departments are. If you know, for example, that Jan Smith's manuals are always deficient, you know that she'll have to be included in every audit. If, however, past history tells you that the engineering department's manuals are always up-to-date, then you won't have to check each of their manuals document-by-document.

One note of caution: The results of your audits should not be taken as an excuse for finger-pointing. That should be left to each individual's manager. The organization's philosophy, policies, and attitudes play a major part in deciding how to handle the audit process and what, if anything, to do about the results of the audits.

SUPPLIES MAINTENANCE

Most of the supplies you'll need will be the same from manual to manual. Only items such as spine inserts and manual pages need to be individualized.

Depending on the size of your organization, its set up, and the number of manuals you have, supplies may be kept in stores or by the manuals coordinating area. Many of these items will become standard stock items or forms. You will need to consider keeping supplies of binders and tab dividers, for example. If your organization has one corporate color, binders could be standard stock items, and stores could supply everyone economically and efficiently.

BIBLIOGRAPHY

GENERAL REFERENCE WORKS FOR ALL WRITERS

Chapman, Robert L. (ed.). *Roget's International Thesaurus,* 4th ed. New York: Thomas Y. Crowell Co., 1977.

Doris, Lilian, and Besse May Miller. *Complete Secretary's Handbook*, 5th ed. Englewood Cliffs, N.J.: Prentice-Hall, Inc., 1983.

Fernald, James G. *English Grammar Simplified.* New York: Harper & Row Pubs., Inc., 1979.

Fowler, H. W., and F. G. Fowler (eds.). *The Concise Oxford Dictionary of Current English.* London: Oxford University Press, 1964.

Kellerman, Dana F. (ed.). *The Living Webster Encyclopedic Dictionary of the English Language.* Chicago: The English Language Institute of America, 1977.

Lewis, Norman (ed.). *The New Roget's Thesaurus in Dictionary Form.* New York: G. P. Putnam's Sons, 1961.

McKechnie, Jean L. (ed.). *Webster's New Universal Unabridged Dictionary*, 2d ed. New York: Simon & Schuster, 1979.

Strunk, William, and E. B. White. *The Elements of Style.* 3d ed. New York: Macmillan Publishing Co., Inc., 1979.

Sykes, J. B. *The Concise Oxford Dictionary of Current English*, 6th ed. London: Oxford University Press, 1976.

Woolf, Henry Bosley (ed.). *Webster's New Collegiate Dictionary.* Springfield, Massachusetts: G. & C. Merriam Co., 1977.

Young, Bruce (ed.). *A Manual of Style*, 12th ed., rev. Chicago: The University of Chicago Press, 1969.

SOURCE BOOKS

Bakewell, K. G. B. *Management Principles and Practice: A Guide to Information Sources.* Detroit: Gale Research Co., 1977.

Carter, Robert M. *Communication in Organizations: A Guide to Information Sources.* Detroit: Gale Research Co., 1972.

Morrill, Chester, Jr. *Systems and Procedures Including Office Management: A Guide to Information Sources.* Detroit: Gale Research Co., 1967.

BOOKS SPECIFICALLY ABOUT MANUALS

Diamond, Susan Z. *Preparing Administrative Manuals*. New York: American Management Association, 1981.

Jackson, Clyde W. *Verbal Information Systems: A Comprehensive Guide to Writing Manuals*. Cleveland: Association for Systems Management, 1974.

Seltz, David D., and Marvin I. Radlauer. *How to Prepare an Effective Company Operations Manual*. Chicago: Dartnell Corp., 1974.

BOOKS ABOUT WRITING, EDITING, AND BUSINESS COMMUNICATION

Bentley, Garth A. *Editing the Company Publication*. New York: Harper & Row Pubs., Inc., 1953.

Bergman, F. L., M. L. Bradford, H. R. Fine, and W. E. Hoth. *From Auditing to Editing*. Washington: U.S. General Accounting Office, 1969.

Communicating Policy and Procedure. Washington: Office of Records Management, National Archives and Records Service, General Services Administration, 1967.

Cowing, Amy. *Writing Words That Work*. Washington: U.S. Department of Agriculture Extension Service, 1961.

Flesch, Rudolph. *The Art of Readable Writing*. New York: Macmillan Publishing Co., Inc., 1949.

Jackson, Clyde W. *Functional Business Writing*. Cleveland: Association for Systems Management, 1977.

Janis, J. Harold. *Writing and Communicating in Business*. New York: Macmillan Publishing Co., 1964.

Klare, George R. *The Measurement of Readability*. Ames, Iowa: Iowa State University Press, 1963.

Lazarus, Sy. *Loud and Clear*. New York: AMACOM, 1975.

Matthies, Leslie M. *The New Playscript Procedure: Management Tool for Action*. Stamford, Connecticut: Office Publications, Inc., 1982.

Morris, John O. *Make Yourself Clear*. New York: McGraw-Hill Book Co., 1972.

Mueller, Robert Kirk. *Buzzwords*. New York: Van Nostrand Reinhold Co., 1974.

Paxson, William C. *The Business Writing Handbook*. New York: Bantam Books, 1981.

Peopleware in Systems. Cleveland: Association for Systems Management, 1976.

Plain Letters. Washington: Office of Records Management, National Archives and Records Service, General Services Administration, 1973.

Reisman, S. J. (ed.). *A Style Manual for Technical Writers and Editors*. New York: Macmillan Publishing Co., 1962.

Style Manual. Washington: U.S. Government Printing Office, 1967.

Turner, Rufus P. *Technical Writer's and Editor's Stylebook*. Indianapolis: Howard W. Sams and Co., 1964.

van Buren, Robert, and Mary Fran Buehler. *The Levels of Edit*. Pasadena: Jet Propulsion Laboratory, California Institute of Technology, 1976.

Wellborn, G. P., L. B. Green, and K. A. Nall. *Technical Writing*. Boston: Houghton Mifflin Co., 1961.

Williams, Cecil B., and E. Glenn Griffin. *Effective Business Communication*. New York: The Ronald Press Co., 1966.

Zinsser, William. *On Writing Well*. 2d ed. New York: Harper & Row Pubs., Inc., 1980.

RELATED BOOKS

Beveridge, W. E. *Problem Solving Interviews*. London: Allen & Unwin, Inc., 1968.

Carrithers, Wallace M., and Ernest H. Weinwurn. *Business Information and Accounting Systems*. Columbus, OH: Charles E. Merrill, 1967.

de Greene, Kenyon B. (ed.). *Systems Psychology*. New York: McGraw-Hill Book Co., 1970.

deMarco, Tom. *Structured Analysis and System Specification*. New York: Yourdon Press, 1978.

Dickinson, Brian. *Developing Structured Systems*. New York: Yourdon Press, 1981.

Dowling, John R., and Robert P. Drolet. *Developing and Administering an Industrial Training Program*. Boston: CBI Publishing, Inc., 1979.

Encyclopedic Dictionary of Systems and Procedures. Englewood Cliffs, N.J.: Prentice-Hall, Inc., 1966.

Freeman, Peter (ed.). *Systems Development Management*. Pennsauken, N.J.: Auerbach Publishers, 1980.

Gane, Chris, and Trish Sarson. *Structured Systems Analysis*. Englewood Cliffs, N.J.: Prentice-Hall Co., 1979.

Gildersleeve, Thomas R. *Decision Tables and Their Practical Application in Data Processing*. Englewood Cliffs, N.J.: Prentice-Hall Co., 1970.

Kindred, Alton R. *An Introduction to Systems Analysis and Design.* Englewood Cliffs, N.J.: Prentice-Hall Co., 1973.

Harper, William L. *Data Processing Documentation: Standards, Procedures, and Applications,* 2d ed. Englewood Cliffs, N.J.: Prentice-Hall Co., 1980.

Hendrick, James G. "Company Manuals," from Victor Lazzaro (ed.), *Systems and Procedures: A Handbook for Business and Industry.* Englewood Cliffs, N.J.: Prentice-Hall Co., 1959.

Holmes, Arthur W., and Wayne S. Overmyer. *Auditing Standards and Procedures.* Homewood, Ill.: Richard D. Irwin, Inc., 1975.

Howell, Murtagh P. *Forms Design Guidelines.* Toronto: Worker's Compensation Board, 1978.

Kahn, Robert L., and Charles F. Cannell. *The Dynamics of Interviewing.* New York: John Wiley & Sons, 1957.

Kelley, William F. *Management Through Systems and Procedures: The Total Systems Concept.* New York: John Wiley & Sons, 1969.

Lazzaro, Victor (ed.). *Systems and Procedures: A Handbook for Business and Industry,* 2d ed. Englewood Cliffs, N.J.: Prentice-Hall Co., 1968.

Lippett, Gordon, and Ronald Lippett. *The Consulting Process in Action.* La Jolla, California: University Associates, Inc., 1978.

Lucas, Henry C., Jr. *The Analysis, Design, and Implementation of Information Systems.* New York: McGraw-Hill Book Co., 1976.

Matthies, Leslie M. *Documents to Manage By.* Stamford, Connecticut: Office Publications, Inc., 1983.

Matthies, Leslie M. *Managing Systems: Part 2—Operating the Program.* Colorado Springs, Colorado: Systemation, Inc., 1966.

Matthies, Leslie M. *Organization As a Base for Systems.* Colorado Springs, Colorado: Systemation, Inc., 1966.

Matthies, Leslie M. *Policy As a Systems Tool.* Colorado Springs, Colorado: Systemation, Inc., 1968.

Morrisey, George L. *Effective Business and Technical Presentations.* Reading, Massachusetts: Addison-Wesley Publishing Co., Inc., 1968.

Pakin, Sandra. *Documentation Development Methodology.* Chicago: Sandra Pakin and Associates, 1982.

Reid, G. A. *Office Procedures.* Toronto: Sir Isaac Pitman Ltd., 1969.

Robinson, John P., and James D. Gravis. *Documentation Standards Manual for Computer Systems.* Cleveland: Association for Systems Management, 1973.

Rubin, Martin L. *Documentation Standards and Procedures for On-Line Systems*. Toronto: Van Nostrand Reinhold, 1981.

Schaeffer, Howard. *Data Center Operations: A Guide to Effective Planning, Processing, and Performance*. Englewood Cliffs, N.J.: Prentice-Hall Co., 1981.

Scherer, Avanell. *Office Procedures: A Project Approach*. Toronto: McGraw-Hill Ryerson, 1976.

Schricker, Karl C. J. "Developing the Standard Operating Procedures Manual." *Handbook of Modern Office Management and Administrative Services*. New York: McGraw-Hill Book Co., 1972.

Sparks, Donald B. *Administrative Improvement Methods*. Houston: Gulf Publishing Co., 1973.

Westgate, Douglas G. *Office Procedures 2000*. Toronto: Gage Educational Publishing, 1977.

Willoughby, T. C. *Business Systems*. Cleveland: Association for Systems Management, 1973.

BOOKS OF GENERAL INTEREST

Brooks, Frederick P., Jr. *The Mythical Man-Month*. Reading, Massachusetts: Addison-Wesley Publishing Co., 1975.

Gall, John. *Systemantics*. New York: Simon and Schuster, Inc., 1975.

Joseph, Earl. *Alternative Futures in Computers, Robots, and Artificial Intelligence*. Sperry Univac, 1982.

Raudsepp, Eugene. *How Creative Are You?* New York: G. P. Putnam's Sons, 1980.

Toffler, Alvin. *Future Shock*. New York: Random House, 1970.

Whisler, Thomas. *The Impact of Computers on Organizations*. New York: Praeger Publishers, 1970.

ARTICLES ABOUT MANUALS AND RELATED TOPICS

Andrews, A. James. "Preparing and Using Administrative Manuals, Parts 1 and 2." *Journal of Systems Management*, Vol. 31, Nos. 3 and 4 (March and April, 1980).

Berry, Elizabeth. "How to Get Users to Follow Procedures." *Journal of Systems Management*, Vol. 31, No. 7 (July, 1981).

Berry, Elizabeth. "Prepare for the Future with Updating Systems." *Journal of Systems Management*, Vol. 32, No. 2 (February, 1982).

Bloom, Stuart P. "Organization of Policy and Procedure Statements." *Journal of Systems Management*, Vol. 33, No. 7 (July, 1983).

Bullen, C. V., J. L. Bennett, and E. D. Carlson. "A Case Study of Office Workstation Use." *IBM Systems Journal*, Vol. 21, No. 3 (1982).

Burrowes, Sharon, and Ted Burrowes. "Do Your Manuals Grow Legs?" *The Computing Teacher*, (October, 1983).

Chamberlin, D. D., O. P. Bertrand, M. J. Goodfellow, J. C. King, D. R. Slutz, S. J. P. Todd, and B. W. Wade. "JANUS: An Interactive Document Formatter Based on Declarative Tags." *IBM Systems Journal*, Vol. 21, No. 3 (1982).

Cowles, Cecelia M. "Pity the Poor Reader: How to Write a Good Manual." *SHARE*, No. 57, Session M253 (August, 1981).

Cryderman, Paula. "How to Set Up a Policy and Procedures Manual." *Dimensions in Health Service*, Vol. 57, No. 11 (November, 1980).

Dean, M. "How a Computer Should Talk to People." *IBM Systems Journal*, Vol. 21, No. 4 (1982).

Gardiner, Julian. "User Documentation: The Key to Successful Systems." *Canadian Datasystems* (April, 1982).

Giuliano, Vincent E. "The Mechanization of Office Work." *Scientific American*, Vol. 247, No. 3 (September, 1982).

Glassford, Bruce. "Executive Guide to Records Management." *Canadian Office* (November/December, 1982).

Goldfarb, Stephen M. "Financial Returns on a Policy and Procedure Manual." *Journal of Systems Management*, Vol. 33, No. 2 (February, 1983).

Goldfarb, Stephen M. "Writing Policies and Procedures." *Journal of Systems Management*, Vol. 31, No. 4 (April, 1981).

Grow, Gerald, "How to Write 'Official'." *Journal of Systems Management*, Vol. 33, No. 9 (September, 1982).

Haga, Clifford I., and Karl C. J. Schricker. "Six Standards of Good Writing." Stony Brook, N.Y.: Manuals Corporation of America, 1976.

Heidorn, G. E., K. Jensen, L. A. Miller, R. J. Byrd, and M. S. Chodorow. "The EPISTLE Text-Critiquing System." *IBM Systems Journal*, Vol. 21, No. 3 (1982).

"How to Measure Manuals." *Popular Computing* (July, 1983).

Jacobus, Stephen F. "The Documentation Hassle." *Journal of Systems Management,* Vol. 33, No. 2 (February, 1983).

James, Vaughn E. "Userfunctional Procedures." *Journal of Systems Management,* Vol. 33, No. 9 (September, 1982).

Kahn, Charles. "Psycho Linguistics and Business Communications." *Journal of Systems Management* (1975).

"Keep it Simple." *The Royal Bank of Canada Monthly Letter,* Vol. 56, No. 5 (1975).

Kellogg, M. Graham. "Preparing the Office Manual." Research Study No. 36. New York: American Management Association, 1959.

"Last Word for the Word Processor." *The Economist* (July 25, 1981).

Laudeman, Max. "Document Flowcharts for Internal Control." *Journal of Systems Management,* Vol. 31, No. 3 (March, 1980).

Lederer, Albert L. "Information Requirements Analysis." *Journal of Systems Management,* Vol. 31, No. 12 (December, 1980).

"Letters That Sell." *The Royal Bank of Canada Monthly Letter,* Vol. 55, No. 5 (1974).

Lum, V. Y., D. M. Choy, and M. C. Shu. "OPAS: An Office Procedure Automation System." *IBM Systems Journal,* Vol. 21, No. 3 (1982).

"Making the Most of Language." *The Royal Bank of Canada Monthly Letter.* Vol. 54, No. 3 (1973).

Matthies, Leslie M. "Preparing a Playscript Procedure." *Systemation Letter* (1963).

Matthies, Leslie M. "Problems With Procedures." *World of Systems* (1976).

Mayo, Harry R. "Putting the System in Writing." *Systems and Procedures Journal,* Vol. 16, No. 3 (May/June, 1965).

Mingione, Al. "Iteration, Key to Useful Documentation." *Journal of Systems Management,* Vol. 33, No. 1 (January, 1983).

"Put It In Writing." *The Royal Bank of Canada Monthly Letter,* Vol. 53, No. 1 (1972).

Rankin, John. "The Productive Office: Evolution or Creation." *Canadian Office* (September/October, 1981).

Schricker, Karl C. J. "Ten Principles to Aid You Avoid Frequent Errors in Writing." Stony Brook, N.Y.: Manuals Corporation of America, 1977.

Schricker, Karl C. J. "Ten Steps for Effective Writing." Stony Brook, N.Y.: Manuals Corporation of America, 1977.

Schricker, Karl C. J., and Gibbs Myers. "Writing Systems Manuals." (ASM Technical Department Report) Cleveland: Association for Systems Management, 1977.

Smith, Donald P. "Cut the Fog About Systems Documentation." *Journal of Systems Management*, Vol. 29, No. 12 (December, 1979).

Stein, Philip. "Process Wording." *Computer Decisions* (March, 1976).

"Writing for All Occasions." *The Royal Bank of Canada Monthly Letter*, Vol. 52, No. 7 (1971).

Zloof, M. M. "Office-by-Example: A Business Language That Unifies Data and Word Processing and Electronic Mail." *IBM Systems Journal*, Vol. 21, No. 3 (1982).

INDEX

H

Headline layout, 121–123; defined, 123; illustration of, 124; typing standards for, 192

Hierarchy, in headline layout, 192

Hole punching, 215–218; illustration of spacing of, for 8½″ × 5½″ paper, 217; illustration of spacing of, for 11″ × 8½″ paper, 216

Hot foil stamping, defined, 225

Housing, 207–231; of binders, 207–219; binder specifications and, 230–231; page lifters and, 227–229; spine pockets and, 229–230; tab dividers and, 226–227

How to use this manual document, 77–82; illustrations of, 79–82; parts of, 77

Hyphenated line, as input/output flow symbol for flowcharts, 148

I

Idiot-proofing, 108

Illustration: illustration of part of a form as an, 196; preparation of, 195–197; printing of, 205–206; use of charts and, 100

Illustration layout, 164–169; defined, 164; illustrations of, 165–167; preparation guidelines and standards for, 168–169; situations in which to use, 164–168

Illustrations index, reports index and/or, 88

Imperative mood, 103

Imperative sentence, 98

Implementation, as presented in a manuals report, 21, 23

Index: combined alphabetic, 55; forms, 83–88; forms, illustration of, 87; illustration of cards for, 86; illustrations of alphabetic subject, 84–85; reading subject material and preparing an, 65; reports and/or illustration, 88; subject, 83; universal, 55–57

Index cards: illustration of, for alphabetizing, 86

Indexing captions, 128

Indices, 10; four types of, in a manual, 10

Ink, table of legibility of paper color and color of, 205

Input/output flow lines, 148; illustrations of, 149–150

Interim procedures: approvals for directives and, 253; defined, 251; deletions of, 253; directives and, 251–253; distribution of directives and, 253; layouts used with directives and, 252; numbering of directives and, 252; paper used for directives and, 253

Interrogative sentence, 98

Interview process, defined, 40

Interviewing: supplementary questions for, 43–44; tools and techniques of, 40–45

Interviews: barriers to good, 40–43; language barriers to, 41; motivational barriers to, 41; overcoming barriers to, 41–43; preparation for, 41; psychological barriers to, 41; supplementing the questions of, 43–44; tools of, 44–45

Introduction: for a manuals report, 21; as presented in a manuals report, 22

Introduction section, defined, 68

Investment, return on, 16–17

Issuing, controlling and: of manuals, 235–239

Iterations, 148; illustrations of, 148

K

Kahn, Robert L., 40

L

Language barriers to successful interviews, defined, 41

Layout: choosing the best, 169–172; defined, 9, 118; directives and interim procedures and, 252; in the draft process, 182; eight types of, 119; examples of notes in, 155; general guidelines for, 119–121; general principles of, 118–121; guidelines for mixing, 172; mix-

ing, 171–172; page format and, 9; summary for, 119; table for choosing the best, 171; types of, 119; typing standards common to all, 188–191; typing standards for bullets used in, 190–191; typing standards for dashes used in, 191; typing standards for multiple notes used in, 188–190; typing standards for notes used in, 188; typing standards for page body in, 188; typing standards for specific, 191–195. *See also* Caption layout; Data flow diagram layout; Flowchart layout; Headline layout; Illustration layout; Matrix layout; Narrative layout; Playscript layout

Legibility, table of ink and paper color in determining, 205

Lensear Write formula, 113–114

Lettering, dry-transfer: defined, 196

Lettering machine, defined, 196

Lists, 111

Logic line, 147; illustration of, 147

M

Mailing, illustration of requisition for printing and, 204

Mailing list, 236–239

Maintenance: amendments and, 242; auditing and, 255–256; authoring procedures and, 241; coordinating responsibilities for, 241; cross-referencing and, 255; directives and interim procedures for, 251–253; distribution and control of, 241; editing and, 241; integrity and, 242; of manuals, 240–257; master and control manuals and, 247–248; responsibilities for, 240–242; revisions and, 242–247; staff changes and, 241; of supplies, 256–257; user education and, 254–255; working relationships and, 255; writer/editor's files and, 248–251

Management: deliverables of, 36; developing a manuals presentation for, 23–27; writing a manuals report for, 19–23

of slant D ring joint position compared to joint position of, 213; table of binder capacity of slant D ring and, 215

S

Scientific symbols, illustration of, 139

Secondary captions, in caption layout, 192

Section, 9, 68; dividing material into tab, subject, and, 68–69; introduction, 68; numbering system for, 70–71

Security, distribution and, 234

Sentence, 98–99; complex, 99; compound, 99; compound-complex, 99; declarative, 98; defined, 98; exclamatory, 98; imperative, 98; interrogative, 98; simple, 98

Sentences, categories of, 98–99

Sequenced action, defined, 169

Sequential numbering, example of, 154

Serif, defined, 185

Set-up: example of, for playscript layout, 152; in playscript layout, 152, 193

Shadow print, defined, 187

Shared resource word processing network, illustration of, 176

Silk screening, defined, 225

Simple sentence, 98

Slant D ring, 210; illustration of round ring compared to, 212; illustration of round ring joint position compared to joint position of, 213; table of binder capacity of round ring and, 215

Solid line, as logic line symbol for flowchart, 147

Spacing, in headline layout, 192

Spacing standards: foot of page and, 187; illustration of page measurements for, 186; masthead and, 187; page margins and, 185–187; typing and, 185–191; typing standards common to all layouts and,

188–191; vertical page measurements and, 188

Specifications, illustration of form for binder and tab divider, 231

Spine: illustration of appropriate type styles for binder, 222; illustration of improper arrangement of lettering on, 224; illustration of inappropriate type styles for binder, 223; illustration of proper arrangement of lettering on, 224; information on cover and, 220–225

Spine pockets, 229–230; defined, 229; illustration of, 230

Staff changes, 241

Stand-alone word processing unit, illustration of, 175

Standards: achieving success with, 38; characteristics of, 38; defined, 39; example of, 39; illustration of policy, procedures, and, in a manuals hierarchy, 40; setting, 38–40

Subject, 9, 68, 98; dividing material into tab, section, and, 68–69; keeping short, 119; numbering system for, 70–71; overview, 90–92; summary for, 119; verb agreement and, 107

Subject content, defined, 65

Subject index, 83; illustration of cards for, 86; illustrations of alphabetic, 84–85; steps in preparing, 83

Summary, 93; in caption layout, 192; defined, 119; every subject has a, 119; example of, for playscript layout, 152; illustrations of, 93; for layouts, 119; overviews and, 90–93; playscript layout, 152, 193

Supplies, maintenance of, 256–257

T

Tab, 9, 68; dividing material into section, subject, and, 68–69; general, 68; numbering system for, 70–71

Tab dividers, 226–227; defined, 10, 226; illustration of, 227; illustra-

tion of specifications for binders and, 231

Tab stops, 52

Table of contents, 73–77; illustration of, 78; illustration of cookbook example of preliminary, 95; illustration of format for preliminary, to the subject level, 94; preliminary, 94–95

Team, manuals, 8

Tense, of verbs, 98

Tertiary captions, in caption layout, 193

Text processing, word processing compared to, 178; defined, 177

Text processing systems, 177. See also Word processing systems

Text processors, desirable features of, 181–182

Text spacing, in caption layout, 193;

Text statements, in playscript layout, 194

Textured vinyl, for binder covers, 226

Time statements, example of, 153

Title page, 72–73; illustration of, 74

Toffler, Alvin, 4

Tools for interviewing, 44–45

Top-down evolution, defined, 31

Transitional words, 106

Transmittal file, 249; defined, 249

Transmittal form, defined, 236

Transmittal log, illustration of, 246

Transmittal notice, 243; defined, 243; illustration of, 244

Transparencies, overhead, 24–25

Triangle, as manual file symbol for flowcharts, 145

Type styles. See Spine

Typing element, 185

Typing standards: common to all layouts, 188–191; dashes and, 191; foot of page and, 187; illustration of page measurements for, 186; masthead and, 187; page margins and, 185–187; spacing and, 185–191; for specific layouts, 191–195; vertical page measurements and, 188

U

Underlining, use of, 109

Universal index, 55–57; characteristics of system to produce, 56

Unnumbered documents: amendment record, 73; management endorsement, 73; title page, 72–73

Unofficial forms, reviewing, 86

Unsequenced action, defined, 169–170

V

Variable data forms, defined, 65

Variable directions, example of, 153

Verb tense, 98

Verbs: active voice of, 102–103; expressing both singular and plural nouns and, 111; imperative mood of, 103; mood, 98; number, 98; as parts of speech, 97–98; person, 98; subject agreement and, 107; tense, 98

Vertical page measurements, 188; illustration of, 189

Vinyl, textured, 226

Vinyl covers, 208–210

Voice, active, 102–103; of verbs, 98

W

Walkthrough, defined, 254

Word processing, text processing compared to, 178

Word processors: desirable features of, 181–182; illustration of, on-line with a computer, 179; linking to computers, 179–181; table of transfer and storage guidelines when using, linked to a computer, 180

Word processing systems, 174–177; defined, 174; desirable features of text and, 181–182; illustration of shared resource, 176; illustration of stand-alone, 175

Words: examples of transitional, 106; as parts of speech, 97–98; table of positive and negative, 106; table of substitutions for avoidable, 101; using positive rather than negative, 106

Word usage, table of, 10

Working paper file, 251

Writer/editors, 33–37; characteristics of, 33

Writer/editor's files: approvals file, 249; archives file, 249; artwork file, 250–251; printing master file, 248–249; transmittal file, 249; working paper file, 251; illustration of flow of documents through, 250

Writers: manuals, 8; rules for, 99–108

Writer's rules, 99–108

Writing, guidelines for, 108–112

Writing costs of manuals, formula for determining, 14–15

Writing guidelines, 108–112

Writing style, 96–117; conversational, 104; introduction to, 96–99; numbering hierarchy and, 110